After the battle of Sedase of the Second Empire, followed by the invest ional Defence set about raising fresh armies. The the capital. The German troops covering the investment were stretched extremely thin until the fall of Metz at the end of October 1870. This released the forces around the city to move north and west to deal with the newly-forming French armies.

The German campaign in the northeast of France was conducted by the First Army led by General Edwin von Manteuffel. Opposing him was the French Army of the North, initially commanded for a short time by General Charles Bourbaki. He was soon replaced by General Louis Faidherbe, who was sent far from Africa.

The campaign was fought to a large extent over the area of the Somme battlefields of the First World War, and the names of the towns and villages are grimly familiar with the resonance of what was to come. In 1914-1918 the direction of the fighting was on an east-west axis; in 1870 - 1871 it was north-south, with the line of the Somme being crucial to the outcome of the campaign.

The first major battle was the battle of Amiens on November 24; fought before Faidherbe's arrival, the Army of the North was led by the Chief of Staff, General Farre. It resulted in a German victory and the capture of Amiens. In December, Faidherbe advanced and took up a strong defensive position along the line of the River Hallue, where a fierce battle was fought on December 23. After the French retreat, Faidherbe regrouped, and advanced again, this time on Bapaume. Another fierce encounter followed on January 3, at the end of which each side believed itself to be defeated. Faidherbe was thwarted in his objective to lift the siege of Péronne, which fell on January 9.

By now the situation at Paris was desperate, and on January 15 Faidherbe began a march eastwards with a view to compelling the movement of part of the investing armies to meet his advance. This resulted in the crucial battle of Saint Quentin on January 19, in which the Germans were now led by the redoubtable General August von Goeben, who won a final and decisive victory.

The author draws on a wide range of rare contemporary sources to describe the campaign, which was fought in appalling weather conditions. The book is copiously illustrated, with specially drawn colour battle maps to demonstrate the course of the campaign, and also includes extensive orders of battle.

is is the latest title in Helion's ground-breaking series of 19th Century studies, and appears in hardback as a strictly limited edition printing of 500 copies, each individually numbered and signed by the author on a decorative title page.

This book is dedicated to the memory of all those who died
in battle on the Somme in 1870-1871 and 1914-1918.

Quintin Barry is a solicitor and retired Employment Judge. He has also held a variety of offices in both the public and private sector, including the NHS and local radio. He is presently Secretary General of an international group of law firms. Throughout his professional career he has maintained his lifelong interest in military and naval history. He has made a special study of the period 1848-78, and has previously published three titles with Helion to wide acclaim – a two-volume study of the Franco-Prussian War 1870–71 and single volume accounts of the Austro-Prussian War 1866 and Russo-Turkish War 1877–78. He is married and lives in Sussex.

The Somme 1870-71

The Winter Campaign in Picardy

Quintin Barry

Helion & Company

Helion & Company Limited
26 Willow Road
Solihull
West Midlands
B91 1UE
England
Tel. 0121 705 3393
Fax 0121 711 4075
email: info@helion.co.uk
website: www.helion.co.uk
Twitter: @helionbooks
Visit our blog http://blog.helion.co.uk

Published by Helion & Company 2014. This paperback reprint 2016

Designed and typeset by Mach 3 Solutions Limited, Bussage, Gloucestershire
Cover designed by Farr out Publications, Wokingham, Berkshire
Printed by Lightning Source Limited, Milton Keynes, Buckinghamshire

Text © Quintin Barry 2014
The author has made every reasonable effort to trace copyright holders of relevant material.
Images © as individually credited
Maps © Helion & Company 2014

Cover: The Prussian 8th Jäger Battalion defends the edge of Tilloy during the Battle of Bapaume, 3 January 1871.

ISBN 978-1-911096-16-0

British Library Cataloguing-in-Publication Data
A catalogue record for this book is available from the British Library

All rights reserved. No part of this publication may be reproduced, stored, manipulated in any retrieval system, or transmitted in any mechanical, electronic form or by any other means, without the prior written authority of the publishers, except for short extracts in media reviews. Any person who engages in any unauthorized activity in relation to this publication shall be liable to criminal prosecution and claims for civil and criminal damages.

For details of other military history titles published by Helion & Company Limited contact the above address, or visit our website: http://www.helion.co.uk

We always welcome receiving book proposals from prospective authors working in military history.

Contents

List of Illustrations   vii
List of Colour Maps & Photographs   xi
Acknowledgements   xii
Preface   xiii

1   The Army of the North   14
2   The advance of the First Army   25
3   The Battle of Amiens   38
4   La Fère   53
5   Rouen   65
6   The arrival of Faidherbe   75
7   The Battle of the Hallue   85
8   Retreat   104
9   The investment of Péronne   110
10   Bapaume   117
11   Goeben takes command   137
12   The fall of Péronne   143
13   Robert Le Diable   153
14   Faidherbe advances again   159
15   The plan to move east   163
16   The march begins   168
17   Tertry – Poueilly   175
18   The eve of battle   183
19   St Quentin: the southern sector   191
20   St Quentin: the western sector   200
21   St Quentin: victory on the left bank   207
22   St Quentin: the end of the battle   214
23   Aftermath   223

Appendices
I   Order of Battle of the First Army, November 15 1870   230
II   Distribution of the German forces for the Battle of St Quentin, January 19 1871   235
III   Order of Battle of the Army of the North, mid-January 1871   239
IV   Moltke's instructions to Manteuffel and Frederick Charles, December 17 1870   243
V   The Chassepôt and the Needle Gun   245
VI   Major Garnier explains himself to General Faidherbe, January 11 1871   247
VII   Report of Colonel Degoutin of the 48th Regiment of the Mobiles du Nord, for January 18 1871   249
VIII   Report of Commandant Hecquet, of the 20th Battalion of Chasseurs, for January 19 1871   251

IX	Report of Lieutenant Belvalette, commanding the Battery Dupuich, for January 18 1871	253
X	General Goeben's orders for the pursuit, January 20 1871	255
XI	Order of the Day from the Commanding General after the Battle of St Quentin, January 21, 1871	256

Notes 257
Bibliography 268
Index 270

List of Illustrations

Gambetta. (Private collection)	15
General Bourbaki. (Hiltl)	17
Lieutenant General Farre. (Rousset/*Histoire*)	18
Bourbaki at Douai, by Tiret-Bognet. (Deschaumes)	21
Lieutenant General Lecointe. (Rousset/*Histoire*)	21
French marine infantry, by Tiret-Bognet. (Deschaumes)	23
General of Cavalry Edwin von Manteuffel. (Rousset/*Histoire*)	26
General August Karl von Goeben. (Rousset/*Histoire*)	27
Lieutenant General Ferdinand von Kummer. (Rousset/*Histoire*)	29
Lieutenant General Albert von Barnekow. (Rousset/*Histoire*)	30
Lieutenant General Georg Ferdinand von Bentheim. (Rousset/*Histoire*)	34
General Faidherbe. (Pflug-Harttung)	36
Lieutenant General Paulze d'Ivoy. (Rousset/*Histoire*)	39
Prussian Jäger at Quesnel, November 23. (Hiltl)	40
A view of the Hangard woods from the German positions. (Duncan Rogers)	43
The village of Hangard from the French positions. (Duncan Rogers)	43
The Battle of Amiens. To the left is the Prussian 44th Infantry Regiment, to the right are guns from the Prussian 7th and 8th Field Artillery regiments. Villers-Bretonneux can be seen in the background. (Hiltl)	44
French attack on the Bois de Hangard, by Pallandre. (Rousset/*Les Combattants*)	45
The Prussian 44th Infantry Regiment storms the railway embankment near Villers Bretonneux during the Battle of Amiens, by Amling. (Fehleisen)	45
The railway cutting at Villers-Bretonneux. (Duncan Rogers)	46
A view from 'Manteuffel's windmill' at Thennes. (Duncan Rogers)	47
Prussian artillery at the Battle of Amiens, by Pallandre. (Rousset/*Les Combattants*)	48
The Füsilier Battalion of the Prussian 70th Infantry storms the churchyard at Dury during the Battle of Amiens, by Röchling. (Lindner)	49
The monument to the Prussian 70th Infantry Regiment at Dury. (Duncan Rogers)	50
German Uhlans at the Battle of Amiens, by Knötel. (Pflug-Harttung)	51
Amiens. (Rousset/*Les Combattants*)	54
German troops enter Amiens. (*Illustrirte Kriegsgeschichte*)	55
Amiens Cathedral. (Pflug-Harttung)	55
The German entry into Amiens, by Knötel. (Pflug-Harttung)	56
Manteuffel receives news of La Fère's capitulation, by Tiret-Bognet. (Deschaumes)	59
The death of Captain Vogel, by Tiret-Bognet. (Deschaumes)	59
Francs-Tireurs with their prisoner, by Bombled. (Grenest)	61
Major General von Zglinitzky. (Priesdorff)	61
General Hermann von Wartensleben. (Rousset/*Histoire*)	64
General Count zur Lippe. (Rousset/*Histoire*)	66

Count von Moltke. (Lindner)	67
The German advanced guard at Bernay, by Pallandre. (Rousset/*Les Combattants*)	73
The Army of the North takes Ham, by Pallandre. (Rousset/*Les Combattants*)	77
Captured Uhlans are brought into Arras, by Leclercq. (Rousset/*Histoire*)	80
Prince Albrecht Junior. (Rousset/*Histoire*)	83
The southern side of Querrieux. (Duncan Rogers)	86
The Battle of the Hallue. In the centre can be seen Querrieux, under attack from the German VIII Corps. In the foreground are guns from VIII Corps, covered by cavalry from the 3rd Cavalry Division. The French positions can be seen along the heights in the distance. (Hiltl)	89
German troops storm Pont-Noyelles. (*Illustrirte Kriegsgeschichte*)	90
Looking from the French positions towards the German lines, near the Faidherbe monument above Pont-Noyelles. (Duncan Rogers)	91
The Faidherbe monument. (Duncan Rogers)	92
The French 33rd Line Infantry Regiment launch a bayonet charge during Pont-Noyelles, led by Captain d'Hauterive, by Tiret-Bognet. (Deschaumes)	93
An episode of the action at Fréchencourt, by Zimmer. (Rousset/*Histoire*)	94
Prussian infantry are chased through woodland near Querrieux, by Bombled. (Grenest)	95
Picquet, a soldier from the Gardes Mobiles of the Pas-de-Calais, shoots a Prussian officer from his horse. An episode from the actions around Pont-Noyelles, by Bombled. (Grenest)	96
An episode from the actions around Pont-Noyelles, by Bombled. (Grenest)	97
Lecointe's attack on Pont-Noyelles, by Pallandre. (Rousset/*Les Combattants*)	100
French Chasseurs and Fusiliers Marines in the streets of Daours, by Pallandre. (Rousset/*Les Combattants*)	101
Streetfighting in Pont Noyelles, by Knötel. (Lindner)	102
A French infantry Regiment on the march, by Detaille. (Rousset/*Histoire*)	105
German hussars skirmishing, by Knötel. (Pflug-Harttung)	106
A scene from the Siege of Péronne, by Pallandre. (Rousset/*Les Combattants*)	115
German prisoners are brought into Péronne, by Tiret-Bognet. (Deschaumes)	116
The combat at Béhagnies, January 2, by Pallandre. (Rousset/*Les Combattants*)	120
Marine Hamel carries a wounded officer to safety during the Battle of Bapaume, by Bombled. (Grenest)	120
An episode of the action at Sapignies, by Leclercq. (Rousset/*Histoire*)	121
Looking towards Bihucourt in the direction of the French advance. (Duncan Rogers)	122
The Prussians defend Biefvillers, by Tiret-Bognet. (Deschaumes)	125
Prussian infantry in action in Biefvillers, by Knötel. (Lindner)	125
A scene from the battle of Bapaume, by Pallandre. (Rousset/*Les Combattants*)	127
Mobiles from Lille during the Battle of Bapaume, by Bombled. (Grenest)	128
The Prussian 8th Jäger Battalion, supported by the 33rd Fusilier 69th Infantry Regiments repel the French from Tilloy during the Battle of Bapaume, by Amling. (Fehleisen)	130
Looking away from Ligny facing the French advance. (Duncan Rogers)	130
The French Fusilier Marines at Béhagnies, by Tiret-Bognet. (Deschaumes)	131

LIST OF ILLUSTRATIONS ix

The 20th Chasseurs are cheered by fellow soldiers due to their actions at Bihucourt, by Bombled. (Grenest)	133
Faidherbe at Bapaume, by Armand-Dumaresq. (Private collection)	134
Faidherbe's headquarters at Boisleux. (*The Graphic*)	135
The Battle of Bapaume - Looking north from the Bapaume monument, towards the French advance. (Duncan Rogers)	135
Von Goeben on the march, by Speyer. (Bleibtreu)	138
A French bivouac, by Tiret-Bognet. (Deschaumes)	141
Captain von Schell. (Priesdorff)	146
Monument to the defence of Péronne. (Rousset/*Histoire*)	148
The Château at Robert Le Diable. (Rousset/*Histoire*)	154
Francs-Tireurs during the assault on Robert Le Diable, by Pallandre. (Rousset/*Les Combattants*)	155
Major General von Gayl. (Rousset/*Histoire*)	158
Troops from the Army of the North on the march, by Pallandre. (Rousset/*Les Combattants*)	160
Charles-Louis de Freycinet. (Rousset/*Histoire*)	164
French troops suffering in the cold weather, by Knötel. (Pflug-Harttung)	171
French Gardes Mobiles on the march, January 16 1871, by Knötel. (Pflug-Harttung)	173
The combat at Caulaincourt, by Pallandre. (Rousset/*Histoire*)	177
Paulze d'Ivoy at Vermand, by Bombled. (Grenest)	178
French infantry during the engagement at Caulaincourt, by Pallandre. (Rousset/*Les Combattants*)	179
French troops repel German cavalry at Vermand, by Bombled. (Grenest)	182
The Canal de St Quentin at Lehaucourt. (Duncan Rogers)	185
The sugar refinery at Neuville St Amand, from a contemporary sketch. (Scheibert)	186
Preparing St Quentin for defence, by Pallandre. (Rousset/*Les Combattants*)	189
Looking at Castres from the road to St Quentin. (Duncan Rogers)	192
The sugar refinery today. (Duncan Rogers)	193
The Prussian 29th Infantry Regiment launches a bayonet attack during the Battle of St Quentin, by Roetzler. (Scheibert)	195
French Chasseurs take German infantry prisoner near the sugar refinery, by Bombled. (Grenest)	195
The defence of St Quentin, by Armand-Dumaresq. (Rousset/*Histoire*)	198
The charge of the Prussian 70th Infantry Regiment at St Quentin, by Röchling. (Rousset/*Histoire*)	199
The French assault on Fayet, by Bombled. (Grenest)	201
Looking towards the rear of the French positions at Francilly. (Duncan Rogers)	202
Looking west from the French lines in front of Fayet towards Holnon, and the direction of the German advance. (Duncan Rogers)	204
The defence of the Bellenglise Canal, by Pallandre. (Rousset/*Histoire*)	205
An episode of the Battle of St Quentin, by Navlet. (Rousset/*Histoire*)	209
An episode of the Battle of St Quentin, by Navlet – a watercolour study. (Rousset/*Histoire*)	209

French engineers deployed as infantry during the Battle of St Quentin,
  by Bombled. (Grenest) — 210
A rather fanciful impression of German cavalry attacking French Gardes Mobiles
  at St Quentin, by Amling. (Fehleisen) — 212
French dragoons form a dismounted skirmish line during the closing stages of
  the Battle of St Quentin, by Bombled. (Grenest) — 216
Faidherbe at St Quentin, by Knötel. (Pflug-Harttung) — 219
French troops in action in the market place at St Quentin, by Knötel.
  (Pflug-Harttung) — 219
The French withdrawal at St Quentin, by Knötel. (Lindner) — 221
The left flank of the German positions on the evening of January 19. The left
  middle distance shows troops from the German 3rd Cavalry Division with
  a battery of horse artillery. To the far right is the road to Péronne, threading
  its way through Savy. The prominent Tout Vent windmill heights can be
  seen just to the left of centre in the distance. (Hiltl) — 222
Exhausted and ill, Faidherbe is carried to his quarters at Cambrai following
  the Battle of St Quentin, by Tiret-Bognet. (Deschaumes) — 225
'The rearguard of the Army of the North', by Sergent. (Rousset/*Histoire*) — 227

Key to Sources

Bleibtreu *Amiens – St Quentin* (Stuttgart 1902)
Deschaumes *L'Armée du Nord (1870-1871), Campagne du General Faidherbe* (Paris, 1895)
Fehleisen *Aus Grosser Zeit! Patriotisches Ehren- und Gedenkbuch aus den Kriegsjahren 1870-71* (Reutlingen, n.d.)
The Graphic
Grenest *Les Armées du Nord et de Normandie* (Paris, 1897)
Hiltl *Der Französische Krieg* (Bielefeld, 1888)
Illustrirte Kriegsgeschichte (Stuttgart, 1871)
Lindner *Der Krieg gegen Frankreich 1870–71* (Berlin, 1895)
Pflug-Harttung *Krieg und Sieg 1870–71, ein Gedenkbuch* (Berlin, 1895)
Priesdorff *Soldatisches Führertum. Die Preussische Generale* (Hamburg, n.d., 10 volumes)
Rousset *Histoire Générale de la Guerre Franco-Allemande (1870–1871)* (Paris, no date, 2 volumes)
Rousset *Les Combattants de 1870–71* (Paris, 1895, 2 volumes)
Scheibert *Der Krieg 1870–71* (Berlin, 1914)

List of Colour Maps & Photographs

Map 1 – The Theatre of War.	B
Map 2 – The Battle of Amiens.	D
Map 3 – The Battle of the Hallue.	F
Map 4 – The Battle of Bapaume.	G
Map 5 – The Battle of St. Quentin.	H
Map 6 – Siege of Péronne.	J
Map 7 – Siege of La Fère.	K
The Battle of Amiens – the village of Hangard from the French positions. (Duncan Rogers)	L
The Battle of Amiens – the railway cutting at Villers-Bretonneux. (Duncan Rogers)	L
The Battle of Amiens – the monument to the Prussian 70th Infantry Regiment at Dury. (Duncan Rogers)	M
The Battle of the Hallue – the southern side of Querrieux. (Duncan Rogers)	M
The Battle of the Hallue – looking from the French positions towards the German lines, near the Faidherbe monument above Pont-Noyelles. (Duncan Rogers)	N
The Battle of Bapaume – looking towards Bihucourt in the direction of the French advance. (Duncan Rogers)	N
The Battle of Bapaume – the Bapaume monument. (Duncan Rogers)	O
The Battle of St Quentin – the Canal de St Quentin at Lehaucourt. (Duncan Rogers)	O
The Battle of St Quentin – looking at Castres from the road to St Quentin. (Duncan Rogers)	P
The Battle of St Quentin – the sugar refinery today. (Duncan Rogers)	P

Acknowledgements

This book springs directly from the two volumes which I published on the history of the Franco Prussian War of 1870–1871. In writing the second of these I had occasion to research the various more or less separate campaigns that followed the fall of the Second Empire and the formation of the Government of National Defence.

I was encouraged to write this study of the campaign in Picardy by my enthusiastic and tireless publisher, Duncan Rogers of Helion. We undertook a short tour of the battlefields together, which was both extremely informative and enjoyable, and perhaps more incident-filled than we had expected. Our tour took us, of course, across the battlefields of the First World War, where we had the deeply moving experience of visiting the many cemeteries there. Duncan is responsible for the illustrations in this book, as he has been in my previous books which he has published, and I am particularly grateful to him for the care with which he has selected them; and also for the many photographs which he took of the battlefields and which we have used.

I drew a great deal of inspiration from Douglas Fermer's brilliant translation of the memoirs of Léonce Patry, published under the title *The Reality of War* by Cassell and Co in 2001. Patry, an outspoken junior officer in the Army of the North, had a great deal to say about the conduct of the campaign, and vividly conveyed the experiences of the troops involved.

I am greatly indebted to Paul Hewitt for the specially dawn maps, which I hope that readers will find to a lucid accompaniment of the text.

I am especially grateful to Tim Readman, who read the book in draft; and to Liz Haywood who typed it from my inexcusable handwriting, about which she made fewer complaints than I deserved. I should also record my gratitude to my wife and family for the patience which they invariably display while I am writing, and which is a perpetual source of encouragement.

Preface

In 1870 the fall of the Second Empire after the battle of Sedan, and its replacement by the Government of National Defence, created a quite unexpected set of problems for Helmuth von Moltke and the leaders of the German armies in France. As a result of the extraordinary efforts of Léon Gambetta and the leaders of the new government in the provinces, large armies, surprisingly well equipped, quickly began to appear. For each of them, their primary objective was the relief of Paris, the investment of which was completed by September 19.

Gambetta's first choice to command the nascent French Army of the North was General Charles Bourbaki who, having left the besieged Army of the Rhine in Metz on an abortive diplomatic mission, had not been permitted to return there. He was, however, too closely associated in the public mind with the Second Empire, and it was not long before Gambetta, who had a great admiration for him, was obliged to accept that he must be replaced. His choice was General Louis Faidherbe, who was serving in Africa; he did not arrive to take up his post until December 3. Thoughtful and determined, he was arguably the most able of the commanders of the new French armies. His service in Africa, however, had seriously damaged his health, and he was utterly worn out by the end of every day of the campaign.

Opposing him was the First Army, commanded by General Edwin von Manteuffel. As Chief of the King's Military Cabinet he had, in the years before the wars of German Unification, wielded enormous political influence in Prussia. As a field commander, he had enjoyed considerable success in the Austro-Prussian War and the first phase of the Franco-Prussian War. His principal subordinate, who was to take over the command of the First Army when Manteuffel was sent to command the forces operating in Eastern France was General August von Goeben. Goeben, too, had distinguished himself previously, in Denmark in 1864, as a divisional commander in South Germany in 1866 and as the commander of the VIII Corps in 1870. He was, perhaps, the ablest of all Prussia's field commanders, and had Moltke's total confidence.

Both Faidherbe and Goeben were literate as well as intelligent commanders; and after the end of the war continued their contest with each other with their pens, each being sharply critical of his adversary's account of the campaign.

It is one of absorbing interest; the French had the advantage of very much superior numbers, and a very much more effective infantry weapon in the form of the Chassepôt, while the Germans had the benefit of extremely well-trained, well-led and battle-hardened troops.

Although, in the end, the campaign ended in a decisive victory for Goeben and his men, there were certainly times when the outcome appeared in doubt.

1

The Army of the North

In 1870 Dr Achille Testelin was a successful physician practising medicine in Lille. Born in 1814, he had been an active member of the Republican opposition during the reign of Louis Philippe. He sat as a Radical in the Legislative Assembly until the coup d'état of 1851. Following this he was, as a spirited opponent of the new Imperial regime, expelled from France. He made his way to Brussels, and practised there until 1859, when the amnesty of that year enabled him to return to France. He took no active part in politics but remained a staunch Republican.

With the overthrow of the Second Empire, he was, as a personal friend of Leon Gambetta, an obvious candidate to take up a responsible position under the Government of National Defence, and he was first appointed Prefect of the Department of Nord, and later, on September 30, as Commissioner for the four Departments of Aisne, Nord, Pas de Calais and Somme. He threw himself energetically into the business of organising the defence of north-eastern France. He faced almost insurmountable administrative and financial problems as he went about the task; but he soon proved that his had been a wise appointment, as he brought intelligence and vigour to the governance of the area for which he was responsible.

The fall of the Second Empire, and the proclamation of a Republic, had left the administration of government in a state of doubtful legality. Clearly, given the prefectorial system by which France was managed, steps had at once to be taken to appoint, as prefects of the departments of France, men who could be relied on to support the new regime and to carry its policies into effect. The scramble for office on September 4 had ended with the 33 year old Leon Gambetta in position as Minister of the Interior, and he was soon confirmed in that post. By September 14 he had appointed new prefects to 85 departments:

> The list of appointments was an illuminating comment upon the make up of the Republican party. Like master, like man: as the majority of the Government of National Defence were either journalists or lawyers, so no less than 44 of the new administrators were, or had been, lawyers, while 14 were primarily journalists. These men, who were to be the keystone of administration in the provinces, were appointed as Republicans, and they seldom failed to show strong party spirit.[1]

A sense of the need to give the government of the provinces some democratic legitimacy had led to a decree on September 17 that municipal elections should be held on September 25 followed by constituent elections for a National assembly on October 2. The date for the latter was brought forward from October 16. The decision to hold municipal elections was greeted with dismay by the newly appointed prefects, including Testelin, who telegraphed: 'Your decree concerning municipal elections is our ruin! You will see all the former Ministers and members of the majority return at the head of the list.'[2]

By now the risk of Paris being cut off had led to a Delegation of the government leaving Paris for Tours. It was headed by Adolphe Cremieux, the 74 year old Minister of Justice, acting with Alexandre Glais-Bizoin, and Admiral Fourichon, the Minister of Marine, and they too protested at the proposed municipal elections. Gambetta was adamant; but since elections could scarcely be held without an armistice, and the talks aimed to achieve this held between Bismarck and Jules Favre on September 19 and 20 proved abortive, it was found necessary to postpone the constituent elections indefinitely, as well as the municipal elections in Paris. The latter decision enabled the Delegation to take the same step in relation to the provincial municipal elections, and the prefects were instructed to deal with the matter by 'the maintenance of the existing municipalities or by the nomination of provisional municipalities.[3] In this way the prefects were able to ensure that a proper Republican constituency could be maintained.

The Delegation, however, now overreached itself by announcing on October 1 that after all constituent elections were to be held in the provinces, in order to reinforce their authority. In Paris, the remaining members of the government were outraged, pronouncing that any such elections should be null and void. Gambetta, who had proposed this, argued that 'a man of energy' should be sent to Tours. On the night of October 1 no agreement could be reached on who should go. Since Paris was now more closely invested than the

Gambetta. (Private collection)

French leaders had expected, the journey could only be made by balloon, and was obviously not without risk. As Foreign Minister Jules Favre had a need to be able to contact foreign governments, and was an obvious choice. Perhaps on the ground of his age – he was 61 – he firmly declined; and the lot fell on the 32 year old Gambetta. After a show of reluctance he allowed himself to be persuaded, and at 11.00 am on October 7 the balloon *Armand Barbès* rose from Montmartre carrying Gambetta, Eugène Spuller, his secretary, and the pilot Tricker. It proved to be an adventurous voyage. A mistake by Tricker caused the balloon to descend rapidly, and it touched the ground before rising again to 2000 feet. The danger was not over; near Creil it had come down to 500 feet over a party of German troops before rising again as they opened fire. Gambetta's hand was grazed by a bullet. The balloon finally passed over the German lines near Montdidier, coming to earth in a forest, from where that evening Gambetta reached Amiens.[4]

Gambetta's escape transformed the situation at Tours. Arriving there soon after noon on October 9 he was, within an hour, in conference with his colleagues. One of the first decisions to be taken was to fill the vacant post of Minister of War, and Gambetta decided to take it himself. Both Crémieux and Glais-Bizoin objected; but Gambetta brought with him the right to two votes in any dispute and Fourichon gave him his vote also. Before nightfall he issued his famous circular to the people of France. In it he gave a distinctly upbeat account of the situation of Paris and of the courage and determination of its defenders, as JPT Bury noted:

> If the truth of his conclusion – 'Paris is impregnable; it can neither be taken nor surprised' – had yet to be proved, it was nonetheless true that the situation and efforts of the capital imposed very definite obligations upon the citizens of the departments: of these the first he declared to be to wage war to the knife, the second – 'to accept as a father's the commands of the Republican authority which has sprung from necessity and from right.'[5]

Gambetta went on to assert that if the Republic was to be preserved, France must repeat the miracle of 1792 and drive back the invader. He ended with a ringing appeal to the French people:

> The Republic appeals for the aid of all citizens; her Government will consider it a duty to employ every brave man and to make use of every talent. It is her tradition to arm young leaders; we shall find them ... No, it is impossible that the genius of France should be veiled for ever, that the great nation should be deprived of its place in the world by an invasion of 500,000 men. Let us rise up, then, *en masse*, and die rather than undergo the humiliation of dismemberment. Through all our disasters and beneath the blows of ill fortune we still preserve the idea of Fench unity and the indivisibility of the Republic.[6]

One of the talents that Gambetta was keen to utilise was that of General Bourbaki, who arrived at Tours on October 15 after his abortive visit to Hastings to visit the Empress Eugénie in pursuit of a possible settlement. Bourbaki, who told Gambetta that Bazaine and his army shut up in Metz still recognised Napoleon III, offered his services to the government, and Gambetta, who was very impressed by him, invited him to take command of the Army of the Loire that was assembling. The two men had immediately taken to each other, although Gambetta quickly reached the conclusion that Bourbaki's strength lay rather in leading troops in the field than organising them for battle. For his part Bourbaki was dazzled by the young politician: 'He bids the paralytics arise and walk, and behold the paralytics arise and walk.'[7] Bourbaki, however, after appraising the hopelessly confused condition of the army and the enormity of the task assigned to it, was sufficiently clear sighted to be firm in his refusal of the post. As the British ambassador Lord Lyons reported to Lord Granville, he had found that the situation was impossible, not least because he 'could not reconcile himself to serving under the eye and the immediate control of the men now at Tours.'[8]

In appointing commissioners to take charge of the various regions in which it was hoped that armies would be formed that would be capable of relieving Paris, Gambetta equipped them with the widest powers to mobilise all the material and human resources available, leaving them with as free a hand as possible. Testelin took full advantage of this. His immediate concern, of course, was to establish with the local military leaders a successful working relationship. Military authority in this region was the 3rd Military Division, and Testelin invested its commanders with all his powers to enable them to organise serviceable military units as a nucleus of an effective army. The results were a fearful disappointment; the officers concerned offered only the negative opinion that the most that could be hoped for was the defence of the fortresses. At the beginning of September the local commander was General Fririon; he was succeeded towards the end of the month by General Espivent de la Villeboisnet. Neither appeared to Testelin to provide the kind of inspiring leadership that would be required.[9] Faidherbe, in his

General Bourbaki. (Hiltl)

short history of the campaign in north-eastern France, described the state of the forces immediately available:

> The improvement of the elements of the defence, which had been disorganised by the despatch of materials to Paris, was not sought. It sufficed to clothe and arm the Gardes Mobiles, without any concern about forming the proper staffs. As to the regulars, they had been drawn from seven or eight regional depots, and detachments from them had been despatched to the centre of the country to be absorbed into other units. Each depot had more than 1,000 men, with incomplete staffs of two companies. By way of artillery there was but one battery at Lille, and that incapable of service. Last, for cavalry the depot of the 7th Dragoons could with difficulty supply several troopers as escorts.[10]

Testelin was by no means content to leave matters in this state, and on October 15 he visited Colonel Jean Joseph Farre, the military governor of Lille. In him, he found a kindred spirit, and he lost no time in appointing him as a member of his Commission. Farre, who was born in 1816, was a career officer who was a distinguished engineer. He had been employed on a number of important construction projects, including Fort Nogent at Paris, and the works around Lyon and Algiers. He took part in the Kabyle expedition of 1857, and was chief of engineers at various times at Le Havre, Toulon and Rome. In 1870 he was director of engineering at Arras and Lille before serving in the Army of the Rhine; when it was invested in Metz he escaped and offered his services to the Government of National Defence, and was posted to Lille.[11]

Lieutenant General Farre. (Rousset/*Histoire*)

THE ARMY OF THE NORTH

Farre certainly fitted Gambetta's specification of a suitable military leader; the latter strongly believed in the importance of engineers in the establishment of the new armies he was raising to fight the Germans. On October 14, the day on which he decreed that the Gardes Nationales should be embodied as an auxiliary army, he issued a separate decree which reflected that belief. Every department which had enemy forces within 100 kilometres of its borders was required to establish a committee of between five and nine persons. Under the presidency of the local military commander, it was to include an engineer officer, a staff officer, a road engineer and a mining engineer. This committee was to have wide powers of conscription, of commandeering supplies and of deploying the Gardes Nationales. At the same time Gambetta also set up an inspectorate to supervise these committees.[12]

Farre, like Testelin, recognised that there was no time to lose if anything approaching a worthwhile army was to be organised, and at once vigorously set about establishing the basic cadres from which units could be formed. Almost immediately he was faced by the defeatist indifference of the officers that constituted the 3rd Military Division, but in spite of this he soon began to make progress, as Faidherbe described:

> The available elements were collected, former soldiers found from whom staffs could be established, an inventory was made of all material in the fortresses so as to understand their resources and more efficiently divide them; last, material was found for the immediate creation of provisional batteries. The zeal of the officials charged with this was stimulated by all means possible.[13]

Bourbaki's refusal of the command of the Army of the Loire had been a great disappointment to Gambetta, but the latter was quick to identify in the nascent Army of the North an alternative opportunity to exploit the general's talents. This post Bourbaki was prepared to accept. He was appointed on October 17 and he made his way northwards to Lille where he assumed the command of all the forces in the Region du Nord. Although the organisation of the army was still in a very primitive state, and his own morale was still low as a result of his experiences in Lorraine, he was not unmindful of the efforts which Farre had made, and he appointed him as his Chief of Staff. Faidherbe described Bourbaki's state of mind as he took up his appointment, which was not very different from his predecessors:

> It must be said that his faith in the efficacy of a prolongation of the defence failed him. He, who had just seen the destruction of magnificent armies, could not pin much hope on a collection of recruits, escaped prisoners and badly armed and very inexperienced militiamen. Moreover, public opinion was unfavourable to him. He was distrusted because of his former intimacy with the court, his command of the Imperial Guard, which he had led at the start of the war, and above all because of his mysterious, fantastic voyage from Metz to London.[14]

Nonetheless Bourbaki worked hard to support and develop Favre's accomplishments, and during the next few weeks a great deal was done to turn the disorganised groups of soldiers into something resembling an army. The bulk of the troops immediately available were regular infantry and Gardes Mobiles. The former were based in the depots, but had few officers and no proper company organisation. The latter were grouped in battalions between 1,200 and 1,500 strong, units which were too large to be managed effectively. An early decision was accordingly taken that battalions were to consist of five companies each of 150 men with three officers.

There were at least as many men available as it was possible to organise and begin to train; but the real problem was in the lack of artillery, about which Bourbaki wrote to Gambetta on October 21:

> To give you some idea ... that to create several artillery batteries it is necessary that we construct the gun carriages, that we buy the horses and their harnesses and that we find artillery men and the cadres of officers.[15]

The only artillery immediately available consisted of two batteries of heavy artillery in the defences each of Douai and Lille. There was also a serious shortage of cavalry. There was a dragoon depot at Lille and three other small detachments of dragoons, but all the rest had been sent away to join the Army of the Loire. Neither artillery nor cavalry could be easily improvised. There were some 80 mountain guns, but these lacked harnesses and, indeed, the horses to pull them; there was also a serious shortage of ammunition.[16]

As to the infantry, the principal source of strength lay in the considerable number of officers who had escaped after being taken prisoner, some at Sedan but the bulk at Metz; it has been estimated that about 400 were available. One of these was Léonce Patry, who got away from Metz and reached Brussels on November 7, from where he made his way to Lille, which he found full of activity:

> It was with real pleasure that I found myself back in the agreeable town of Lille where I had been garrisoned three years previously. It was full of unwanted bustle occasioned by the extraordinary agglomeration of troops and service units intended to form the future Army of the North, by the movement of officials and travellers of every sort which its standing as capital of the northern region and virtual seat of an independent government drew to it; and by the boost given to its population by the numerous refugees from Paris.[17]

Patry, who had been promoted to the rank of captain while at Metz, on November 13 took command of a company in a battalion of the 75th Regiment; he was able to choose a friend as his second lieutenant and also to hand pick the NCOs, nearly all of whom had escaped imprisonment.

With surprising speed the infantry available were being formed into effective units, and soon after Bourbaki had arrived at Lille a brigade was constituted under Colonel Lecointe, who had been the commander of the 2nd Grenadier Guard Regiment and was another escapee from Metz. Lecointe was a veteran of Algeria, the Crimea, Italy and Mexico. The cavalry, such as it was, sufficed only to form two squadrons of dragoons; later, these grew to five. The regional gendarmerie was put together to provide two more squadrons. Progress was made with the artillery; one battery was recalled from Mézières, while others were established and manned by gunners from the navy, and also from the Garde Mobile.[18] In addition the navy furnished some 50 pieces of heavy artillery for the defence of the fortresses.

THE ARMY OF THE NORTH 21

Bourbaki at Douai, by Tiret-Bognet. (Deschaumes)

Lieutenant General Lecointe.
(Rousset/*Histoire*)

It was well understood by Bourbaki and Farre, and all those concerned with organising the Army of the North, that time was extremely short; Patry, however, had been struck that in spite of the fact that it was well known that the First German Army from Metz was heading northwards, 'a very carefree attitude reigned among the inhabitants, who seemed to me just as inclined to enjoy themselves as in the past.' In spite of this, considerable progress was made; further brigades were constituted, consisting of seven battalions, made up as to one battalion of *chasseurs à pied*, a provisional regiment of three infantry battalions and a provisional regiment of the Garde Mobile. The second brigade to be formed was under the command of Lieutenant Colonel Rittier; this, with Lecointe's brigade, constituted the 1st Division.[19]

The geography of the region was by no means unhelpful to the defence, as the German Official History observed:

> The numerous fortresses situated towards the Belgian frontier offered to the foe excellent bases for assembly and support, from which, favoured by the fortified passages of the Somme at Ham, Péronne, Amiens and Abbeville, he could at any time move forward for the relief of Paris, and threaten the right flank of the First Army advancing in a westerly direction, before the front of which the deeply sunken valleys of the tributaries of the Seine offered strong lines of defence. A network of well maintained roads intersects the densely populated district now under consideration, but the bye-roads, on account of the prevailing chalky soil, speedily become difficult for traffic after bad weather. In the fertile closely cultivated valleys, the villages, consisting chiefly of clay-built houses, are confined within narrow limits and are surrounded by extensive meadows and gardens enclosed by walls and hedges; the more elevated villages on the other hand consist almost exclusively of isolated farmsteads which are still more completely separated by high earthen walls.[20]

This was the region towards which the First Army was advancing. When it arrived, however, it would face an enemy no longer led by Bourbaki. On November 19 he received orders to give up his command and return to Tours. The reason was a fundamental disagreement with his civilian colleagues, as the leading French historian of the campaign has described:

> Ever since his arrival at Lille, the difficulties of his situation had increased. His ideas as to the future mission of the army did not accord with those of M. Testelin. He thought only of creating a small army corps that would operate between our fortresses and go to the assistance of those threatened by the enemy. On the other hand the Commissioner, and the bulk of the population, regarded the defence of these places as entirely secondary. In their eyes, the Army of the North, after assembling all its forces, must attempt to relieve Paris, the object on which the attention of the whole of France was solely fixed.[21]

There had been a stormy meeting of the war council at Amiens on November 8, when the extent of the disagreement became entirely clear. The civil authorities demanded immediate action against the modest German forces in their immediate vicinity.

French marine infantry, by Tiret-Bognet. (Deschaumes)

Bourbaki strongly objected; there was no point, he said, in advancing to occupy points that must immediately be abandoned when the enemy developed his strength. The dispute was referred to Gambetta, who supported the demand for an offensive, and Bourbaki reluctantly began to plan for an operation in the direction of Paris, in response to the suggestion that he should synchronise his advance in conjunction with the Army of the Loire. It was not the first conflict that Bourbaki had had with the Republican leaders; convinced that it was on the Loire that the decisive action would be fought, they had been sending off units, as soon as they had been formed, to reinforce the Army of the Loire. Bourbaki was only able to put a stop to this by threatening resignation.[22] And, highly suspect in the public mind as one of the leading generals of the Second Empire, he had had to face abuse in the street from hostile demonstrators following the fall of Metz. It was an unhappy time for him, but he was still resolved to do his duty. Orders had already gone out to begin the planned movement when he received on November 19 the order to report to Tours. He set off at once, taking with him a large part of his personal staff. This left the unfortunate Farre in charge of the army, the high command of which had thus been completely disorganised on the eve of its first battle. It was not a promising start to its campaign.

Bourbaki subsequently gave an account of his meeting with Gambetta when he arrived at Tours:

> M. Gambetta did not conceal from me that I had been relieved from command as a political measure and that, still having full confidence in me, he believed it necessary to displace me in order to send me to take command of the 18th Corps. I replied that I was sure that I could gain the confidence of the population of the Nord; but that if several clubs, more concerned with political manoeuvres than the national interest, were sorry to see me given the high command at Lille, I should still have been supported by the government; that my removal was an expression of disrespect, and that under such conditions it was impossible for me to accept a command.[23]

A few days later, however, Bourbaki changed his mind, and declared that he was, after all, prepared to accept a new command under the Government of National Defence.

2

The Advance of the First Army

By the second half of October it had become clear that the capitulation of Metz could not be far off, and on October 23 Moltke issued his preliminary instructions for the future tasks of the First and Second Armies following the fall of the fortress. These, for the First Army, foreshadowed the campaign which it was to conduct against the Army of the North:

> The First Army (I, VII and VIII Army Corps, 3rd Reserve Division) will garrison Metz, besiege Thionville and Montmédy, take charge of the captured army and send the prisoners off under escort of the Landwehr troops. A return of the latter is not be expected for the present, as there are no other troops momentarily available to guard the prisoners at home; other Landwehr battalions may perhaps be brought up later ... Two army corps at least of the First Army will march to the line St Quentin – Compiègne, the leading troops of which will start immediately after the capitulation has taken place.[1]

The First Army had been without a commander since the erratic and self-willed General Karl von Steinmetz, who had caused Moltke a good deal of trouble since the start of the war, had been removed and sent to become Governor of Posen. Thereafter, during the investment of Metz the several units of the army had been under the direct command of the Second Army. Now, on October 27, General of Cavalry Edwin von Manteuffel, the commander of the I Corps, was appointed to the command of the First Army as it prepared to undertake the mission laid down for it. He was an obvious choice for the command, having led his corps successfully in the battles around Metz, although he remained in the eyes of many a controversial figure.

Karl Rocher Edwin von Manteuffel was born at Magdeburg in 1809. He joined the Guards Dragoon Regiment at the age of 17. In 1848, while serving with the rank of Major as adjutant to Prince Albrecht, the brother of King Frederick William IV, he found himself during the March Days in the royal palace in Berlin. There, he impressed the King by his firmness during the disturbances, and he was thereafter always close to the monarchy. When, having reached the rank of major general, he became Chief of the Military Cabinet in 1857, he assumed a position of enormous political influence, which he applied relentlessly to the furtherance of his extreme monarchical principles. He was also head of the Personnel Division of the War Ministry, and in this position considerably enhanced the efficiency of the Prussian army by his ruthless weeding out of ineffective officers. This earned him the enmity of many of those he displaced; but he never courted popularity. Perhaps, in his personnel function, his most notable contribution to his country's history was when he recommended the appointment of Moltke as

Chief of the General Staff in 1857. His strongly monarchist principles inspired confidence in him on the part of both Russian and Austrian governments, and he was sent on a number of diplomatic missions to St Petersburg and Vienna when sensitive issues arose. He was hated by the liberal members of the Landtag for his vigorous support for Prussian army reform. His refusal to entertain any dilution of Roon's plans endeared him to King William but severely hampered the flexibility with which Bismarck when he came to power sought to manage the crisis. His repeated policy conflicts with the Minister President led ultimately to his being sidelined in 1865 when he was appointed to the position of Governor of Schleswig.

During the Austro-Prussian war in 1866 he led his division competently as part of the army under the command of General Vogel von Falckenstein, before succeeding that particularly incompetent commander when Moltke was finally asked to get rid of him. Thereafter Manteuffel led the Army of the Main to a series of victories that led to the comprehensive defeat of the Middle States.

General August Karl von Goeben, the commander of the VIII Corps, was especially well regarded by Moltke. He was born in 1816, and joined the Prussian army at the age of 17; however, after three years he became bored with peacetime soldiering and resigned his commission. He made his way to Spain to take part in the Carlist Wars there, rising

General of Cavalry Edwin von Manteuffel. (Rousset/*Histoire*)

swiftly to the rank of colonel. In the course of the four years that he spent there he was wounded five times. At the end of this period he returned to Germany; penniless, he published in 1840 an account of his adventures in Spain. In 1842 he rejoined the Prussian army. Compared to the relatively slow promotion of many of his colleagues he rose rapidly; in 1864 he successfully commanded a brigade in the Schleswig Holstein War and two years later served, like Manteuffel, as a divisional commander in the Army of the Main. He reached the rank of General of Infantry at the outset of the Franco Prussian War when he was appointed to the command of the VIII Corps.[2]

The third of the corps commanders of the First Army was General Dietrich von Zastrow, the commander of the VII Corps. Seventy years old in 1870, he was beginning to show his age. He had taken an almost entirely passive part in the battle of Spicheren, when his divisional commanders had largely taken matters into their own hands. At Gravelotte, he had acquiesced in the rash attack ordered by Steinmetz in the mistaken belief of a French retirement, a movement so foolish that Fritz Hoenig wrote that 'in short, General von Steinmetz and von Zastrow destroyed here in a few hours the whole of the glory of their great lives.'[3] It was to be the VII Corps that was assigned the less dramatic aspects of the campaign of the First Army, overseeing the transfer of French prisoners from Metz and the sieges of Thionville and Montmédy.

General August Karl von Goeben. (Rousset/*Histoire*)

The need to take action against the forces being assembled by the Government of National Defence had been evident for some time. On October 9 Goeben had written personally to Moltke, a letter which took ten days to arrive, to suggest that the forces around Metz be reduced by two corps which would be able either to strengthen the army of investment of Paris, or to operate on the Loire. Moltke wrote a characteristically thorough response to Goeben's proposal:

> Assuredly, it would be extremely advantageous for us to have another corps before Paris, for our investment line is very thin. But if, just at the moment we are not considering weakening the army of Metz, it is because, since Sedan, we reckon that it is at Metz that must be found the decisive result of the whole campaign. A successful assault by Bazaine would have much greater consequences than a partial break in our line of blockade.[4]

Moltke went on to set out in some detail the present situation as he saw it, and his strategic intention, remarking that it would be necessary to destroy quickly the resistance that was being organised at Amiens and at Rouen.

Before however it was possible to carry out this part of Moltke's strategy, the problems arising from the fall of Metz had to be dealt with. These were considerable. Hermann von Wartensleben, acting at this time as Chief of Staff of the First Army, calculated in his history of this part of the campaign the numbers required to deal with prisoners:

> As a rule, 100 prisoners require as escort 10 infantry, and one cavalry soldier. If we take this number as basis, and treble it, so as to be able to relieve guard during the period of watching the prisoners in their camps, we find that 173,000 prisoners require in round numbers 55,000 men to guard them. This was at that time the whole effective strength of the First Army, including the Landwehr.[5]

Because the effective strength of the VII Corps, and of the 3rd Reserve Division (von Kummer) which also formed part of the First Army, had been so reduced by sickness and casualties, these units were not by themselves sufficient both to garrison Metz and escort the huge number of prisoners. For the moment, therefore, the march of the First Army towards Amiens and Rouen could not begin. By the beginning of November the various units of the army were widely scattered. One division of the VII Corps garrisoned Metz and the forts. The Landwehr battalions of the 3rd Reserve Division were escorting prisoners to Saarlouis, and its Combined Brigade (von Blanckensee) was similarly occupied on the Saarbrücken route. The 60th Regiment, 8th Rifle Battalion and a company of pioneers from the VIII Corps had gone to join the siege of Verdun. The 3rd Cavalry Division was at Fresnes. On October 31 Moltke ordered that a division of the VIII Corps be sent to reinforce the troops in front of Mézières; the 1st Division (von Bentheim) was assigned to this task. The rest of the army was for the moment guarding the camps established for the prisoners; it could not set off on its mission until these had been largely cleared.[6]

The process of detaching units for other duties continued; the 4th Brigade (von Zglinitzki) was ordered to proceed to La Fère, and undertake the siege of that place. It set off on November 9, accompanied by a squadron of cavalry and a battery of corps artillery. Manteuffel, meanwhile, had been completing his plans for the departure of the First Army, and had on November 6 issued orders to Zastrow setting out his future responsibilities. These were first, to settle all security issues arising in and around Metz, then the creation of an army reserve under Major General Schuler von Senden which was to follow the First Army as soon as possible, and finally the taking of Thionville and Montmédy. The army reserve was to consist of Blanckensee's Brigade, the 3rd Reserve Hussar Regiment and the 1st Reserve Dragoon Regiment, which were to be led by Major General von Strantz; and three reserve batteries.[7]

For the coming campaign Goeben would have two very experienced divisional commanders. Leading the 15th Division was the fifty-four year old Lieutenant General Ferdinand von Kummer. His early career had followed the usual pattern of the Prussian army; he was a captain by 1848 and a major seven years later. He was promoted to colonel in 1861, when he took command of the 37th Infantry Regiment. In 1865 he became major general, and in the following year served in the Army of the Main under first, Vogel von Falckenstein, and later under Manteuffel. He was promoted to lieutenant general in 1868. In 1870 he commanded the 3rd Reserve Division during the siege of Metz with distinction, and after the fall of the fortress was provisionally appointed its governor. However, the 3rd Reserve Division was then broken up, and he was assigned to the command of the 15th Division.

Lieutenant General Ferdinand von Kummer. (Rousset/*Histoire*)

Albert Christof Gottlieb von Barnekow was born in 1809. He was 37 before he reached the rank of captain and it was not until 1852 that, promoted to major, he took command of a battalion. His slow climb to higher rank continued with his promotion to lieutenant colonel in 1858; two years later he became colonel, commanding the 68th Rhineland Infantry Regiment. During the Danish campaign of 1864, by now a major general, he commanded the 2nd Infantry Brigade; he was still leading that brigade in 1866, when it took part in the battle of Trautenau. In 1870 he became commander of the 16th Division with the rank of lieutenant general, taking part in the battles of Spicheren, Rezonville – Mars la Tour and Gravelotte – St Privat, and in the siege of Metz.

The first stage of the First Army's advance was from Metz to Rheims. Manteuffel, very conscious that the problems at Metz had delayed his departure, was determined to press on as fast as he could. He himself was to accompany the advance guard. He was, at this time, quite seriously physically handicapped, having had a fall with his horse on September 6, soon after the battle of Noisseville, in which he had fractured a bone in his foot. This had to be bandaged daily throughout the autumn and winter campaigns. As a result, Manteuffel had to use a walking stick, and could not mount his horse without assistance. In spite of this, and in spite of the fact that he was sixty-three years old, he continued to carry out almost all the marches on horseback, however long and fatiguing

Lieutenant General Albert von Barnekow. (Rousset/*Histoire*)

they were.[8] The march began on November 7. Precise instructions were issued to the units of the army for its conduct:

> The march will be performed on as broad a front as the necessity for guarding against any attacks of the enemy's free corps will permit, so that the troops may be furnished with good quarters. During the march all places will be searched for arms, which, when found, are to be confiscated. Although the greater part of the country we have to pass through has been already traversed by Prussian troops, and some points are permanently occupied, still attempts have been made to organise a partisan war, particularly in the Argonnes district. The security of the cantonments, the trains, etc, must be particularly attended to.[9]

Concern about the franc tireurs' operations in the Argonne had led to the 3rd Cavalry Division (Lieutenant General von der Groeben) being sent on ahead to deal with these. Count Georg Reinhold von der Groeben was born in 1817 into a large and well-connected military family. First lieutenant at the age of 25, he served as adjutant to Prince William in the Baden Campaign of 1849. In the following year he was made captain, serving in the 1st Garde Uhlan Regiment. Appointed *Flügeladjutant* to King Frederick William, he reached the rank of major in 1855; was commander of the 3rd Hussar Regiment in 1858; and next year was a lieutenant colonel. It was not a meteoric rise; but it was relatively brisk, and no doubt owed something to his proximity to the Royal family. In 1861 he was promoted to colonel, and was *Flügeladjutant* to King William in 1864; next year he was major general. In 1866 he commanded a cavalry brigade at Königgrätz, and at the outbreak of war in 1870 he took command of the 3rd Cavalry Division with the rank of Lieutenant General. Meanwhile the surrender of Verdun had relieved the First Army of one at least of its many responsibilities, and made available to it for further operations the troops which had been detached there.

Sir Randal Roberts, who had been accompanying the headquarters of the First Army as an observer since the start of the campaign, was, as always, impressed by the efficiency with which quarters were found for him with the staff. At Varennes, where he went to inspect the house in which Louis XVI had been seized in 1791, he found that his quarters had been temporarily occupied by a number of his colleagues:

> Upon my return, my room was a picture which Maxwell would have liked to draw with his imaginative pen. The staff of Manteuffel and von Goeben were there, sitting upon beds, washstands, chairs, stools – in fact on everything on which it was possible to sit. We were in the land of champagne – why should we not drink the vintage of the neighbourhood? And we did it. 200 francs was the little bill which welcomed us into the heart of France. Delightful was it – while it lasted.[10]

As Roberts looked out of his window, however, there was a foretaste of the hardships to come; snow had begun to fall in thick heavy flakes.

The I Corps was to take the road to Réthel, and thence via Laon towards St Quentin; the VIII Corps was to march by Étain, around Verdun and then by Rheims and Soissons to Compiègne. Von der Groeben's cavalry was to keep between them and half a day's march ahead. The intention was to reach the line Réthel – Rheims by November 16 and St Quentin – Compiègne by November 22. Although advancing on a broad front, after reaching Reims the army had to be ready to concentrate rapidly if occasion arose. In addition, Moltke had ordered that as the First and Second Armies moved away from Metz they should relieve the Landwehr troops that had been covering them, so that the latter could assume *Etappen* and garrison duties.[11] Although Verdun had fallen, the First Army still had to deal with Mézières, and also La Fère.

The country along the Meuse which the First Army must now advance was gradually becoming more hilly:

> At a short distance from the left bank of the river rise the wooded heights of the Argonnes, in several parallel ranges of hills, filling the space between the rivers Meuse and Aisne. The woods are of beech and oak, with, for the most part, dense undergrowths, and were on November 11 sprinkled with the first fall of snow. The roads crossing the mountain country are good, and, as is everywhere the case in France, macadamised, but lead mostly through long defiles, without crossroads. The Argonnes, therefore, form an impediment well known in military history – that is to say, supposing forces to be at hand on the plains westward of the forest, ready to fall upon the heads of the columns when they debouch from the mountainous and wooded district. There was no chance of this during the march of the First Army, so that the beauties of this landscape, which were perceptible even in the month of November, could be fully enjoyed.[12]

Meanwhile the army reserve under Senden had been assembled and was ready to start after the army. This gave Manteuffel the opportunity to relieve Bentheim's 1st Division from its commitment before Mézières; Senden's detachment, weaker in infantry but stronger in cavalry than the 1st Division, was better fitted to act as a corps of observation of the triangle of fortresses Mézières – Rocroi – Givet, which was all for the moment that was required. On November 14, therefore, Manteuffel placed Senden under Zastrow's orders for this purpose. He was explicit about what was to be done about Mézières:

> The siege of the fortress of Mézières must not be commenced until means sufficient to ensure success have arrived and can be brought to bear on it. Until this is the case I forbid any half-measures, such as bombarding the town and the like, which only cause loss of life and destruction of property, without obtaining any military result.[13]

Bentheim, to whom this order was sent, was instructed to pass it on to Senden. The forces in front of Mézières were for the moment to confine themselves to covering the First Army's right flank and its communications, and protecting the siege park and other matériel as it successively arrived.

On November 15 and 16 Zglinitzki invested La Fère on both banks of the River Oise. La Fère was found to be garrisoned by some 2,000 troops, under the command of naval Captain Planche, who clearly intended to put up a fight to defend it. As the 4th Brigade deployed, it came under a heavy but largely ineffectual fire from the fortress; siege operations were delayed because the siege train could not yet be brought up from Soissons. This was to come by road; however, all the German armies in France were heavily dependent for supplies and munitions upon the railways, and it was necessary for the Royal Headquarters to issue stern instructions as to their use, proportionate to each army's actual needs.

The other commitments of the First Army obliged Manteuffel somewhat to revise his plans for the continued advance. On November 16 he issued orders for the advance to the River Oise, directing that the right wing was not as originally intended to extend as far as St Quentin but only to Guiscard. The 3rd Brigade was to pass to the South of La Fère, reaching Noyon by November 21, from where it was to send forward patrols towards Amiens. Meanwhile Goeben's VIII Corps was to advance from Reims to reach Compiègne on the same day. It was to push forward advance guards towards Montdidier and Beauvais, and also establish contact with the rear areas of the Army of the Meuse around the north of Paris. On the right flank of the army, von der Groeben's 3rd Cavalry Division, reinforced by the 8th Rifle Battalion and a horse artillery battery from the VIII Corps, was to occupy Guiscard, and reconnoitre towards both Amiens and St Quentin.[14]

Roberts described the arrival of the headquarters staff of the VIII Corps at the imperial palace of Compiègne on November 21:

> At one o'clock General von Goeben and his staff rode into the palace-yard. Dismounting from our horses, we ascended the great staircase in the centre of the quadrangle, and entered the magnificent hall, embellished by those two grand efforts of the Prince de Talhouët. His Excellency's staff occupied the left, that of General Manteuffel the right, wing of the palace. In the centre are the chambers of audience, the magnificent ballroom, the famous Don Quixote gallery, and the imperial apartments. The last were unoccupied and remained only open to view. Every care had been taken of the furniture and other belongings, and not a single article had been damaged in any way.[15]

The immediate objective for the First Army had been laid down by Moltke in an order received on November 20:

> The command of the army is hereby informed that His Majesty the King, approving of the operations hitherto carried out, has been pleased to command that the First Army continue its advance from the line Compiègne – Noyon, in the direction of Rouen. Whether or not, in so doing, the main forces of the army follow the Amiens road, will depend whether the considerable forces of the enemy (about 18,000 men), said to be assembling in that neighbourhood, remain there, or, as is most likely, retreat on the advance of the First Army. At all events Amiens is of itself sufficiently important a place to justify its being occupied, and held by a strong detachment in either case.[16]

This was the first reference by Moltke to the size of the 'considerable forces' in the north available to the French with which to oppose Manteuffel's advance. He was now beginning to receive a good deal of intelligence as to their strength, although obviously not their intentions.

It seemed to Manteuffel that although given the green light for offensive operations against the Army of the North, it was not necessary to embark on these immediately. His troops were exhausted by the long marches from Metz; a number of detachments could now be brought up to join the main body; and it would be as well to undertake further cavalry reconnaissance to discover what and where the French forces actually were. For all these reasons he gave the army a break, indicating that for the moment he did not expect to resume his advance beyond the Oise before November 24. The VIII Corps was concentrated around Compiègne, while the bulk of the I Corps was in quarters in and around Noyon. Manteuffel had hitherto retained direct command of the I Corps, but he now handed this over to Bentheim, who was succeeded in command of the 1st Division by Major General von Falkenstein.[17] Lieutenant General Georg Ferdinand von Bentheim was born in 1807. He was aged forty before he reached the rank of captain. He took part in the First Schleswig War; he became major and second in command of a Guard Landwehr battalion in 1852. Five years later he was promoted to lieutenant colonel and in 1859 reached the rank of Colonel. He fought throughout the Danish war of 1864, and was wounded in the storming of Düppel. After the war he was promoted to major general. In 1866 he had the command of a combined Landwehr infantry division. Following this he took command of the 1st Division, with the rank of lieutenant general, and he held this post until he was now appointed to lead the I Corps.

Lieutenant General Georg Ferdinand von Bentheim. (Rousset/*Histoire*)

Wartensleben described the terrain now entered by the First Army:

> The country between the Aisne and the Oise is covered for many miles by the dense forest of Compiègne, which is bounded on the east by the valley of Pierrefonds, with the spa of the same name, and an imperial castle, perched on a high rocky ledge, and rebuilt after the plan of a castle destroyed in the time of Richelieu. Between this remarkably picturesque spot and Compiègne reigns the deep solitude of the dark forest. This wood is intersected by broad avenues which cross a central hill, from the summit of which anyone looking westwards beholds the imperial palace of Compiègne at his feet, and beyond it, on the other bank of the Oise, the ancient county of Picardy.[18]

The total strength of the First Army at this point, including the 1st Division which was arriving from Mézières and the 4th Brigade which was still before La Fère, amounted to 38,244 infantry, 4,433 cavalry and 180 guns.[19] While the army was taking its breather, von der Groeben's cavalry had moved forward in the direction of Amiens. Reports from its patrols suggested that the French had concentrated some 17,000 men in the city. These included the garrison of Ham, some 1,500 strong, which had evacuated that town on von der Groeben's approach. The cavalry had been picking up all sorts of rumours as to the French intentions, including contradictory reports as to whether Bourbaki was still in command; one story, that it was not intended seriously to defend Amiens but retreat on Lille was, in the light of other reports, dismissed as very unlikely.

The order from Tours relieving Bourbaki from his command had named General Louis Léon Faidherbe as his successor. Born in 1818 in Lille, Faidherbe joined the engineers and was posted to Algeria. After a spell working on Fort Josephine, in Guadeloupe, he returned to Africa in 1850. He became Deputy Director of Engineers in Senegal, where he led a number of expeditions against hostile native tribes before becoming Governor of the colony in 1854, where he was responsible for the construction of the port of Dakar and much of the supporting infrastructure. Ill health led to his giving up the post in 1860 but after two years in Algeria he returned to Senegal as Governor. Again, however, ill health drove him from the post, and he took up the command of a division in Algeria. In July 1870, while on sick leave at Lille, he applied to join the Army of the Rhine; he was, however, known to be a strong republican, and he was sent back to Algeria. He was still there when he received the order assigning him to the Army of the North, and he at once made his way to Tours to meet Gambetta, who told him: 'You have carte blanche. Do your best for France, for the Republic!' Faidherbe, already having been put in the picture as to the general situation, replied, somewhat doubtfully: 'I will do my best.'[20] To do his best required a major physical effort. His health was quite broken down, and he was perpetually wracked with fever, and constantly exhausted. He was often obliged to go to bed at 5.00pm and to rise again at midnight to dictate his orders.[21]

It would not be until December 4, however, that Faidherbe would arrive to take up his command, and in the meantime Farre had to do the best he could. Having lost a lot of his staff when Bourbaki left, Farre had been fortunate to find in Lieutenant Colonel de Villenoisy, another engineer, an officer who gave him loyal and efficient support.

Mamès Cosseron de Villenoisy was an engineer officer of strong personality. Born in 1821, he had served in Algeria and at the siege of Sebastapol. In 1869 he had the temerity

General Faidherbe. (Pflug-Harttung)

to co-author a paper criticising the fortification theories of the renowned Belgian engineer Henri Brialmont, to which the latter delivered a thunderous response. In 1870, when war broke out, Villenoisy was serving as professor of fortification in the officers' school at Metz. Following the surrender of the fortress he was determined not to be taken prisoner and escaped on foot, dressed as a civilian, and made his way via Luxembourg to Brussels. There, he published anonymously four articles denouncing Bazaine's capitulation, before making his way to Lille to join the staff of the nascent Army of the North.

Lecointe, too, proved to be a tower of strength, and he was promoted to general. Alongside his 1st Brigade of the 1st Division was the 2nd Brigade, led by Colonel Derroja. Farre also had available the 1st Brigade of the 2nd Division under Colonel du Bessol.

Both brigade commanders were among those that had escaped from Metz. Jean Barthelemy Xavier Derroja, born in 1822, had seen a good deal of service in a military career that included North Africa and the occupation of Rome, after which he reached the rank of captain. In the Italian Campaign of 1859 he fought at Robechetto, Magenta and Solferino. As a lieutenant colonel he commanded an infantry regiment in the 4th Corps in 1870 at the battles of Borny, Rezonville – Mars la Tour and Gravelotte – St Privat and later at Servigny and Noisseville. He escaped from Metz at the time of the capitulation, and made his way through Belgium to Lille. He was first appointed Commandant of Cambrai before becoming a brigade commander.[22]

Joseph Arthur Dufaure du Bessol had followed a very similar path. Born in 1828, he began his career with the Foreign Legion. He distinguished himself during the Siege of Sebastopol after which he returned as captain to North Africa. He then took part in the

Italian Campaign in the Imperial Guard and then went as part of the ill-fated expedition to Mexico. In 1870 he was seriously wounded at the battle of Rezonville – Mars la Tour, and later served during the siege of Metz where he reached the rank of lieutenant colonel. He escaped from Metz at the capitulation, after first burning his regiment's colours, and arrived in Lille via Belgium, where he was given the command of a regiment du marche before being appointed to his brigade.[23]

The 2nd Brigade of the 2nd Division was still in the course of formation, commanded by Colonel Rittier. Its Chasseur battalion and two other newly formed battalions were sent from Lille and Arras to cover the Somme crossings between Péronne and Corbie together with two heavy batteries. Farre was, as has been seen, especially weak in cavalry, having only two squadrons of dragoons and two squadrons of gendarmes. He had six batteries (four of which were equipped with 4-pounders and two with 12-pounders); at the last minute he was joined by another 12-pounder battery. There was one engineer company. The whole amounted to 17,500 men, but he could also count on the garrison of Amiens under General Paulze d'Ivoy which provided another 8,000 together with 12 heavy guns.[24]

Pondering the reports sent in by his cavalry, it appeared to Manteuffel and his staff that the situation did now call for an immediate advance on Amiens, in order to break through the centre of the forces which the French were evidently concentrating there. In addition to the military considerations, there was also a political dimension to be taken into account. The battle of Coulmiers, and the retreat from Orleans which followed, had increased French self-confidence enormously, and in the last couple of weeks there had been no significant counter measures taken by the German forces. There was some concern that this might have some influence on the attitude of the neutral powers, so a decisive blow at Amiens just now might be very useful.

By the afternoon of November 23 Manteuffel had made up his mind to strike at Amiens at once, without waiting to complete the concentration of his army. The rest of the 1st Division ought in any case to come up soon. Accordingly he issued orders at once that the VIII Corps should advance to Montdidier and be in position there by November 25. By the same day the I Corps was to echelon all its troops between Noyon and Roye, bringing up its later arrivals through Noyon. Roye, which was to be occupied, was to form the right wing of the army. Meanwhile the 3rd Cavalry Division was to maintain a garrison at Ham, and cover the right flank, while breaking up all the railways radiating from Amiens. By November 25 the bulk of the division was to be at Moreuil.[25]

3

The Battle of Amiens

The country which the First Army was now entering would of course become acutely familiar to the British and German Armies in 1916. Wartensleben described its principal features:

> The district between the Oise and the ocean, the Somme and the Epte – ancient Picardy – is a highly cultivated hilly country, crossed in all directions by good roads, and containing numerous towns, villages and other localities. The woods mostly consist only of small patches. The sweeping undulations of the ground which intervene between the different streams, form in many cases broad open plateaus, easy to be overlooked. This is especially the case with the plateau of Sains and Dury, between the Noye and the Celle, in the immediate neighbourhood of Amiens, which town lies at the foot of the plateau, and is completely commanded by it. On the other hand, Picardy is intersected by numerous watercourses, which, from the nature of the adjoining country, bear the type of military positions. The most important one of these is the River Somme, which rises in the neighbourhood of St Quentin. This river is for the most part accompanied by a broad tract of swampy meadowland, and canalisation has divided it into several channels, which sweep in a bend southwards past Ham and Péronne, and then flow past Corbie and Amiens to the ocean.[1]

Tributaries of the Somme rising in the south, such as the Avre, the Noye and the Celle tend to be separated by heights which are steeper and more wooded, and come together near Amiens, so that the intervening country spreads out from the town, making difficult the co-operation of different columns approaching Amiens from the south.

Amiens itself was an extremely wealthy city of some 62,000 inhabitants; its economy was based on linen and woollen goods. It had broad and handsome streets and squares. Its ancient walls had long since become promenades, and the only part of the fortification which remained was the citadel, a bastioned pentagon in design, the north front of which was particularly strong. To the south of the city a connected chain of entrenchments had been constructed, running from the valley of the River Celle below Salouel in a curve as far as a point on the height above the village of Cagny on the River Avre. The strength of these fortifications was later a matter of some dispute. Faidherbe noted that although they were well placed they were incomplete and their profiles were low and their extent enormous. On the other hand, Captain Seton, who accompanied the First Army throughout its campaign, noted that they 'were for the purpose of covering artillery and infantry, as also for sweeping the ground in front, both thick and commanding, though the exterior slopes were hardly, if at all, scarped.'[2] This position was defended by the 8,000 troops of the Amiens garrison under Paulze d'Ivoy. Advanced posts were thrown forward towards Hébecourt.³ Farre posted four battalions of Derroja's brigade at Boves and St Nicholas, with the Chasseur battalion in a forward position at Fouencamps and the remaining two battalions in reserve at Longueau, halfway between Boves and Amiens. Further east the brigade of Bessol occupied the villages of Gentelles, Cachy and Villers-Bretonneux. Lecointe's brigade for the moment remained in the city. It was in these positions that Farre awaited the advance of the enemy.⁴

Meanwhile the First Army had continued its march. While the main body was moving forward, on November 23 a detachment of the 3rd Cavalry Division had a brisk engagement at Quesnel, where the 14th Lancer Regiment, a company of rifles and two guns encountered two companies of gardes mobiles. It soon chased the enemy out of the village and pursued them as far as Hourges, in the direction of Amiens. Next morning, the advanced guard of the detachment, consisting of one squadron and a party of riflemen was attacked by about 1,000 gardes mobiles. Colonel Lüderitz, the commander of the detachment, brought up the rest of the rifle company, which held the village until three French battalions advanced on it, supported by a further three battalions and some artillery. Heavily outnumbered, Lüderitz fell back through Quesnel to Bouchoir. Von der Groeben sent forward reinforcements to cover his retreat, and as night fell he had restored the position. Lüderitz lost 24 men in this encounter.

Lieutenant General Paulze d'Ivoy. (Rousset/*Histoire*)

Prussian Jäger at Quesnel, November 23. (Hiltl)

That night, as Manteuffel digested the news of this, he received intelligence from Berlin to the effect that the French had concentrated some 46,000 men around Amiens, with 42 guns, which if true meant that he would be outnumbered. For the moment, however, he did not, however, consider that it justified any change of plan, and on November 25 the main body of the First Army reached the line Roye – Breteuil. Only the 3rd Brigade from the I Corps had so far come up to Roye; other units were echeloned back as far as Noyon and beyond, and much of the infantry would not reach the Oise before November 27.[5]

As the cavalry patrols continued to probe forward it was found on the morning of November 25 that the enemy was still in possession of Moreuil; it was also reported that the French, with both infantry and artillery were at Boves, Gentelles, Cachy and Villers-Bretonneux, firmly holding the country between the Luce and the Somme. Von der Groeben, riding forward with his advance guard, concluded that his force was not strong enough to hold his ground in the face of the strong French force at Moreuil; he stationed his main body at Quesnel, and his advance guard on the ridge between Beaucourt and Fresnoy. Meanwhile the right wing of the VIII Corps had moved beyond Montdidier, driving back into Moreuil the enemy troops encountered to the south of that place. On Goeben's left flank the 16th Division had reached Rocquencourt and Breteuil.[6]

It so happened that on the afternoon of November 25 Goeben was himself in Montdidier. Asked by Manteuffel for his opinion as to the action to be taken, Goeben unhesitatingly argued for an immediate advance on Amiens. Wartensleben, too, was strongly in favour, and at 8.30 pm that night Manteuffel issued the necessary orders.

The VIII Corps was to push the 15th Division forward to Ailly and, with the left flank detachment, towards the cross roads at Essertaux. Meanwhile the advanced units of the I Corps were to move up to Quesnel, with the corps artillery behind at Bouchoir. The rest of the 1st Division, as it came up, was to assemble at Roye. Von der Groeben was to command the right wing until Bentheim arrived. The 3rd Cavalry Division was to continue to operate against the railways in the French flank and rear.[7]

During November 26 there was sporadic fighting as some of the advancing units of the First Army made contact with the enemy. The VIII Corps reached its objectives for the day without meeting any resistance, although in the late afternoon, probing beyond Moreuil, the 30th Infantry Brigade encountered weak detachments of the French which retired along the Avre. Other contacts were made at St Nicholas, Domart and Hangard, where a succession of attacks by French infantry were driven back. On the right, the leading units of the 3rd Infantry Brigade moved on through Le Quesnel to Cayeux, while other units of the I Corps were arriving between Bouchoir and Coucy. Patrols of the 3rd Cavalry Division reached Caix, with the main body at Rosières. Reconnaissance had shown that the French were in some strength to the north of the Somme.[8]

It seemed clear to Manteuffel and his staff that the French would limit their action to the defence of Amiens, and he decided to shorten his line by moving closer to the French position on November 27. He certainly did not anticipate that a battle would be fought on that day, since he intended to await the arrival of the main body of the I Corps.[9] The I Corps was to close up to the Luce, while the 3rd Cavalry Division (now put under Bentheim's orders) was to reconnoitre to the north of the river. The VIII Corps was to take up a position between the Noye and the Celle and with its advanced guard watch the enemy around Fouencamps and Hébecourt.[10]

As General Palat, who wrote under the pseudonym Pierre Lehautcourt, pointed out, the First Army was much more widely scattered than its opponent. In addition, when making his dispositions, Manteuffel was not well informed about the position taken up by the enemy:

> These dispositions meant that a general action was brought on a day earlier than Manteuffel would have wished. Our troops were further advanced from Amiens than he supposed from the erroneous reports provided by his cavalry, in spite of their large numbers. On the other hand General Farre was exactly informed of the dispositions of the enemy. The mayors of the places around took the greatest trouble to keep him well informed.[11]

Receiving reports that franc-tireurs had been seen in the villages of Hailles and Gentelles, either side of the road to Amiens, Goeben decided to go and see for himself, as Sir Randal Roberts reported:

> With the King's hussars in front, and patrols from the same regiment thrown out on both flanks, we advanced at a good trot. We had just got as far as the village of Thennes, when the patrol to our left flank received fire from a small wood on the other side of the River Noye, a branch of the Somme. Then came a halt, and glasses were put into requisition; but the mist hung so thick upon the hills, that it was impossible to make out anything. Just then an orderly galloped up to say

that the village of Hailles, some three-quarters of a mile to our left front, was held by a battalion of chasseurs à pied. The mist at this moment cleared away, and we perceived a body of men retreating upon Hailles along the ridge of the mountain on the other side of the river.[12]

Roberts also recorded that when the Prussian troops approached Hailles, the inhabitants waved white flags, but when the unsuspecting troops advanced, fire was opened on them from the houses, inflicting a number of casualties; Roberts remarked of this incident that his experience of franc-tireurs was anything but pleasant, and that they were capable of 'any atrocity he or they may see fit.'

On November 27 the direction taken by Goeben on the left and Bentheim on the right meant that the two wings of the army were effectively separated by the marshy valley of the River Avre, so that the ensuing battle was effectively fought in two distinct actions. Manteuffel's original intention for the conduct of the battle was that Bentheim should take up a position between Thézy and Démuin on the River Luce. However, as the advance guard of the I Corps moved forward along the Amiens road from Quesnel and Bouchoir, it reported French concentrations at Gentelles, Cachy and Marcelcave, while the woods of Domart and Hangard appeared to be occupied. On the other hand there appeared to be no enemy units on either side of the Amiens road beyond Domart, and as it developed, Bentheim's advance swung more and more to its right towards Cachy and Marcelcave. Meanwhile on the left the VIII Corps was advancing between the Noye and the Celle. This widened the space between the two corps so that in the German centre at Thennes, on the right of which Manteuffel and his staff had taken up their position, there was now a gap which should have been filled by the left flank of the I Corps.

The advanced guard of the I Corps was led by von Pritzelwitz, the commander of the 2nd Division, and consisted of the six battalions of the 3rd Brigade, with three squadrons and two batteries. Pritzelwitz reached the Luce at about 10am. Advancing in three columns, he pushed forward the 4th Regiment towards Domart and the 44th Regiment towards Hangard. The 4th Regiment soon cleared the Bois de Domant of the enemy, and moved on Gentelles. There a French chasseur battalion was posted which opened a brisk fire. It was, however, obliged to retreat to Cachy when the 5th Heavy Battery came up, unlimbered in a clearing, and opened fire on Gentelles. The fusilier battalion of the 4th Regiment occupied the village and took up a position along its north-eastern edge, facing towards Cachy. Meanwhile a squadron of the 10th Dragoon Regiment trotted forward along the main road to Amiens to reconnoitre, although it encountered no sign of the enemy there. The French troops facing Pritzelwitz were from Bessol's 3rd Brigade; Farre intended that they should be supported by Lecointe's 1st Brigade, which had spent the night in Amiens before moving up to the front.

On the right a rigorous engagement had begun in the Bois de Hangard, into which Bessol had advanced from Cachy. His progress was halted by the 44th Regiment under Major Dallmer, which occupied the eastern portion of the wood towards Démuin and then pushed forward through the Bois de Morgemont, leaving one battalion in the Bois de Hangard. As it did so it encountered strong bodies of the enemy on the road between Marcelcave and Cachy, and particularly along the railway embankment near Villers-Bretonneux. There, a redoubt had been constructed, together with a line

THE BATTLE OF AMIENS 43

A view of the Hangard woods from the German positions. (Duncan Rogers)

The village of Hangard from the French positions. (Duncan Rogers)

The Battle of Amiens. To the left is the Prussian 44th Infantry Regiment, to the right are guns from the Prussian 7th and 8th Field Artillery regiments. Villers-Bretonneux can be seen in the background. (Hiltl)

of entrenchments covering the railway. After extending his line Dallmer launched an attack, as described by the Official History:

> The 44th advancing by rushes approached to within 300 paces of the enemy's left flank, and then, after a brisk file-fire, dashed from all sides with a cheer upon the entrenchments, during which movement the left flank company further west made its way towards the railway embankment. After a short but embittered hand to hand struggle, the French retreated, followed by the fire of the victors, who, in view of the hostile masses assembled at Villers-Bretonneux, at once arranged the captured position for defence, and brought the 6th Light Battery into action to the east of it.[13]

Lecointe's brigade was by now moving into action, and Pritzelwitz's advanced guard, which was stretched in a line nearly five miles in length, was facing mounting pressure as the French attempted to recapture their lost ground. Manteuffel, who had been monitoring the progress of the I Corps from the heights above Thennes, moved forward to a point south of Gentelles. This brought his headquarters staff further into the space between the I and the VIII Corps. It looked to Manteuffel that at this point the lack of troops in the centre of his position might enable the French to seize the opportunity of pushing forward from the Bois de Gentelles and capturing the crossing over the Luce at Thennes:

> It seemed necessary at all events to show some troops here also, in order to hide this state of affairs from the enemy. Accompanied by his whole staff, and sending

THE BATTLE OF AMIENS 45

French attack on the Bois de Hangard, by Pallandre. (Rousset/*Les Combattants*)

The Prussian 44th Infantry Regiment storms the railway embankment near Villers Bretonneux during the Battle of Amiens, by Amling. (Fehleisen)

The railway cutting at Villers-Bretonneux. (Duncan Rogers)

forward hussar patrols in all directions, General Manteuffel therefore ascended the plateau north of the Luce. He kept his station here from midday upon a conspicuous height between the two high roads leading to Amiens and opposite to the wood of Gentelles. In order still further to conceal the weakness of the centre, the battalion of the 28th Regiment was also brought forward and stationed in a neighbouring dell. A slow skirmishing fire was sustained with the enemy in the Gentelles wood, the latter returning the fire at first only feebly but afterwards with much vigour.[14]

Several casualties were sustained among the headquarters staff, and Major Koppelow, the battalion commander, was among the wounded. At about noon, also anxious about the threat to the left of the I Corps, Manteuffel sent an appeal to Goeben to assist, if possible, by sending forward reinforcements through Fouencamps.[15] Goeben was, however, obliged to reply that for the moment all his troops were now engaged.

For a while a stalemate existed in this part of the battlefield, and it seemed that the action might be coming to an end. However, the deployment of Lecointe's brigade, together with several batteries in support, enabled the French, who still held Cachy, to renew their attacks with such force that at about 3.00 they re-entered Gentelles, the garrison of which was running out of ammunition. The two battalions of the 44th Regiment which had been in support to the east of the village had moved somewhat to their right. A fierce artillery exchange followed, in which the newly arrived French batteries were engaged by four batteries of Bentheim's Corps artillery to the east of the Bois de Hangard. In addition, two horse artillery batteries, located to the north of Domart, came into action, and the further advance of the French infantry was stalled. The order to evacuate Gentelles did not reach all the German units, and an officer and 16 men were captured there, and triumphantly carried off to the citadel at Amiens.[16]

In the centre, the French advance again seriously threatened Manteuffel and his staff:

> Late in the afternoon, when the enemy began to press upon the left wing of the 3rd Brigade, the general was in some danger of being cut off from the bridge at Thennes, and of being forced back upon the almost impassable Avre. He therefore withdrew shortly before twilight set in to the windmill hill south of Thennes, followed by his escort, the infantry of which occupied the passage over the Luce, whilst the hussars held their ground on the other side of the stream for some time, though often pressed by the enemy.[17]

At about 3.30 Lieutenant Colonel von Hüllesheim, with the three battalions of the 41st Regiment and one squadron and one battery of the 1st Brigade, arrived on the battlefield; Bentheim directed him to occupy Domart and Thennes. He moved two battalions of Colonel von Massow's 1st Grenadier Regiment to the east of the Bois de Hangard, principally to cover the corps artillery. They drove the French from a small copse in front of the wood, and then, supported by the 2nd Heavy Battery, stormed the left flank of the earthworks at Villers Bretonneux. Simultaneously detachments advanced against the position from the Bois de Hangard; with loud cheers and drums beating all the German troops in this part of the field charged towards Villers-Bretonneux, and the French fell back in disorder towards the Somme at Corbie. In Villers-Bretonneux 9 officers and 320 men unwounded were taken prisoner, together with about 800 wounded.[18]

A view from 'Manteuffel's windmill' at Thennes. (Duncan Rogers)

Further to the right, von der Groeben's 3rd Cavalry Division had reached Bayonvillers at about 8 am, with its advanced guard at Lamotte-Warfusée, to the east of Villers Bretonneux along the Roman road to St Quentin. Patrols were sent forward to reconnoitre the Somme crossings between Corbie and Bray. These were held by units of the 75th Regiment which had been sent down from Lille. Léonce Patry, whose battalion had been leading a rather pleasant garrison life in the city, recorded the bewilderment of the officers when they were roused at 1.00 am on the morning of November 27 and loaded with another battalion on to trains to Albert, which they reached at about 6.00 am before marching to Bray. Here they passed a peaceful afternoon listening to gunfire coming from the south. Major Tramond, in command of the two battalions, was intensely frustrated, seething at not being able to march towards the sound of the guns:

> He had strict orders to guard the passage of the Somme between Corbie and Péronne very closely with his two battalions. Joining him on the high ground, we listened without seeing anything, straining every fibre of our being towards this sound which seemed stationary. But we could not make even a light reconnaissance to inform ourselves about the fighting on the far bank because the bridge over the Somme had been destroyed several days ago.[19]

While Bentheim's I Corps had, ultimately, got the better of the brigades of Bessol and Lecointe, Goeben's 15th Division (Kummer) had been engaged with Derroja's 2nd Brigade and the 16th Division (Barnekow) advanced on the Amiens garrison under Paulze d'Ivoy. The operations of the two divisions were themselves almost entirely separated, as Goeben himself pointed out; overall the extended line of the First Army was

Prussian artillery at the Battle of Amiens, by Pallandre. (Rousset/*Les Combattants*)

almost 15 miles long with the result that inevitably at various points in its length the Germans were extremely thin on the ground.[20]

Paulze d'Ivoy, having occupied the entrenchments south of Amiens, pushed forward advanced patrols as far as St Sauflieu, where they were encountered early on November 27 by the leading units of the 32nd Brigade (Colonel Beyer von Kargow) from Barnekow's division, which drove them back to Hébécourt. The brigade had been advancing in two columns, on the left from Essertaux through St Sauflieu and on the right through Rumigny. It now aimed to attack the French in Hébécourt, where several battalions of chasseurs were in position in and on either side of the village and in a copse to the rear. The inhabitants also took part in the ensuing fighting as the 32nd Brigade forced its way into the village and the copse, and drove the defenders northward. Barnekow pushed on through Dury; to the north of the village he found himself facing a strongly fortified position consisting of carefully constructed entrenched batteries connected by rifle pits. From this position the French kept up a vigorous rifle fire and, soon after, heavy fire from the batteries. Barnekow moved close up to the position, two companies of the 70th Regiment carrying a cemetery at the point of the bayonet only 300 yards from the French line, but thereafter settled down for the night, remaining in occupation of Dury and the cemetery.[21]

Goeben and his staff had been accompanying the advance of their right wing, the 15th Division under Lieutenant General von Kummer. The advanced guard of the division, the 30th Brigade (Major General von Strubberg) had assembled early in the

The Füsilier Battalion of the Prussian 70th Infantry storms the churchyard at Dury during the Battle of Amiens, by Röchling. (Lindner)

The monument to the Prussian 70th Infantry Regiment at Dury. (Duncan Rogers)

morning of November 27 at Hailles, from where two battalions of the 28th Regiment (Colonel von Rosenszweig) were dispatched as outposts to Fouencamps; the rest of the brigade was posted to the east of Dommartin. A company reconnoitring beyond that village ran into several battalions of Derroja's brigade. The 28th Regiment deployed, and Strubberg brought up artillery from Dommartin together with 68th Regiment (Colonel von Sommerfeld). The fire of the German guns caused the French to evacuate Le Paraclet Farm, in which they had taken up a position; this was promptly occupied by the 68th Regiment, which also seized the crossing over the Noye at Cottenchy.

At this point Strubberg learned of the situation facing the I Corps, and of the request for support made by Manteuffel, and he decided to advance, at about 1.00 pm, upon Boves and St Nicholas. He reinforced his right with the fusilier battalion and the two companies holding Le Paraclet with the 2nd Battalion of the 68th Regiment. Supported by the guns of the 2nd Heavy Battery, the brigade advanced and at 2.30 pm, with drums beating, stormed the village of St Nicholas. Strubberg's left wing moved on Boves, and from there established connection with the 29th Brigade (Colonel von Bock).[22]

Bock had advanced during the morning from a point between Moreuil and Ailly, encountering no opposition. Having reached Sains, at about 1.00 pm he pushed forward two battalions towards St Fuscien. It was at this point that Goeben and Kummer received news of Strubberg's progress, which was confirmed by the roar of artillery from that direction. Goeben had by now also received news of Barnekow's success on the left:

German Uhlans at the Battle of Amiens, by Knötel. (Pflug-Harttung)

> With a smile of his face, the general rode forward until he came opposite the French position, whence we could see the French troops retiring upon Boves before General Strubberg from the wooded ground about St Nicholas. Here the staff awaited the advance of the troops. The 33rd Regiment – that is to say, two battalions – marched forward to the ravine between St Nicholas and Boves, to storm the village and French position.[23]

Within half an hour the French were driven from their position, heavily shelled by the German artillery as they fell back down the road to Amiens.

Roberts later received a first hand account of the attack of the 33rd Regiment on Boves:

> It appears that an English officer witnessed it from the French side, having taken up his position in a church tower in rear of Boves. He told me that when he saw the regiment advancing he never witnessed anything so fine in his life. They only wanted red coats to make them an English regiment; and when they stormed the position and drove the French into the village, and from that in the Amiens road, forgetting the lofty observatory in which he stood, he took off his hat and threw it into the air, and had consequently to trudge back into the town without one.[24]

As night had fallen, Goeben, having carefully reconnoitred the French positions, rode back to St Sauflieu. It was far from clear to him whether the French intended to make a further stand in front of Amiens, and that night he rode over to Moreuil to see Manteuffel, whose headquarters were in the magnificent chateau of the Comte du Plessis. Here he learned that a report had been received early in the evening from Zglinitzky to the effect that La Fère had capitulated that same day. The night was wet and windy, and the staff had had great difficulty in reading reports as they came in, 'by the help of lucifer matches lighted under shelter of the windmill.'[25] It was still not apparent to Manteuffel and Goeben that the French would abandon Amiens, although reports from the right wing arrived during the night with news of the victory at Villers Bretonneux. It was Goeben's view that the French position on the Dury plateau could be taken, if at all, only with a very heavy loss. To attempt to do so would be inexcusable, and the orders issued by Manteuffel were accordingly very circumspect. Back at St Sauflieu Sir Randal Roberts reflected gloomily as to arrangements for the following day, fearing that daylight would 'usher in another day of blood and massacre.'[26]

4

La Fère

There was, however, to be no further defence of Amiens. Farre himself, who had gone to Corbie when his troops retreated, had every intention of renewing the battle on the following day. However, that night a council of war was held in the city attended, among others, by Lecointe, Derroja, Villenoisy, Bessol, Charon and Paulze d'Ivoy. With the exception of the last named, all were in favour of a retreat, and these opinions were telegraphed to Farre. After a long period of deliberation, he reluctantly acquiesced, and gave the necessary orders.[1]

The prefect of the Somme Department issued an apologetic proclamation to the population:

> Citizens: The day of trial has come. In spite of the incessant efforts made by me for three months, to the feeble extent of my means of action, the chief town of the department falls in its turn into the hands of the enemy. The council of superior officers has just determined on the retreat of the Army of the North and the disarmament of the national guard. I am absolutely obliged to leave you, but in the firmest hope of an early return. Calmness and confidence! France will be saved. Vive la France! Vive la République!
> (Signed) The Prefect of La Somme, J Lardiere, Amiens, November 28, 1870

This left the unfortunate Mayor of Amiens holding the baby, and, evidently unimpressed with M. Lardiere's effort, he immediately issued a mournful proclamation of his own:

> The generals entrusted with the defence of Amiens have suddenly departed with the troops, and, considering them too feeble, have abandoned us. The military committee has not been consulted. The prefect quitted Amiens tonight. As for me, I remain with my municipal council in despair, but without forces against the enemy: Devoted to my fellow citizens, and ready for all sacrifices in their behalf, The Mayor.[2]

Early on the morning of November 28, there was an unusual silence from the French positions; finding no enemy troops before him, Barnekow ordered a cautious advance. Encountering no opposition, his troops entered the city, and he immediately sent a report:

> When the news reached General von Goeben, he could scarcely credit it; nor indeed, could any of us; and, in fact, orders had been given to remain on the defensive. We awaited an attack from the enemy, whose numbers were too great to admit

Amiens. (Rousset/*Les Combattants*)

of our attempting a forward movement until the 1st Army Corps should have had time to deploy to the right between Gentelles and Cachy.[3]

Still incredulous, Goeben rode forward to confirm the news, riding through the entrenchments defended on the previous day by the Amiens garrison under Paulze d'Ivoy. After some delay, and accompanied by the three battalions of the 40th Regiment, Goeben made his way to the city centre, where the infantry marched past him. He then repaired to the Hotel de France for breakfast.

The victory had not been bought cheaply, for the French had put up a much more spirited resistance than their lack of experience and training might have justified. Total German losses were 1,270, of which 230 were killed and 1,140 wounded. French casualties were put by Faidherbe as 266 killed, 1,117 wounded and about 1,000 missing. In addition, many gardes mobiles had left the columns.[4]

The French retreat was, so far as the regular troops were concerned, conducted in good order. This was not entirely true of the gardes mobiles; Faidherbe records that among those who left for home were some of their officers. As the columns left Amiens, the retreat beginning at 5.30 am on November 28, some disaffected gardes nationales fired off their rifles before breaking them, causing disorder among the troops who were at that time being issued with cartridges. The retirement was carried out in four columns; the first, under Lecointe, went towards Doullens; the second, under Paulze d'Ivoy, towards Pas d'Artois; the third was led due north by Farre. The fourth column made its way along the railway line to Albert and Achiet le Grand.

German troops enter Amiens. (*Illustrirte Kriegsgeschichte*)

Amiens Cathedral.
(Pflug-Harttung)

The German entry into Amiens, by Knötel. (Pflug-Harttung)

There remained the citadel of Amiens, constructed to protect the city to the north. 22 smoothbore guns, including 8-pounders, 12-pounders, 16-pounders, howitzers and mortars had been installed on the ramparts to cover the glacis and sweep the ditches. The 1st battery of the Gardes Mobiles de la Somme had been assigned to work these guns, supported by the two depot companies of the 43rd Regiment; the latter, however, were ordered to rejoin their battalion and retreat to Arras so there were only the 130 artillerymen left. Their commander, Captain Woerhaye, then obtained the 1st, 2nd and 7th companies of the Garde Mobiles du Nord from Paulze d'Ivoy to replace them, bringing the total strength of the garrison to about 450. At about 10.00 am the mayor and his municipal council went to the commandant of the citadel, Captain Vogel, to see what he intended; he promised them that he would remain on the defensive.[5]

This reassurance did not suffice to set the mayor's mind at ease, and he visited Goeben to ask him to persuade Vogel to capitulate. Goeben was certainly happy to attempt this, since the citadel was sufficiently strong to be a tough nut to crack. It consisted of a pentagonal bastion, dating originally from the seventeenth century. The walls were in a good state; at a height of some 80 feet from the bottom of the ditch they were too high to be taken by escalade. A bombardment by field artillery would not have produced a decisive result, since there were sufficient bomb-proof shelters to accommodate the garrison.[6]

The strength of the citadel came as a surprise to Goeben and his staff:

> While studying on our approaching Amiens the maps of that district, we had indeed noticed that citadel. As meanwhile we could procure no more accurate information as to its condition, also one of our officers, who in course of a journey had touched at Amiens, on searching his memory recollected only an old high mass of masonry beyond the Somme, we assumed that it was in ruins, and all the more because the maps of the French General Staff, in which we found it shown, were very old.[7]

The surprise was not however, altogether a disagreeable one; Goeben was in no doubt that he should soon take it, and thereby acquire a strong base which would, he thought, be 'of extraordinary value in the task allotted to the army.' He, therefore, resolved not to open fire on the citadel, and at noon sent forward a parlementaire to open negotiations. Vogel lowered the drawbridge and met the Prussian officers; in the discussions which followed, he refused to surrender even on the favourable terms offered, but said that he would not take any hostile initiatives. The Prussians retired, leaving observation posts around the citadel, and not much else happened during the day apart from the desertion of 50 gardes mobiles who abandoned the advanced post in front of the citadel.

That night Goeben sent a letter to Vogel, praising his courage and patriotic sentiments but suggesting that there was no point in continuing an impossible resistance, now that he had been abandoned by the Army of the North. Vogel again refused to surrender, and Goeben reluctantly gave orders for the preparation of an attack; the walls and roofs of the houses around the citadel were pierced during the night.[8]

Next morning at about 11.00 am Goeben, still hopeful of avoiding the need for an assault, sent a third summons to surrender; when Vogel again refused, he was warned that fire would be opened in 15 minutes. This duly occurred, and an exchange of fire ensued, in the course of which the citadel's artillery took part, although the German artillery did not reply. Vogel toured the ramparts, encouraging the garrison:

> Finally, towards midday, he had just ended his dangerous round when he arrived at Bastion No.5, the most threatened. There he spoke to Sergeant Major Savary, ordering him to cease fire on the town since the enemy artillery was not responding. The latter explained that the bastion was so overlooked by the tax office in front of the embrasure that it was impossible to show oneself without being fired on, and that for that reason it appeared to him to be necessary to demolish it. The

Commandant replied that that was a different matter and went forward to examine the position of the building. But barely had he arrived at the embrasure when he was seen and was mortally wounded by a bullet which hit him in the right side and went through his body.[9]

Sporadic rifle fire continued to be exchanged during the rest of the day, although the Germans pulled back in the evening. It now seemed clear that if a surrender could not be negotiated to deal with the citadel, a full assault would be necessary, and during the night of November 29/30 bridges were thrown over the river at Longpré, just below Amiens, and by dawn 66 guns were in position ready to open fire. Woerhaye, who had taken command on the death of Vogel, had however already been urged by the surgeon and the chaplain to surrender and as day broke a white flag was seen. At 8.00 am on November 30 Woerhaye agreed to an immediate capitulation. The officers and the Gardes Mobiles du Amiens were pardoned; those of Nord were made prisoners of war. The small detachment which had been taken prisoner at Gentelles during the battle of Amiens had been kept prisoner in the citadel; they were agreeably surprised when the German troops entering the citadel knocked on the door of their room and released them. The guns and material were handed over; less than a month later they would be in action against the French at Péronne. Captain Vogel was buried by the Germans with full military honours in the citadel.[10]

Goeben, in his comments on Faidherbe's history of the campaign, dealt comprehensively with the French claim that the failure to pursue the beaten Army of the North was a proof of the magnitude of the German losses. Observing that the burden of responsibility, if a pursuit had been at all practicable, should be laid on him rather than Manteuffel, he pointed out that no one had expected the French would on November 27 abandon Amiens without a further struggle. It had been settled that no attack would be made early on November 28, but that the arrival of the rest of the I Corps would be awaited. As a result, when the retreat of the French was discovered, the bulk of the VIII Corps could not be ready to advance until the afternoon. In addition, the occupation of the citadel, which commanded the existing bridges over the river, meant that crossings further up and down river would have to be utilised, and cavalry patrols reported that these had been destroyed:

> On November 28 then any pursuit was in fact impossible. On the following day however, such a movement, as it would have had no prospect, would have therefore had no sense; then it was necessary at once to prepare for fulfilling the second task allotted to the army: the march on the Seine against the French army formed in that quarter, which had recently shown a very threatening aspect.[11]

And Goeben was especially severe on Faidherbe's suggestion that heavy losses had precluded a pursuit, remarking caustically that 'even the more prominent leaders came forward repeatedly as well with the most peculiar military ideas, as with the most surprising ignorance of the army opposed to them'.[12]

* * *

Manteuffel receives news of La Fère's capitulation, by Tiret-Bognet. (Deschaumes)

The death of Captain Vogel, by Tiret-Bognet. (Deschaumes)

The capture of La Fère had been a high priority for the First Army as soon as its advance brought it close to contact with the enemy. La Fère lies on the main road from Laon through Compiègne to Paris, and is the place where the roads from Cambrai and Amiens meet. The Laon-Paris railway passed close to the south, going west from there to Tergnier, where northbound lines branched off. The Crozat Canal runs close to the west of the town, as does the River Oise. La Fère was therefore a crucially important communications hub, and as long as the French held it the operations of the First Army would be gravely hampered.

The town had about 5,000 inhabitants, and had formerly been the site of a famous artillery school. The fortifications consisted of a high town wall on the pattern of the Middle Ages:

> The deep ditches in front of this wall are flanked by towers – some half-round, some half-angular – or by flanks in the escarp. On the west, north, and east, this town wall is covered from direct fire by an earthen parapet of weak profile and irregular trace. Before the introduction of rifled guns of long range, and of indirect breaching fire, this may have sufficed, but now the town walls, in spite of the earthen parapet, can be got at from great distances. The passages over the Oise and the Crozat canal are covered by a little redoubt made like a bridgehead.[13]

In preparation for a siege, the Oise had been dammed, creating extensive inundations in the meadows around the town, and represented a key part of its defences, being about a mile wide close to the fortress, but broader to the north and south. On the east and west however there are gently sloping heights which would give a besieger excellent locations for batteries. At the south-eastern corner of the fortress the French had in modern times thrown up several bastioned earthworks to cover the railway station.[14]

The overall effect of these natural and artificial defences was to offer reasonable protection to the fortress on all sides except to the east, where the village of Danizy lay close to the enceinte; the houses in the Notre Dame suburb were less than 300 yards distant. The town was thus very much exposed to an enemy bombardment. There was a lack of bomb proof cover for the defenders; in early August the chief of the engineers had unsuccessfully called for the construction of this, and had at the same time pointed out that the magazines were vulnerable to enemy fire from all directions.[15]

At the start of the war the commandant of the fortress was Colonel Delmas de Lacoste, who made few preparations for defence, partly due to the lack of resources. On orders from Farre, he had even begun removing material which exceeded the town's strict requirements, a step which provoked among the population suspicions of treachery; in the face of these public protests the process was abandoned. On November 9 Delmas had been replaced as commandant by naval Captain Planche who, on taking over, announced his intention of defending the place 'jusqu'à la dernière gargousse'.[16]

To support these brave words, Planche had a garrison of about 2,700 men. He had, however, only 40 fully trained gunners; for the rest, he had three battalions of gardes mobiles from the Pas de Calais and one from Guise; three companies from Saint Quentin; two batteries of gardes mobiles from Soissons and Vervins; a half battery of volunteer former artillerymen, and three companies of francs-tireurs. The fortress was equipped with 113 heavy guns, of which 36 were rifled.[17]

Francs-Tireurs with their prisoner, by Bombled. (Grenest)

Major General von Zglinitzky. (Priesdorff)

Zglinitzky arrived in front of the fortress on November 15 with his 4th Infantry Brigade, having arrived by rail at Soissons on November 11 and 12 from Pont à Mousson. On arrival he picked up a complement of siege guns, together with a pioneer company and several artillery companies. While the siege guns were being brought up, Zglinitzky at once invested La Fère, in which task he was not impeded to any extent by the garrison.[18] He immediately identified the south-east front of the fortress as the point to attack. His situation was not, however, entirely comfortable:

> Far in advance of the head of the army to which he belonged, surrounded by an irritated and excited population, in the midst of hostile forces in process of formation, the task of Major General von Zglinitzky was no easy one. Great prudence was required, for the detachment had to be so placed round the fortress that it could at any moment front either way.[19]

For the first few days the garrison merely responded to the investment by a brisk but largely ineffective fire, but thereafter embarked on a number of small sorties without achieving very much. On November 20 a battalion of gardes mobiles with four guns sent from Amiens, and a battalion of francs-tireurs, advanced from Ham against the rear of the line of investment. The force was commanded by Colonel Krafft and was 1400 strong. It was attacked at Vouël by the 1st Battalion of the 5th Regiment, and after an engagement of three hours was forced to retreat, leaving an ammunition wagon in the hands of the Germans. The battalion of francs-tireurs, the Volontaires de la Somme, had advanced into Vouël having taken no precautions on the strength of the mayor's information that the village was not occupied so far as he knew; when the Prussian infantry opened fire from the houses, the francs-tireurs turned and fled, saving their guns with great difficulty. The gardes mobiles, directed towards Tergnier, did no better, and the whole force went back to Ham.[20]

Meanwhile the siege train had been arriving from Soissons, consisting of 32 guns. Once this was in place, Zglinitzky set about reducing the fortress with ruthless efficiency. On the night of November 24/25 seven batteries were constructed, four being located to the north of Danizy, one in that village (interestingly, this consisted of six French 22 cm mortars), and two to the south of the village. The location of the batteries was determined by the need to conceal them as far as possible from the view of the fortress by placing them behind small undulations of the ground. There was, however, one important obstacle which must be overcome during the night of November 24/25, while the pioneers were constructing the batteries:

> First Lieutenant von Roeszing, with the remainder of the pioneers, undertook to remove the trees which stood in the midst of the inundation, at about 400 paces from the fortress, and almost entirely masked the fire of the batteries. The men dropped down the Oise in a boat to the place, and then the pioneers, standing up to their middles in water, and in constant danger of being carried off into the river, began to saw the trees, which were upwards of half a metre in diameter. There were about 60 trees and by 6.00 am all were down. The French did not disturb the work, although parties of them in boats approached close to the place.[21]

At 7.30 am on November 25 the bombardment commenced. The garrison did not respond for half an hour; thereafter the artillery exchanges continued throughout the day. The siege guns soon began to inflict heavy damage on the enemy, but the garrison's fire produced little effect:

> Soon the town was on fire in several places, and the distress there was the greater, because there were no cellars in which the inhabitants could take refuge. The garrison was entirely without bomb proof cover of any sort, the only barracks in the place were soon in flames, several magazines caught fire, the gate of the fort towards Laon was shot to pieces, and the fronts attached were seriously damaged.[22]

By now many of the inhabitants had had enough, and called on Planche to capitulate, a demand which at first he refused. The German bombardment continued, more slowly, throughout the night and the following morning, without reply from the garrison; the artillerymen now refused to go on to the ramparts. At about midday on November 26 the white flag was displayed, and negotiations began for a capitulation. While this was going on a party of gardes mobiles made their escape through the Saint-Firmin gate. On November 27, at noon, the Germans entered La Fère. 78 officers and 2,234 men were taken prisoner and 113 guns, 5,000 rifles and a considerable quantity of material captured. The 4th Brigade had sustained losses of 7 men killed and wounded during the investment and siege.[23]

Manteuffel accordingly now turned to the implementation of the second phase of Moltke's orders, which had made it clear that after taking Amiens he should press on towards Rouen. He was concerned about reductions in his strength that might arise as a result of the capture of fortresses. When Moltke, after the fall of Thionville, ordered that the siege of Montmédy begin at once, to free the line of the railway between Thionville and Sedan, Manteuffel's reaction had been on November 26 to express some anxiety about the responsibility of his army for the captured garrisons of Thionville and, when it fell, La Fère. He did not want to weaken his army to take care of these while he was operating in open country. Moltke replied on November 30, pointing out that the First Army would have both the 14th Division (of Zastrow's corps) and Senden's detachment for the sieges of Montmédy and Mézières. He went on:

> A simultaneous advance against these two places is most desirable. For the attack on Mézières, the high command will be able to employ in addition the men and siege artillery materiel etc which have been used against La Fère. The destruction of the works at La Fère must be prepared in such a manner so as not to expose the inhabitants of the town to any danger; this destruction can then be carried out as soon as ordered by the General Staff.[24]

To carry out the advance to Rouen was not a straightforward option for the First Army, since there were other military considerations to take into account. These, however, were firmly regarded as secondary, as Wartensleben explained:

> The main idea which had given rise to the operations against Amiens was to disturb the organisation of the enemy's armies. In order to follow up this idea it became

General Hermann von Wartensleben. (Rousset/*Histoire*)

a necessity, consistent both with the instructions of November 18, and with the general military situation, not to allow the army to be enticed to follow the enemy and entangle itself among the northern fortresses, thereby leaving the army in Normandy free scope, but rather now to turn against the latter. The march to Rouen was therefore decided on.[25]

While preparing for this operation the Germans took steps to exploit the victory at Amiens, not only by sending patrols to follow the retreating enemy, but by establishing a large force in and around Amiens to overawe the civilian population. For the moment it was intended to act on the defensive along the line of the Somme, to secure that river against any further attempts southwards by the Army of the North.

5

Rouen

The Germans had been able to collect a good deal of intelligence at times about the forces being raised by the Government of National Defence. Unsurprisingly, however, much of it was inaccurate. With new units coming into existence on a daily basis, and with no orthodox orders of battle, it was difficult to assess the strength of these forces. The intelligence that had been collected about the French army in the neighbourhood of Rouen put it at about 44,000 men, 11,000 of whom were troops of the line, with 94 guns, mostly of heavy calibre.[1] This was a gross overestimate. The Official History accepts the figures given by Rolin, in *La Campagne de 1870-1871: La Guerre dans l'Ouest*, which puts the total strength of the force at about 22,000 men with 32 guns.[2]

It was commanded by General Briand. Contrary to the intelligence reports received at German headquarters, it was almost entirely composed of gardes mobiles. Without the stiffening of regular troops, it was much less effective than the Army of the North. However, Briand resolved to attempt to bar the way of any advance on Rouen, and occupied an entrenched position at Isneauville, about three miles to the north-east of the city centre, with advanced posts as far forward as the line Lyons/ la Forêt – Argeuil –Forges – Neufchatel.[3] During the days following the battle of Amiens, contact had been made with Briand's advanced troops by cavalry patrols from units of the Army of the Meuse, temporarily attached to the First Army, moving through Beauvais and Gisors. The Guards Dragoon Brigade had found the line of the Epte at Gournay to be occupied by the French. On November 27 and 28 the Saxon Cavalry Division, reconnoitring to the west of Gisors, was in contact with a body of French infantry and cavalry, which fell back to Richeville. On November 29 the commander of the Saxon Cavalry Division, General Count zur Lippe, sent forward strong reconnaissance detachments which occupied Etrepagny and Les Thilliers. The 5th Company of the 100th Regiment, which was quartered in a building to the west of Etrepagny, was at 1.30am surprised by a strong French column advancing from Ecouis; most of the German troops were taken prisoner. The rest of the detachment succeeded in breaking out, and retreated to Gisors. In their engagement the German losses amounted to 150 killed, wounded and captured; the French lost about 50 men.[4] Another French column which had advanced on Les Thilliers found the German troops there better prepared, and was beaten off and retreated to Ecouis.

Meanwhile the First Army was preparing to advance against Rouen. A detachment was to be left behind under the command of Lieutenant General von der Groeben, consisting of the 3rd Infantry Brigade (Colonel von Busse), the 6th Cavalry Brigade (von Mirus), two batteries, 8 squadrons and 18 guns, with a pioneer company, and a siege artillery company brought up from La Fère to garrison the citadel. Von der Groeben was given a very strict set of instructions by Manteuffel as to the tasks he was to perform.

General Count zur Lippe. (Rousset/*Histoire*)

First, he was to cover the march of the army; secondly, to occupy and hold Amiens; thirdly, to cover the line of the Amiens – La Fère railway; and finally, and importantly, to keep the French in ignorance of his strength.[5] This last was essential; the force available to von der Groeben was barely adequate for the tasks allotted, and might well be seen as a tempting target by the Army of the North. In addition to his primary tasks, therefore, von der Groeben was also to be active beyond the Somme:

> For this purpose the Amiens – Arras and La Fère – Cambrai lines of railway and telegraph must be destroyed at a point at least two days' march distant from their termination, therefore beyond Albert and St Quentin. Both these latter towns and other suitable localities are to be alternately and temporarily garrisoned by flying columns. Similar measures will be taken with regard to the Abbeville railway. Péronne must be watched, and I look forward to receiving a report whether and by what means it may be possible to gain possession of the place.[6]

This task was, as Manteuffel told von der Groeben, 'of an essentially defensive character, but one requiring at the same time a considerable amount of activity and initiative.' It was indeed a very demanding task, as events were to show. The immediate step that was necessary was to put the citadel of Amiens into a defensible state; Manteuffel had instructed von der Groeben that it would provide a firm point *d'appui*, and would 'enable the detachment to employ the greater part of its forces further forwards, because in case of eventualities it will suffice to hold the town in subjection.'[7]

The advance on Rouen began on December 1. For this operation Manteuffel had the VIII Corps, the I Corps less the 3rd Infantry Brigade, but with the 4th Infantry Brigade from La Fère, and the 5th Uhlan Regiment. In addition Moltke assigned the Guard Dragoon Brigade to the First Army for this operation, while the Saxon Cavalry Division acted in conjunction with it. Altogether Manteuffel had 43 battalions (amounting to 30,000 men) 31 squadrons and 168 guns.[8]

The temperature had been falling, and the march began on the first frosty day for some time. The immediate objective was to reach the line of the Epte by December 3. The VIII Corps took the road through Poix and Formerie, while the I Corps moved by way of Conty to pick up the main road between Breteuil and Rouen. By December 3 the advanced guards of each corps had reached the Epte at Forges and Gournay without making contact with the enemy, Briand having pulled back from this line during the previous night. Still in expectation that a vigorous defence of Rouen would be made, Manteuffel ordered Goeben on the following day to advance to Buchy, while Bentheim moved to Lyons la Foret and La Haye. He retained the 30th Brigade as the army reserve, which was to halt at Argeuil. Meanwhile cavalry patrols from the Saxon Cavalry Division were to reconnoitre as far as Fleury and Les Andelys, while the Guard Dragoon Brigade, attached for this task to Goeben's corps, was to cover the army's right at La Ferté. Major General von Sperling, Manteuffel's Chief of Staff, who had been off sick and for whom Wartensleben had been deputising, could not bear any longer to remain absent, and although not fully recovered rejoined the First Army headquarters on this day.[9]

Count von Moltke. (Lindner)

Advancing from the Epte, Goeben had his 31st Brigade (Colonel Mettler) on his right, and soon received a report that it had encountered the French to the south of St Martin Osmonville. Little opposition was put up, however, and the enemy retreated to Rocquemont, followed up closely by the 29th Regiment, which immediately stormed the village and captured most of its defenders, who did not get out in time. Another column of the 31st Brigade, advancing through Saint Saens, turned south through Bosc Berenger to support the rest of the brigade. Finding that this was not needed, the column turned west and drove a French detachment out of Bosc le Hard.

Meanwhile Kummer, with the 29th Brigade, on the left, had encountered the French in some numbers between Forgettes and Liffremont. Three batteries opened fire on these, to which the French replied briefly with four guns before falling back in the face of an attack by the 65th Regiment. They were pursued by parties of hussars who broke up the retreating French units, chasing them beyond Buchy.[10]

The cavalry of the I Corps had met with substantial detachments of the enemy as it probed westward along the road from Gournay to Rouen, and it appeared likely that they intended to defend the crossings over the Andelle. Accordingly Bentheim advanced no further than La Feuille, where it took up quarters for the night. Further south the Saxon Cavalry were in contact with the enemy at Le Thil en Vexin, about six miles to the west of Gisors.

The Germans were now advancing into very different countryside, as they crossed the River Epte, which flows south past Gourney and Gisors to reach the Seine at Vernon:

> Where the lines of march of the First Army crossed the river, it forms the boundary between the ancient provinces of Picardy and Normandy, now termed 'Département de la Somme' and 'de la Seine Inférieure'. Immediately beyond Gournay the landscape changes from the table-land and the mostly open plains of Picardy to the hilly and intricate country of Normandy, which greatly resembles the east part of Holstein. The pasture grounds, fenced in with hedgerows, abound with large herds of cattle that seek and find ample nourishment in the meadows until late in the autumn and winter. Here, as well as in Picardy, numerous seats of the ancient nobility are seen, often most picturesquely situated and in extent and style truly deserving of the name of 'château', an appellation of which the French are known to be very prodigal.[11]

The German headquarters staff were, therefore, not likely to be in want of comfortable quarters.

That, however, had not been the case for Goeben's staff on the night of December 4/5; Sir Randal Roberts described their advance on the following morning:

> With the ice on the hard frozen road crackling under the horses' feet, the staff left its anything but comfortable quarters at Buchy as the clock struck half past eight in the morning of December 5 – the red rays of the frosty December sun throwing a rosy light upon the frost bespangled trees on either side of the way. General von Goeben had received instructions to make a reconnaissance upon the Rouen road, and not to attack the enemy if he found that they had taken up a position behind earthworks.[12]

Manteuffel, meanwhile, who had been overnight at Argeuil, accompanied the I Corps as it similarly probed towards Boos after crossing the Andelle.

Goeben accompanied the leading units of Barnekow's 16th Division as they advanced to St André, about five miles west of Buchy. When he went on to Quincampoix he found Barnekow there. A patrol had made prisoner the mayor of the village as he was driving out of Rouen, and he had told his captors that 35,000 French troops had been at Quincampoix the previous night, but had remained only for an hour before departing to Rouen. It was his understanding that the intention was not to defend the city. Goeben and his staff were at first inclined to take this with a pinch of salt; it seemed entirely possible that this was a tale intended to deceive. However, after a short discussion with his Chief of Staff, Colonel von Witzendorf, and Major Bumke, he made up his mind to advance to Rouen, and sent a message to Manteuffel announcing his intention.

Meanwhile two squadrons from the 7th Hussar Regiment, reconnoitring ahead of the 29th Brigade, had found that the entrenched position at Isneauville was unoccupied, and pushing on into the city found that Briand's force had disappeared from there as well. Ignoring the extremely hostile demeanour of large bodies of workmen in the streets, they rode on to the market square, where they were joined at about 2.30pm by two battalions of the 32nd Brigade, which Goeben had sent on ahead. An hour or so later Goeben rode into the city with the rest of the brigade. Later that evening the 29th Brigade marched in, while the 31st Brigade and the Guard Dragoon Brigade occupied the villages north and west of the city.[13]

Sir Randal Roberts had ridden on ahead of Goeben's troops, and described his approach to the city:

> Riding through the suburb of Rouen, on the north-east side, among the luxurious villas and summer residences of the rich citizens, we arrived at that bend of the road from which the traveller gets the first glimpse of the old town. Rouen lies in a basin, surrounded on all sides by high hills. Through the town flows the Seine, then unusually full. No troops had yet entered, beyond a patrol of hussars; and, as we stood upon the height overlooking the city, strange sounds were carried to our attentive ears. Here and there a shot, a discordant shout, then a hollow rumbling noise as of a huge body of wooden shoed men in movement.[14]

What he was hearing was the noise of a mob of workmen who had occupied the square of the Hôtel de Ville. Soon after this, a magistrate – 'a tall, thin old man with the ribbon of the Legion of Honour on his coat' – appeared and asked for the Germans to help restore order. The mob were armed with weapons abandoned by the gardes nationales, and appeared to be trying to shoot the mayor:

> They were firing upon the Hôtel de Ville – firing in that sort of drunken, miserable way in which a French mob delights. Already the facade of the Hôtel de Villle was pitted with bullets, the windows were broken, and the members of the Commune huddled together in a back room, were, to use their own expression, *au désespoir*.[15]

The German troops soon brought things under control. One battalion of the 40th Regiment was stationed in the Place Cauchoise, with two guns; the rest of the regiment, with the 70th Regiment, moved into other parts of the city. Before nightfall Goeben, standing in the Place de l'Hôtel de Ville beside the statue of Napoleon I, took the salute as the 16th Division marched past him.

Moltke received the news of the fall of Rouen with satisfaction; but perhaps mindful of the lack of any effective pursuit after the taking of Amiens, his first reaction was a telegram that same evening: 'Commence the pursuit on Le Havre and solidly occupy Rouen. Special instructions for your subsequent operations will be sent tomorrow'.[16] He repeated the instruction that the pursuit was to be 'as energetic as possible' during the night of 6/7 December, and a couple of hours later sent off a letter to Manteuffel with the promised special instructions:

> Rouen will be occupied, and from there the left bank of the Seine will be observed. Liaison with the 5th Cavalry Division (with headquarters at Dreux) must be maintained. The main body of the First Army will continue its offensive against the enemy troops still in the field in the north-west of France. His Majesty regards it as immediately essential to pursue vigorously the troops of General Briand, which have fallen back on Le Havre. The commander in chief will decide on the spot whether to attempt a *coup de main* against this place ... In any case, His Majesty does not wish to see the First Army undertake any prolonged operation against Le Havre. It should on the contrary always have as its principal aim the dispersal of any enemy troops that again take the field, and from this point of view a renewal of operations against the troops beaten at Amiens should be not be neglected if they advance from their present points of concentration around Arras etc.[17]

Moltke's instructions came as no surprise to Manteuffel and his staff, who had already anticipated what would be required of them. Immediately the need was to follow up Briand's retreating forces. It was supposed at first that these had retreated down the right bank of the Seine, but it soon appeared that the bulk of the enemy had crossed the river and moved down the left bank, largely by rail, in the direction of Pont Audemer and Bernay. The orders issued on December 7 directed the I Corps to send mixed columns in brigade strength towards Vernon and Evreux; the VIII Corps was to pursue Briand on both sides of the Seine. Manteuffel had also, on December 6, ordered Major General zu Dohna, the commander of the 7th Cavalry Brigade, to take his two regiments, with two battalions of infantry and a horse artillery battery and march on Dieppe, disarming the country as it advanced and destroying the coastal telegraph line.[18]

The weather was growing colder. By the end of the first week of December, during which there was a heavy snowfall, there was a prolonged period of alternating frost and thaw, turning the muddy country roads to a quagmire. This impeded the progress of the columns radiating out from Rouen, but they all attained the objectives set for them.

Of Bentheim's I Corps, Pritzelwitz with six battalions, three squadrons and two batteries had crossed the Seine at Les Andelys, beneath Richard the Lionheart's Château Gaillard, and marched with little hindrance on Vernon. This column encountered only a party of 60 gardes nationales, who were taken prisoner. Colonel von Massow, with five battalions, three squadrons and two batteries, crossed the river at Pont de l'Arche, and reached Louviers on December 8. He entered Evreux next day, finding that a detachment of the 5th Cavalry Division from the Army of the Meuse had got there before him;

this force, under Colonel von Trotha, marched off to Chartres, and Massow occupied Evreux on December 10. The only intelligence he was able to gather was to the effect that a force of between 12,000 and 14,000 gardes mobiles, with 9 guns, had been there, but had removed to Cherbourg via Conflans.[19]

Goeben sent Colonel von Bock across the Seine at Rouen with the 29th Brigade. After a nine-hour march through deep snow Bock reached Bourgachard on December 8, sending cavalry patrols forward to Pont Audemer. Next day he moved forward to that place, finding that Briand's main body had indeed passed that way and gone on to Honfleur, where they had apparently recrossed to the right bank of the Seine. This was confirmed by the advance patrols on that side of the river from Brandenburg's Guard Dragoon Brigade which, reinforced by two battalions and one battery from the 16th Division, had reached Bolbec on December 9. The cavalry continued to probe towards Le Havre, finding the line Gaineville – Montivilliers to be occupied, evidently to cover the moment across the river of Briand's main body. Brandenburg continued to reconnoitre Le Havre, which was fortified on its land side; information obtained suggested that at least 25,000 troops were assembled there, and one estimate was as high as 50,000.[20] Dohna's force had moved rapidly towards Dieppe, which it reached on December 9. There, it spiked 27 guns in the shore batteries, and broke up the telegraph line along the coast before taking up a position at Auffray.

In order to carry out the tasks set out in Moltke's order of December 7, Manteuffel split his force. Bentheim, with the I Corps and the Guard Dragoon Brigade, was to be responsible for Rouen and the Lower Seine, while Goeben, with the VIII Corps and the 3rd Cavalry Division, covered Amiens and the line of the Somme. Before Goeben went back to Amiens, however he was first to move on Le Havre, and then, if he concluded that a *coup de main* was not feasible, along the coast as far as St Valéry.[21]

Rouen, in fact, presented particular difficulties, as Wartensleben noted:

> Rouen is completely overlooked by the neighbouring heights on the right back of the Seine. This situation of the town may well have been one of the reasons which induced General Briand to abstain from defending the town itself. These local considerations became of still greater weight now that we had to hold a hostile town of more than 100,000 inhabitants, among whom were 30,000 unemployed workmen. Even now this easily excited mass of human beings crowded to the quays with ill disguised hopes whenever a gun or cannon shot was heard in the neighbourhood, and might have proved an absolute danger if our troops had been obliged to pass the town on a retreat.[22]

On the left bank the situation was no better. Although the ground was more level, 'a labyrinth of detached buildings and gardens' stretched out into the countryside, and the approach of an enemy would be screened by the extensive forests. South of the nearest of these, at La Grande Couronne, lay the large town of Elbeuf, with another large and very discontented working class population.

The I Corps had therefore, in defending Rouen and the Lower Seine, to cope with the bocage, the unusual feature of the Normandy countryside which was, seven and a half decades later, to shape the campaign following the Allied invasion:

The intricacy of the whole country on the left bank of the Seine increases towards the south and south-west. Hedgerows, so characteristic of Normandy, are only found here and there on the right bank of the Seine, but abound on the left bank. By reason of this peculiarity of the country, connected operations of large bodies of troops were attended with great difficulty; cavalry and artillery, the two arms in which we were superior to the enemy, could be made but little use of. On the other hand, the locality was favourable to single combat, and to guerrilla warfare.[23]

Soon after the occupation of Rouen, Manteuffel had commissioned his artillery and engineer commanders, Lieutenant General von Schwartz and Major General Biehler, to report on the defensive capabilities of the city. Their conclusions were not encouraging; the defensive perimeter around Rouen would have to be nearly 13 miles in length, based on 15 redoubts, and its defence would require at least one whole corps. To commit Bentheim to this task would destroy Manteuffel's freedom of action in the western sector of his area of operations, and was plainly not feasible. The energetic movements out of the city against any reported enemy were, he reasoned, the more effective way of defending it.[24]

Meanwhile the German troops occupying Rouen had been found by the inhabitants to be a good deal less disagreeable than had been expected. However, this was probably not the view of M. Nion, from the mayor's office, who was interviewed on December 7 by the First Army's Intendant, who explained that in addition to all the horses in the city being collected before the Hôtel de Ville, 40,000 pairs of boots would be required within six days, together with 20,000 pairs of socks within three days. 'Monsieur, je vous assure ce n'est pas possible,' cried Nion. The Intendant was implacable: 'After this I shall only trouble you for 2,000 flannel shirts, 10,000 blankets, and 10,000 good cigars:'

> At the last demand M. Nion, who had been carefully noting the various items, threw down his pen in despair, pulled off his glasses, stretched his legs to their full extent under the table, and groaned once more, 'Monsieur, c'est impossible'. 'I am very sorry to hear it, Sir,' answered the imperturbable Intendant; 'for in that case His Excellency will impose upon the city a fine of three times the value of these articles.' The Intendant bowed; M.Nion also bowed, shrugged his shoulders, and said, 'Je ferai mon possible'.[25]

And, in the event, no fine was required, for all the requisitions were supplied.

Pushing westwards from Evreux, Bentheim sent his 2nd Brigade towards Bernay on December 11. Next day it advanced on Serquigny, finding that the gardes mobiles that had been reported there had already fallen back. Information gathered by patrols suggested that there were now of the order of 12,000 to 15,000 gardes mobiles at Bernay. Massow, commanding the 2nd Brigade, occupied Brionne and posted his troops in echelon on the road back to Rouen, where the rest of the I Corps was now concentrated, with the exception of the units that had been left in Amiens, and part of the 4th Brigade, which had moved towards Le Havre in support of the Guard Dragoon Brigade.

Meanwhile Goeben had advanced with his corps towards Le Havre, reaching Yvetôt and Caudebec with Barnekow's 16th Division on December 10. There were, however, already signs of increasing activity on the part of the Army of the North, so Goeben

The German advanced guard at Bernay, by Pallandre. (Rousset/*Les Combattants*)

ordered Strubberg's 30th Brigade, at Maromme, not to follow the 16th Division but to march eastwards towards Amiens. Kummer's other brigade, the 29th Brigade under Bock, which was at Pont Audemer, was ordered to take the same direction. Goeben himself moved on with the 16th Division to Bolbec on December 11, where he reviewed the reports of the cavalry reconnaissance of Le Havre. The enemy, he learned, was busily throwing up entrenchments around that place, and appeared to intend to hold a line between Harfleur and Montivilliers. It was quite clear that an attempt at a *coup de main* was not practicable, and Goeben's orders precluded any extended operations against Le Havre. Quite apart from anything else, to start such operations, only to break off and return to Amiens and the line of the Somme would be construed as a defeat. Goeben decided, therefore, having thoroughly reconnoitred Le Havre and Briand's dispositions there, to head back to the area assigned to him, going by Dieppe. It was a prudent decision; the most reliable subsequent account on the French side put the defenders of Le Havre at 40,000 men with several field batteries while the forts were armed with 137 heavy guns.[26]

Unknown to the Germans, the situation in Le Havre had become somewhat confused. Soon after the arrival of Briand's troops, an order had come from Tours requiring the despatch of 4,000 men, and an appropriate number of guns, to Cherbourg. When the news got out it was very ill received:

This created a furious scene of riot and disorder. Vast crowds paraded the town, protesting against the order, which the authorities were about to carry into effect. The guns had been shipped, but the mob proceeded to the harbour and compelled the commander of the transport vessel to unship them. Finding that no other course would appease the populace, both the civil and military authorities resolved to disobey M. Gambetta's order, and issued all over the town a proclamation to the effect, that in their opinion he was not in so good a position as themselves to judge of the local necessities of the defence.[27]

Leaving the Guards Dragoon Brigade to observe Le Havre, for which purpose it now passed under Bentheim's command, Goeben set off for Dieppe, which was reached by the 32nd Brigade on December 14. Behind it, the 31st Brigade was at St Laurent en Caux, while the corps artillery was at St Saens. In Dieppe, there was a substantial English population, and Roberts was interested to see how it reacted to the arrival of the German invaders:

> General von Goeben treated the English residents of Dieppe with every kindness consistent with the customs and necessities of war; and I do not think there is a single person who has a word of complaint to make upon this subject. In every possible way the Prussian officers endeavoured to show the respect they had for Her Majesty's subjects; and when the men were quartered in an English resident's house, their conduct was beyond all praise.[28]

The German troops were not, however, allowed to enjoy this English hospitality for long; on December 15 the march towards Amiens was resumed, and the next phase of the operations against the Army of the North was about to begin.

6

The Arrival of Faidherbe

On December 3 Faidherbe arrived at Lille to take up his command. He was very mindful of the need to impose discipline on his inexperienced troops, and two days later issued a ringing Order of the Day to his army. After paying tribute to Farre's conduct of the army, he went on:

> Minister Gambetta has proclaimed that in order to save France he asks of you three things: discipline, strict moral standards and a contempt for death. I will require that discipline to be merciless. If all cannot attain strict moral standards, I ask for at least dignity and especially temperance. Men under arms for the deliverance of their country have been given too sacred a mission to allow themselves the smallest public disturbance. As to a contempt for death, I demand it in the name of your salvation. If you do not expose yourself to a glorious death on the battlefield, you will die of misery, you and your families exposed to the merciless yoke of the foreigner. I have no need to add that court martials will deal with cowards, for there are none among you.[1]

Not all his troops were inspired by this kind of thing; Leonce Patry was especially unimpressed, observing that 'death, danger, privation and the strength of the enemy are subjects which one should take care never to broach with soldiers if you want to keep them in a good state of morale.'[2]

The troops available to Faidherbe were now organised as the 22nd Corps, consisting of three divisions. The 1st Division (Lecointe) had as its brigade commanders Derroja and Pittie; the 2nd Division (Paulze d'Ivoy) had the brigades of du Bessol and de Gislain. The 3rd Division was commanded by Admiral Moulac; his 1st Brigade was led by naval Captain Payen, and his 2nd by naval Commander Lagrange. The 3rd Division was organised rather differently from the first two; its 1st Brigade was composed of a battalion of chasseurs, a regiment of three battalions of fusiliers marins and a regiment of gardes mobiles, while the 2nd Brigade was composed of gardes mobiles and gardes nationales. Four new batteries had been created, so that each division had three, with two in general reserve. At the beginning of December, the total strength of the 22nd Corps amounted to 30,000 men with 60 guns.[3]

Faidherbe wasted no time in taking the field. The absence of the bulk of the First Army, for the time being operating in the Rouen area, left an obvious opportunity for a movement against the line of the Somme. On December 5 the units comprising the advanced guard of Lecointes corps began to move south, in biting cold. Their objective was Fins, where the force would be assembled under the command of de Gislain. The force consisted of three line battalions, one each from the 65th, 75th and 91st

Regiments, plus the 17th Light Infantry Battalion and six guns. By December 7 the force had reached Roupy and next day entered St Quentin. Leonce Patry's battalion was part of the force, and he recorded the high morale of the troops:

> We were all full of confidence and desirous of redeeming our failings at Metz by a great show of vigour and willing spirits. We passed the day at Saint Quentin in pleasantly renewing acquaintances and in gossip in which the hope of forthcoming success was the major topic.[4]

While de Gislain's force was moving towards the Somme von der Groeben had been endeavouring to carry out the tasks allotted to him. At Amiens he brought up four captured French rifled guns from La Fère, and installed them in the citadel. He formed a number of small detachments, each comprising one company and one squadron, and sent them into the country north of the Somme. Other detachments were sent to break up the railways which might be of use to the French should they attempt to advance; three railway bridges were blown up between Arras and Albert. Reconnaissance in the Péronne area found that the French had occupied villages on both banks of the Somme, and von der Groeben concluded that it would be inadvisable to attempt a *coup de main* against the fortress.

On December 3 he had despatched a strong detachment of two battalions, two squadrons and two guns under Major Bock to St Quentin. This force passed through Ham next day. On December 5 Bock reached St Quentin, encountering considerable hostility from the population before he overawed them by firing two shells into the main street. After blowing up the railway bridges at St Quentin and at Essigny le Petit, Bock marched back, reaching Ham on December 7 and Amiens on December 9. In Ham he left a party of the 3rd Field Railway Division, supported by a detachment of infantry, with the task of repairing the Laon-Amiens railway line.[5]

Lecointe's original intention had been to make a wide movement through Saint Simon and the Chauny and Nesle roads towards Peronne, but he received information from M. Martine, the mayor of Villiers-St. Christophie, which led him to change his plan.[6] Patry recorded the arrival of Martine at St Quentin on December 9 with intelligence which indicated that Ham might be an attractive target:

> We were all gathered at the same table eating lunch at a hotel next to the main square, when a man entered the dining room briskly and asked to speak to the officer in command of the troops, which was Major Tramond. He told him in a perfectly confident tone that the town of Ham, 18 kilometres from Saint-Quentin, was occupied by two weak German companies and that nobody suspected that we were in the vicinity.[7]

At any rate, the French troops were soon put in motion, marching through thick snow. After night had fallen, the march was halted outside Ham. At 6pm the French entered the town from all sides, taking its German occupants completely by surprise. Most of them succeeded in taking refuge in the castle; but by 2.00am it was obvious that further resistance was impossible, and they capitulated, only a few officers and men being able to escape.

The Army of the North takes Ham, by Pallandre. (Rousset/*Les Combattants*)

The news of the capture of Ham reached Amiens during December 10, and was immediately forwarded to Manteuffel's headquarters at Rouen. Von der Groeben was ordered at once to send out a force to retake Ham, and since it was considered possible that its defenders might still be holding out in the castle, he sent a force of one battalion, one squadron and four guns under Captain Luckowitz to its relief that evening. On December 12, near Eppeville, about six miles west of Ham, Luckowitz encountered what the Official History describes as 'superior hostile forces', and fell back through Roye en route to Amiens. Patry, in a sardonic description of this encounter, remarked that Luckowitz 'utterly lacked boldness and even the most elementary flair'. Even if he had not attacked but had sought to discover his enemy's strength he could, thought Patry, have entered Ham straight away.[8] When Manteuffel heard of this he sent a peremptory order on December 13 to von der Groeben to retake Ham straight away, and to find out whether the whole of the Army of the North was on the move.

This movement appeared to Moltke at Versailles to indicate a possible French threat to the German line of communications, a view which was strengthened by an approach to La Fère on December 12 by a force of several battalions supported by artillery. That day, too, the French cut the telegraph wires between La Fère and Reims. Moltke sent an order direct to von der Groeben to emphasise that the appearance of French troops near La Fère required his immediate intervention. Reflecting on all this, Moltke wrote to Manteuffel on December 13 to explain that it was not intended that there be a permanent occupation of the whole of north-western France; all that was necessary was to disperse any forces that might be assembled to raise the investment of Paris. He accordingly directed that the First Army should be concentrated at Beauvais, from where it could support the advanced forces at Rouen and Amiens. Moltke concluded by saying that the army could move up to Amiens again 'as soon as the present situation of affairs shall have cleared up.'[9]

It seemed to Manteuffel, and separately also to Goeben, on the basis of the reconnaissances that had been carried out in the direction of Abbeville and of Péronne, that Faidherbe's intention was to move with the bulk of the Army of the North from Arras through Bapaume, Péronne and Ham and the roads further east. To operate against this movement there were immediately available von der Groeben's forces with Kummer's 15th Division further west at Forges and La Feuillée.

Von der Groeben had received the order to retake Ham on December 13 at about midday; his response, which Manteuffel grudgingly accepted, was to say that he could not advance until December 16, when he had reassembled all the detachments he had sent out. In acknowledging this, Manteuffel added that a sufficient force must be left in Amiens to ensure the security of the city. To this the harassed von der Groeben replied that in that case he could not send more than two battalions with four squadrons and a battery on the expedition to Ham. Meanwhile Kummer was ordered to concentrate his division at Montdidier as soon as possible, and pending Goeben's arrival from Dieppe was to take von der Groeben under his orders.

Moltke's order of December 13 reached Manteuffel at Rouen on the following day. The instruction to concentrate at Beauvais necessitated the issue of revised orders to the various units of the First Army, which went out on December 14. Von der Groeben was to leave three battalions, two batteries and one regiment of cavalry at Amiens, and set off to Roye on December 16 with the rest of his force, including Dohna's brigade. Kummer was still to go to Montdidier but Barnekow was to make directly for Beauvais. The orders for Bentheim were unchanged, although on December 17 he was instructed to occupy Gisors and keep in touch with Beauvais from there.[10]

Bentheim had, during the past few days, been operating well to the west of the Seine. After a series of brief contacts he pushed forward the 1st Division on December 16, reaching Bourgtheroulde, with the advanced guard at St Denis des Monts. He found that the French had occupied the heights on the left bank of the Rille beyond Brionne in considerable force, making the strike which he had intended between the Rille and the Seine too risky, and he accordingly pulled his troops back to Rouen, establishing a line of defence on the left bank between Grande Couronne and Pont de l'Arche.[11]

Meanwhile the operations of Bentheim's engineers had gone a long way towards the creation of an international incident. Charged with protecting Rouen from an attack up the River Seine by gunboats, they resolved to create a barrier across the river. A suitable location was found for this at Duclair, to the west of which there is a hill well adapted as a position for batteries to command the Seine. The only way to construct a barrier, however, was by sinking seagoing ships. There were no French ships available; there were, however, a number of English ships which could be requisitioned. French gunboats moved upriver on December 17 and shelled some of the detachments of the 2nd Division, and it was decided to create the barrier at once. Over the energetic protests of their captains a total of nine English ships were requisitioned, and sunk in the river, between December 19 and 23, with torpedoes (mines) placed in front of them:

The tops of the masts of all the nine ships were cut off on December 24; but still fastened to the ships by the tackle, were left to float about, and it was hoped would be sufficient to bring up a ship trying to pass through a gap of the barrier. Altogether it made a very fair obstacle. Covering batteries and shelter trenches were thrown up on the right bank, and would have made it very difficult to reconnoitre the barriers, or to make an opening by aid of boats.[12]

The incident aroused violent hostility in the British press at first and not surprisingly the French press did all it could to stir up trouble. The *Journal de Havre* sanctimoniously observed:

We are convinced that England, so proud of the privileges of her citizens, will enquire quickly into this affair. In it her honour, her dignity, and her security are at stake. If she allows such an act to be committed with impunity, she will lower herself in the rank of nations to the fourth order.[13]

It soon became clear, however, that the early reports were exaggerated and that there had been no breach of international law. The Prussians had given the owners a bond of full indemnity in respect of their loss. 'A regard for British susceptibilities induced Bismarck to show himself very amenable in the affair,' as one historian has written, and the matter was peaceably resolved in the following year when the German ambassador formally accepted all the claims made.[14] As usual Bismarck was pragmatic; he was not always as sensitive to the demands of the British Government; on one occasion, soon after Sedan, he had reacted to a request from Lord Granville for an early response to an enquiry about a possible armistice by telling his staff: 'There is no hurry to reply to this rubbish.'[15]

The reconnaissance patrols sent out from Amiens had established pretty conclusively that a large number of French troops had been moved southwards from Arras. However, the decision to bring the VIII Corps back to the area of Amiens and the Somme had already been taken before the surprise of Ham or the appearance of the Army of the North before La Fère. Faidherbe, perhaps understandably, recorded that these events 'gave concern to the enemy generals, since they believed it to have been destroyed on November 27. Orders went out for a concentration of force and VIII Corps was promptly recalled from Normandy.' He added that he 'had therefore attained his goal.'[16] Wartensleben, however, points out that the order to Goeben had been issued on December 9; what is surprising is that Goeben took the roundabout route through Dieppe rather than proceeding more directly, and more swiftly, to the threatened area.

What Faidherbe actually intended was far from clear at Manteuffel's headquarters. From La Fère it was learned that the French forces that had appeared in front of the fortress, amounting to 5,000 men and 18 guns, had withdrawn in two columns, towards Moy and Noyon. On December 15 further reports came in, suggesting that the Army of the North was marching in three columns on Abbeville and Amiens, that there were 20,000 men at Lens, north of Arras, and that another large force was at St Omer. Events were to show that these reports were greatly exaggerated, but it was obvious that the French were rapidly increasing their strength.

Other reports were of French skirmishes on the road from Albert to Bapaume, and of columns marching from there to Péronne, while Roye was found to be occupied by

Captured Uhlans are brought into Arras, by Leclercq. (Rousset/*Histoire*)

the enemy. All this suggested that Faidherbe was concentrating behind the Somme, under cover of Péronne; but what was not evident was the direction he would then take. Meanwhile Kummer was by December 16 making good progress in his march towards Montdidier from Rouen, the 30th Brigade having reached Breteuil and the 29th Brigade Marseille-le-Petit.

Manteuffel was therefore feeling reasonably comfortable about the position until the early evening of December 16, when he received a very nasty surprise indeed. First Lieutenant Sulzer, the officer assigned to the duties of prefect of Amiens, rode into his headquarters at Rouen with a totally unexpected letter from von der Groeben:

> This letter showed that, according to the view he took of the situation, the general had deemed it advisable to leave only two companies of infantry, with the garrison artillerymen and pioneers, in the citadel, and to march with the whole remaining force early on the 16th to join the 15th Division at Montdidier. This proved that the army orders of December 14 were not yet in the hands of the general when he took this step.

As a result, the Inspector-General of the Etappen troops had also pulled out of Amiens, taking the military chest to Conty, while the German civil authorities were on their way to Rouen by rail.[17]

Manteuffel was furious; Wartensleben tactfully conceded that von der Groeben's orders 'did not certainly set aside the possibility of Amiens being momentarily given up', but quite apart from military expediency the move had all the appearance of a serious setback. Manteuffel had 'set great store on maintaining the German occupancy of Amiens as long as possible ... it was not wished to make any alterations in the state of affairs there without cogent military reasons.' Just at this moment, it would be very undesirable if the French were to be buoyed up by the appearance of a victory if Amiens were to be retaken.[18]

The citadel there was commanded by Captain Hubert, who had the 7th and 8th Companies of the 44th Regiment, the 8th Company of the 11th Fortress Artillery Division and the 3rd Field Pioneer Company from the I Corps. It was with this force that he settled down to overawe the population of Amiens, and discourage it from getting any ideas of hostile activity. In the task he was reasonably successful; the leaders of the civil community had themselves issued placards calling for 'quiet and prudence', and insisting that the hospitals left in the town should be respected. A few hundred workmen assembled in front of the citadel, but a short burst of rifle fire was sufficient to disperse them. Hubert warned that he would bombard the town if any attack was made on the citadel.

The news from von der Groeben electrified the First Army headquarters. It was essential that the situation at Amiens be restored at once, if possible before the French got there in force. Two mounted orderly officers with escorts rode out from Rouen that evening, one going straight to Bréteuil (61 miles in a direct line) and the other by rail to Forges and then by road to Bréteuil. They both reached there at about 7.30am on December 7 and reported the situation to Kummer. He was to send Major General von Mirus to Amiens at once with three battalions or, if he thought it necessary, the whole of the 3rd Infantry Brigade with a cavalry regiment and two batteries. Von der Groeben, who was by now not Manteuffel's favourite person, reverted to the command of the 3rd Cavalry Division, which was to be reconstituted as soon as Dohna got back from Dieppe. Kummer was ordered to concentrate his own 15th Division at Montdidier and await the arrival of the 16th Division, which was ordered to march there directly rather than through Gournay, as originally intended.[19]

Manteuffel had planned to move his headquarters to Beauvais, the point of concentration specified by Moltke's order of December 12, but it now seemed clear that it would be the Somme where the crucial events would take place. Accordingly, he reported by telegraph to Moltke on the morning of December 17:

> According to Your Excellency's instructions the position at Beauvais was to have been occupied, in order to cover the north investment of Paris, and, in case of eventualities, to push forward to Rouen or Amiens. The latter is now the most pressing. I therefore shall not let the 16th Division march to Beauvais, but shall assemble the bulk of my army on the line Bréteuil – Montdidier, whereby the troops will be spared a detour and will move at hand for Amiens or for assuming the offensive northward.[20]

Next day Manteuffel rode eastwards, in bitter cold, reaching Marseille-le-Petit by nightfall, after a ride of over 30 miles; he went on to Bréteuil on December 19. By then the situation at Amiens had been restored; Kummer had wasted no time in sending Mirus forward to the city by way of Ailly with five battalions, four squadrons and two batteries, and the city was reoccupied without opposition on December 18. Manteuffel was pleased to learn of the co-operative attitude taken by the French authorities there during the city's brief abandonment, and in gratitude for this remitted a contribution which Hubert had imposed on the city. It had, however, been a narrow squeak; on December 18 Faidherbe, accompanied by Favre, had arrived on the heights of the Noyon suburb of Amiens to reconnoitre, and a number of units of his army were in easy striking distance.[21] Ever since December 14 they had been moving from the Oise valley in the direction of Amiens, led by Lecointe's division, with the rest following. By December 16 Faidherbe's headquarters were at Corbie; the divisions of Lecointe and Paulze d'Ivoy were between that place, Villers-Bretonneux and Foucaucourt; that of Admiral Moulac was in and around Pertain. Behind them, at Albert, were being assembled a number of battalions of gardes nationales, which were intended to form a fourth division.[22]

Faidherbe was realistic about the needs of his men, as Lehautcourt wrote:

> Our movement was carried out in the best conditions. The cold was not at all excessive. In addition, Faidherbe arranged quarters for his troops each day. He then abandoned the tente-abri, which the routine of the African wars still imposed on most of our troops, to their great detriment. The Army of the North did not regret it.[23]

As he moved westwards, it had been Faidherbe's intention to throw his three leading divisions to the south of Amiens, while keeping the gardes nationales back at Albert. By the time he got to the suburbs of Amiens, however, this plan no longer appeared feasible, and an attack on the city would in any case have led to its partial destruction. In addition, a movement south of Amiens would have been threatened by the German troops known to be concentrated in and around Montdidier.

By December 18 the French intention to march along the Somme towards Amiens seemed much clearer, and Kummer pushed the 30th Brigade forward from Montdidier to the Avre at Davenescourt. The 29th Brigade reached Montdidier on the same day. The 3rd Cavalry Division (minus the 7th Lancer Regiment, which was with Mirus in Amiens) was also moved north. To the east, Roye was now held by one battalion and half a squadron from the 30th Brigade. By December 19 Goeben had concentrated the whole of his corps in the rectangle Conty – Moreuil – Montdidier – Bréteuil. Contemplating the strength of the enemy which he had to face, with the I Corps still at Rouen, Manteuffel was in no doubt that he was outnumbered, and he looked about for reinforcement. He thought he had found it in the 14th Division, which had been assigned to the task of besieging Mézières; now, he submitted to Moltke, his need for it was greater than the commencement of the siege there. Moltke would have none of it:

> In reply to the letter you addressed to me on the 15th inst, I have the honour to make known to Your Excellency that the questions raised on the subject of the immediate commencement of the siege of Mézières have received the most serious examination. However, the general interests of the army, which needs the opening of a second railway line, have led His Majesty the King to order the 14th Division to undertake and execute the siege of Mézières as rapidly as possible.[24]

Prince Albrecht Junior. (Rousset/*Histoire*)

However, he was prepared to allow Senden's detachment to rejoin the First Army, and it was to set off on December 19 with a view to reaching St Quentin by Christmas Day. In addition, Moltke created another Guards Cavalry Brigade, under Prince Albrecht Junior, consisting of the Guards Hussar Regiment, the 2nd Guard Uhlan Regiment and a horse artillery battery; this he sent off to join the First Army to arrive at Beauvais on December 22.

The uneasiness among Manteuffel's headquarters staff was increased by a report from Versailles to the effect that some intelligence suggested that Faidherbe had as many as 62,000 men in the field, while Briand had about 40,000 at Le Havre. During his ride to Bréteuil Manteuffel had paused for a conference with Goeben at Crèvecoeur at his headquarters in a vast chateau there. They agreed that it was desirable that the whole of the VIII Corps should close up to Amiens in the face of the French advance westward. Next day Goeben, who now had command of all the troops on the Somme by which Faidherbe would be opposed, rode into Amiens and established his headquarters there.[25]

That day Mirus had sent a battalion of the 44th Regiment, supported by a detachment of cavalry and two guns, on a reconnaissance down the road to Albert. This force ran into serious trouble in the neighbour of Allonville, close to Querrieux. As it pushed towards the opposite border of a wood to the south-west of Querrieux it became involved in a lengthy skirmish with superior forces. The battalion fell back to a farmstead called Les Alençons and there defended itself against an attack from four battalions before retiring to Amiens with the loss of 50 men killed and wounded. While never in contact with the enemy's main body, this reconnaissance strongly suggested that it was now located in the area between the Somme and the Hallue.

The enemy activity on the perimeter of the circle around the investment of Paris, albeit at a considerable distance from it, led Moltke to ponder the overall situation and, after having done so, to convey his conclusions to his senior commanders. His object was to ensure that they thoroughly understood what it was they should be trying to achieve and what were the difficulties to be overcome. The letter which he wrote to Prince Frederick Charles and to Manteuffel on December 17 was one of the most important instructions which he issued during the course of the war:

> The general situation renders it desirable that the pursuit of the enemy, after the victory which has been gained, should only be continued to the extent necessary mainly for the dispersion of his masses, and for the prevention of their reassembly for a considerable period. We cannot follow him to his last points of support, like Lille, Havre and Bourges, nor permanently occupy distant provinces like Normandy, Brittany, or La Vendée, but must make up our minds to evacuate again even places which we have won like Dieppe, and eventually also Tours, so as to concentrate the bulk of our forces at a few main points. These latter should be occupied as far as possible by entire brigades, divisions, or corps. From them the neighbourhood, but only the immediate neighbourhood, should be cleared of franc tireurs by moveable columns; at them we must wait until the hostile levies have become again embodied into formed armies, so as to proceed to their encounter by short offensive movements. By these means our troops will presumably be guaranteed the long rest of which they stand in need, so that they may recover strength, bring up their reinforcements of men and ammunition, and replenish their equipments.[26]

For the First Army, Moltke repeated his prescription that the main body should be concentrated at Beauvais, while Amiens, Rouen and St Quentin were to be occupied. Senden's division would shortly go to St Quentin. The left bank of the Seine was to be abandoned, although the river was to be watched as far as Vernon. Moltke ended his letter thus:

> To the Army Headquarters all further arrangements (also as regards the Detachment of His Royal Highness the Grand Duke of Mecklenburg) are herby committed with the very respectful remark, that the preceding observations are only intended for the information of the Headquarters of Armies, and, consequently, should only be communicated to the Corps' Headquarters, to the extent that it may be desirable for the execution by the latter of the tasks allotted to them.[27]

Presumably he did not want the less senior commanders to feel that they had a free hand to interpret these instructions as they wished.

7

The Battle of the Hallue

Captain Seton, who had taken his leave of the VIII Corps soon after the battle of Gravelotte, had intended to rejoin the Corps headquarters staff in the autumn, but in the event he did not catch up with them until December 19. Next morning he obtained renewed permission to accompany the corps from Goeben, 'whom I found kind and pleasant as ever, though he struck me as looking somewhat worn by the exertion and cares of the last five months.'[1] At Amiens, he set off to the Hotel du Rhin, where the landlord told him there was no room as it was all taken up by Manteuffel; but in the event he managed to get in. He found the wealthier citizens of Amiens to have been apprehensive, during the German withdrawal, as to the likely conduct of the large number of working class unemployed.

It was evident that Faidherbe meant to offer battle. He described the position which he had taken up:

> The French army posted itself on the right bank of the Somme, which presented a series of heights overlooking the left bank. There it was completely covered towards the south by the river and the canal, with their vast swamps which were very difficult to cross. All the bridges had been broken. A battle line was adopted which faced the citadel, the only point of passage left to the enemy, in the Hallue Valley, where lay the villages of Daours, Bussy, Querrieux, Pont Noyelles, Bavelincourt, Béhencourt, Vadencourt and Contay. The majority of the troops were billeted there. The rest occupied the length of the railway line by the town of Corbie, where headquarters were established, and the neighbouring villages.[2]

The Army of the North had now undergone a further reorganisation, with the establishment of an additional infantry division composed of the gardes nationales. The army was now divided into two corps, each of two divisions. Apart from the garde nationales division, the other three each had two brigades, each of four line battalions and three of gardes mobiles. Lecointe, promoted to lieutenant general, was appointed to command the 22nd Corps, with Derroja and Bessol as his divisional commanders; each of them was promoted to major general. Paulze d'Ivoy and Farre also made lieutenant general. The former took over the 23rd Corps; his 1st Division was led by Admiral Moulac and his 2nd Division by Major General Robin (who had been a naval captain of marines). General Robin, who had fought at Sedan and subsequently escaped from the prisoner of war camps, had a pronounced reputation which had preceded him, being known for incompetence, womanising and corruption; his division of gardes nationales was to prove extremely unreliable.[3] The Army of the North now had 78 guns; but it was still woefully deficient in cavalry. Lecointe's corps was posted along the Hallue, from Daours to Contay. Moulac's division was in and around Corbie, while Robin was in a second line in the villages southwest of Albert, having detached a regiment to Bray to watch the line of the Somme.

To the east of Amiens, the country is open, and it was commanded in 1870 to a considerable extent by the citadel, from which fire had been opened on any French column that got too close. Wartensleben reviewed the strength of the position that the French had taken up:

> Four miles and a half further on towards Albert, the high road passes through some woods of no considerable dimensions. A mile before reaching Querrieux, the plateau again becomes perfectly open, and falls in gentle slopes down to the Hallue, in itself an unimportant rivulet, but accompanied by wet meadows, and therefore in general only to be crossed by the bridges in the numerous villages. The latter form groups of villages lying partly on both banks of the stream. On the opposite bank of the Hallue the eastern slopes of the hills rise without a break, and often in very steep ascents, to a considerable height. From thence every part of the west side ... was commanded.[4]

Faidherbe could not have found a stronger position in which to stand and fight. He may have had, as Howard points out, little hope of defeating Manteuffel, but he had by his choice of ground given his inexperienced troops every chance to give a good account of themselves. The bare, open chalk slopes which the Germans must assault gave admirable fields of fire for the French infantry.[5]

The southern side of Querrieux. (Duncan Rogers)

Manteuffel, of course, still had to concern himself with Briand as well as Faidherbe. Bentheim had reoccupied the line La Bouillée – Elbeuf – Pont de l'Arche on the left bank of the Seine, while on the other bank Pritzelwitz, with the 4th Brigade and the Guard Dragoon Brigade held a line between Duclair – Barentin – Clères. Downstream from Duclair, where the English colliers had been sunk, the French could freely cross the river. Although there were no signs that the considerable forces facing Bentheim were contemplating an advance, they were well placed to do so if they chose. Having regard to Moltke's instructions of December 17, there was no longer any need to occupy a position on the left bank at all, however, and that being the case it seemed to Manteuffel reasonable to bring back from Rouen to Amiens by rail six battalions to reinforce Goeben. If the worst came to the worst, and Briand did advance in force, Bentheim was instructed to fall back in the direction of Beauvais rather than towards Paris.

The first part of this reinforcement, two battalions of the 3rd Regiment, arrived at Amiens on December 22; the rest followed in the next two days. The only other immediate accession to Goeben's strength would be the newly formed Guard Cavalry Brigade under Prince Albrecht Junior, which was to reach Amiens by way of Moreuil on December 24. Senden was also on his way, and reported that he should reach St Quentin by December 24.[6]

On the morning of December 22 Manteuffel convened a conference at his headquarters to review the situation, attended by Goeben, Sperling and Wartensleben. Although the French had taken up a position close to Amiens, it certainly did not look as if an attack was intended, and there was a case to be made for standing on the defensive. There were, however, some good reasons for taking a more aggressive line. Manteuffel had, as Wartensleben recorded, 'great faith in the moral element', and felt that simply to stay put and see what happened would stimulate the enemy and depress his own troops. In addition, such a policy might prompt the French to become more active on the Seine to such an extent that, weakened by the detachments he had made, Bentheim would have to abandon Rouen. This alone was enough to demonstrate that an assault should not await Senden's arrival at Amiens; in any case, it was thought that the French would themselves be able to bring up further reinforcements if there was further delay.

It was, of course, apparent that an immediate attack on the Army of the North must necessarily be with inferior forces. The Germans were not yet aware of the French reorganisation into two corps, but their intelligence reports had put enemy strength as high as 60,000 men. Acknowledging that this may have been an exaggeration, Wartensleben suggests that the true figure for Faidherbe's four divisions must have been at least 40,000 to 45,000 men, organised in 56 battalions. Howard puts the figure at about 40,000 men. On the Prussian side, including all the battalions brought up or en route from Rouen, and taking into account the weak effective strength of each battalion at that time, Wartensleben states that the total strength 'numbered very little more than 20,000 fighting men'; Howard puts the figures at about 25,000.[7]

The four men had little difficulty in eliminating the possibility of an attack on Faidherbe from the south, across the River Somme. It would be extremely difficult to cross, and even if an assault were to succeed, it would only push the enemy back along his natural line of retreat. There appeared to be two viable alternatives; to attack from

Amiens, advancing eastwards and aiming for Faidherbe's right flank, or to pull out of the city and march along the south of the Somme before crossing the river and coming at him from the east. The latter option would enable the First Army to pick up Senden's force, but since it would postpone the day of battle, it could also give Faidherbe the opportunity of bringing up reinforcements. After much discussion it was resolved to advance direct from Amiens across the Hallue. What was not known was whether the French position there was the main position, or merely a flank guard of the main position along the Somme.[8]

The conference soon reached agreement on the plan of attack, which was fixed for the following day:

> General Goeben was to advance with the VIII Corps and three regiments of the Cavalry Division by the roads leading to the Hallue. This right flank division would, if possible, first drive the enemy back behind the Hallue, then establish itself on this line and hold the enemy fast in the front. His left flank division and the cavalry would take the road to Acheux, and then press and attempt to turn the enemy's right flank, which was expected to be in that quarter. The Commander in Chief would hold the remaining troops in reserve, and employ them as circumstances might demand.[9]

As Goeben was soon to find, the position on the Hallue was indeed Faidherbe's main position. In the front line, along the crest of the hills to the east of the river, stood Lecointe's Corps. Derroja held the section from Contay and Vadencort southwards as far as Béhencourt, and Bessol continued the line down towards the river at Daours. Moulac's division was held in support at Corbie; Robin, with Paulze d'Ivoy's other division, which had been quartered in Albert, moved down the high road during the morning of December 23 and took up a position to the east of Béhencourt.[10] Early on December 23 Moulac's division moved out of its billets in Corbie to take up a position in and around Daours.

Patry, with his battalion, had been posted on the right of the French position at Contay. The effect of the reorganisation was to allocate his battalion to a newly formed regiment, the 67th Regiment de Marche, and was part of the 1st Brigade (Aynès) of Derroja's 1st Division of Lecointe's 22nd Corps. There was little happening at Contay during the days immediately before December 23, although on one of them there was a distinguished visitor there:

> One morning during lunch, however, we saw a disreputable cabriolet with its hood lowered pull up in front of the château, and from this boneshaker descended a tall gentleman dressed in blue smock, wearing a fur cap, his nose adorned by a pair of spectacles with very thick lenses. He asked to speak to the colonel. He was shown in, and it was none other than our commanding general, General Faidherbe, who after a reconnaissance which he had pressed for some distance had come to ask us for lunch. He shared his plans and intentions with us. I was all eyes and ears. But I could not stop wondering why, instead of going to do his reconnaissance quite peacefully on horseback with a good escort, he had adopted this disguise which, despite myself, I found absurd because it was unnecessary.[11]

Apparently Faidherbe used a carriage when reconnoitring in order to accommodate Admiral Moulac, a poor horseman, although the latter's division was of course located at the other end of the line.

December 23 dawned bright and clear. It was bitterly cold as Goeben's troops began to file over the bridges over the Somme. The 15th Division, the Horse Artillery Division of the corps artillery, and Dohna's 7th Cavalry Brigade crossed over pontoon bridges constructed above Amiens, at Camon and La Neuvville, before advancing on and to the right of the high road to Albert. The progress was delayed for an hour when the bridge at La Neuville sank. The 8th Rifle Battalion (Major von Bronikowsky), ordered to wait until the main body was across, moved from its position opposite Corbie at 9.00am, and once over the river moved on the extreme right of the army towards the villages of Vecquemont and Daours. The 16th Division, with the rest of the corps artillery, crossed the river by the bridges inside Amiens. Barnekow was to take the roads north and northeast towards Poulainville and Rainneville, concentrating at Pierregot before swinging to the right with a view to turning Faidherbe's flank.[12] Dohna's cavalry brigade would operate as a link between the two infantry divisions, and advanced towards Cardonnette. Far out on Goeben's left, Lieutenant Colonel von Pestel, with the 7th Uhlan Regiment, ensured that no threat to Amiens was to be feared from this direction; during the day he remained in position at Picquigny, watching enemy troops that had appeared down river near Longpré-les-Corps Saints.

Although Faidherbe's main position, very well chosen, ran along the heights on the east of the Hallue, his advanced guards occupied the villages on the river in some force; there were also detachments at Allonville and Bergerie on the main road, but these fell back during the morning to Querrieux.

Goeben had ridden forward with his staff with the leading troops of Kummer's division towards Allonville, before pausing to watch the infantry of the brigade march by.

The Battle of the Hallue. In the centre can be seen Querrieux, under attack from the German VIII Corps. In the foreground are guns from VIII Corps, covered by cavalry from the 3rd Cavalry Division. The French positions can be seen along the heights in the distance. (Hiltl)

Roberts, in Goeben's party, wrote that it was 'a magnificent sight to truly behold the troops advancing:'

> Steadily, as if on parade, marched the compact masses of infantry, the skirmishers in front, with their supports to the right and left of the Albert road. They took possession of the woods beside Allonville; in a moment the village was occupied; still not a French soldier was to be seen. Had the enemy, then, retreated? No; an orderly galloped up to say that the village of Querrieux was strongly held by the French troops. We mounted our horses and rode straight up the road to that village.[13]

Kummer's division was led by the 29th Brigade, which had been joined by the 1st Heavy and 1st Light Batteries of the divisional artillery, and by two squadrons of the 7th Hussars. Bock's brigade reached the eastern end of the Querrieux wood without encountering opposition; but the infantry posted in and about Querrieux, and the French artillery on the far bank of the Hallue now opened fire. To this the two batteries with the 15th Division responded, opening fire at about 11.15am. The rest of the divisional artillery, which had accompanied Strubberg's 30th Brigade to Les Alençons Farm, was quickly brought up in support, and the four batteries pounded the French positions across the river. At noon Bock pushed forward the 3rd Battalion of the 33rd Fusilier Regiment and the 2nd Battalion of the 65th Regiment in an assault on Querrieux. The 33rd Regiment (Lieutenant Colonel von Henning) stormed into the village, driving its defenders back over the river into Pont Noyelles; when the 65th came up this village was also taken, and the French fell back up the slopes to their position along the hills, leaving many wounded and 200 unwounded prisoners in German hands. The 2nd Battalion of

German troops storm Pont-Noyelles. (*Illustrirte Kriegsgeschichte*)

the 33rd Regiment also came up to occupy Pont Noyelles together with a large part of the 65th Regiment's Fusilier Battalion.

Henning's remaining battalion had been aimed towards the village of Bussy les Daours, a village which straddled the river. There, part of the 1st Battalion of the 33rd Regiment, together with the 4th Squadron of the 7th Hussars, had taken up a position on the southern outskirts of the village. At about 1pm an attack from both battalions drove the defenders across the Hallue, and a skirmishing line was formed along the river.

Manteuffel had remained in Amiens with the reserve under Mirus, which consisted of the five battalions of the previously arrived 3rd Brigade from Rouen and the 5th Uhlan Regiment. This force, to which would be added units of the 2nd Brigade as they began to arrive from Rouen, was under orders to march out of the city at 11.00am and take up a position under cover south of the Querrieux wood on a line with Les Alençons, and Manteuffel accompanied them. Meanwhile the 2nd Battalion of the 3rd Regiment which had arrived at Rouen on the previous day had been posted at 10.00am at La Motte Brébière, on the Somme, with one squadron and one battery, at 10.00am with orders to hold the bridge there against any advance of the enemy along the right bank of the river.

In Bussy, Colonel von Dörnberg, the commander of the 65th Regiment, had four companies of infantry, together with the detachment of the 33rd Regiment which had participated in the capture of the village. He now moved south-east down the road to Vecquemont, a sprawling village on the west bank of the Hallue at its junction with the Somme. In this attack he had the co-operation of Colonel von Löe's force which had, in accordance with instructions, been moving along the bank of the Somme towards Vecquemont. The village's defenders put up an energetic defence, and little progress was made until at about 3.00pm the troops at La Motte Brébière came forward to

Looking from the French positions towards the German lines, near the Faidherbe monument above Pont-Noyelles. (Duncan Rogers)

The Faidherbe monument. (Duncan Rogers)

join in the struggle.. This had been on the direct orders of Manteuffel who, seeing the lack of progress, ordered Major von Lewinski of his staff to lead forward these troops. Lewinski interpreted his instructions literally; with Löe he rode ahead of their troops into Daours to see if the French were still there. As they made their way into the centre of the village there was a shout of 'Qui vive?' and a column of chasseurs appeared and opened fire on them. Löe and Lewinski galloped back, both unhurt. Meanwhile, the battle for Vecquemont had become a bitter house-to-house fight. The French had also now brought up to Daours, on the other side of the river, the units of Moulac's division which were to constitute the left of Faidherbe's position, resting on the Somme. By 4.00 however the troops of Löe and Lewinski had succeeded in taking first Vecquemont and then Daours.[14] At 4.40 Lewinski attempted to advance out of Daours, since its occupants were under heavy fire from the French infantry on the heights to the north of the village. Pushing both battalions up the steep slopes, Lewinski soon realised that there could be no chance of taking the position without suffering very heavy losses, and he fell back into Daours.

Hozier described one incident in the battle for Vecquemont and Daours:

Here both sides fought hard, appealing to the bayonet to settle the disputed possession of the villages, whose capture in fact formed one of the most remarkable incidents of the battle, as it was accomplished by the Rhenish rifle battalion against a whole division of the French army. With only about 800 men, Major Bronikowsky waited till the heavy columns of the enemy who came to attack him were within 90 paces. The Germans had every one waiting at this point with the eye on their enemy and the finger on the trigger; and when their commander gave the word 'Nun! Kinder, schnell feuer!' they sent such a volley into the ranks of the French as to leave upwards of 40 dead in one place.[15]

Further up the valley there had been bitter fighting around Pont Noyelles. For the defenders of the village a particular problem was a wood on the high hills to the north, which jutted out like a bastion. These heights commanded all the ground beneath them, and French batteries were soon in action from this very favourable position. As early as 1.30pm Kummer had ordered Strubberg to take his brigade northwards to Fréchencourt and from there attempt to assault the wooded height from the other side. Once that attack was launched an assault could be made up the slopes from Pont Noyelles.

Strubberg accordingly pushed forward Rosenzweig's 28th Regiment along the Fréchencourt road from Querrieux. It soon came under fire from the crest of the hills immediately opposite on the other side of the Hallue, and was obliged to halt and return fire. Strubberg, following behind with the 68th Regiment, swung past and entered Fréchencourt at the double just as a large body of French troops began to descend from the hill with the evident intention of occupying the village. The acting commander of

The French 33rd Line Infantry Regiment launch a bayonet charge during Pont-Noyelles, led by Captain d'Hauterive, by Tiret-Bognet. (Deschaumes)

the regiment, Major von Olszewski, was able to beat off the vigorous attack to hold the village. He then attempted to assault the wooded height that had caused so much trouble, but failed to dislodge the enemy. One hill was surrounded by densely lined rifle pits and was crowned by batteries firing from behind parapets, while the terraces on the slopes of the hill made it difficult of ascent.[16]

Kummer now held the line of the Hallue and the villages along its length from Daours to Fréchencourt. His division was, however spread out over a position some four and a half miles long, and he had no reserves of his own to commit to meet any French counter attack. He and Goeben were anxiously awaiting news of Barnekow's division and its attempt to turn the right flank of the French position. By about 2.00pm, however, it seemed to Goeben that Barnekow's movement might be having some effect on the enemy, as Wartensleben noted:

> Movements which the latter made towards his right wing tended to prove this. When this state of affairs was reported to General Manteuffel, he moved the reserve more to the front, so as to have them nearer at hand, either to support the 15th Division or to assume the offensive if these impressions were confirmed. General Manteuffel and his staff then joined General Goeben on the windmill hill at Querrieux.[17]

An episode of the action at Fréchencourt, by Zimmer. (Rousset/*Histoire*)

Prussian infantry are chased through woodland near Querrieux, by Bombled. (Grenest)

The anxiety felt by the staff of the VIII Corps was still considerable, and at 2.40pm Roberts rode north from Querrieux to see what was happening. As he did so, the sound of Barnekow's artillery greeted him, and he saw Gneisenau's troops moving southwards down the road from Contay towards Montigny and Béhencourt. He rode back to give the news to Goeben. After this he went into Querrieux to visit a wounded friend:

> Whilst I was in the house in which he lay a furious fire was opened upon the village, and my orderly came rushing up to tell me that, if we did not make haste, we should be taken prisoners, as the French had again attacked Querrieux, and the 65th were retiring. As I got to the street door, the last sections of the 65th were slowly falling back, whilst at the other end of the village I could see the dark uniforms of the chasseurs advancing. I made a rush at my horse, and scrambled into the saddle; but just at that moment the French chasseurs received a murderous fire from the 33rd, who advanced upon them from the cross streets with the bayonet, and once more drove them back pell mell out of the village.[18]

The French had also been threatening Pont Noyelles, the garrison of which consisted of four battalions. Enemy infantry had moved up close to the edge of the village. Henning, who was in command here, launched the 2nd Battalion of his 33rd Regiment, together with the 9th Company and some other troops, in an assault on the wooded height to the north, in order to relieve the pressure:

> With a vigorous rush, the 33rd gained the edge of the heights; detachments of the 5th and 8th companies led by Vice-Sergeant-Major Kising made a sudden dash on two guns in action, and captured them. But as considerable reinforcements now took part in the struggle on the French side, the East Prussian Fusiliers found themselves forced to retire, and were also compelled, after a brave resistance, to surrender again to the foe the two captured guns, one of which had been spiked.[19]

Barnekow's march north from Amiens had reached Rubempré by about 1.00pm, when he received Goeben's orders to march to his right on what was presumed to be Faidherbe's right flank. The direction which he was to take was to Beaucourt and Contay, although what would be his own right wing was to march through St Gatien. Barnekow left two companies of infantry and a troop of cavalry in Rubempré and set off at once. His left

Picquet, a soldier from the Gardes Mobiles of the Pas-de-Calais, shoots a Prussian officer from his horse. An episode from the actions around Pont-Noyelles, by Bombled. (Grenest)

flank was covered by the 9th Hussar Regiment. The first of his troops to come into action were the battalions of Gneisenau's 31st Brigade, which Roberts had seen advancing; these moved rapidly forward to Montigny and Béhencourt. Dohna's cavalry, who had been covering their sector, now moved further north, bringing their horse artillery into action against the French guns across the valley.

Léonce Patry's battalion had been well forward during the days preceding the battle, but he was surprised by the orders which came early on the morning of December 23:

> We took up our arms and, instead of taking position on the ground to the west and south-west of Contay that we had become familiar with for three days past, we were marched across to the left bank of the Hallue where we took position half way up the hills. As the enemy had not yet appeared in front of us we kept our men in ranks, well in hand. Major Tramond strongly criticised this way of doing things. According to him, instead of submitting to the enemy's moves and awaiting him passively, we should have gone forward and advanced squarely to meet him. Besides raising the morale of our young troops, by doing so we would have had the advantages of taking the enemy by his left flank while he was making a frontal attack on the line of the Hallue at Pont Noyelles.[20]

An episode from the actions around Pont-Noyelles, by Bombled. (Grenest)

Barnekow's division had meanwhile been engaged in the task first of seizing Bavelincourt, Montigny and Béhencourt and then, if possible, pushing forward to Franvillers to relieve the pressure on the left wing of the 15th Division. Before Béhencourt could be taken, the French launched an attack through the village which was only beaten back by a sharp struggle. The Fusilier Battalion of the 29th Regiment (Colonel von Blumroeder) endeavoured to follow up the retreating enemy but could not get across the river, the bridges having been destroyed. While the 1st Battalion extended the regiment's right to Fréchencourt, the fusiliers, under heavy fire, laid foot bridges across the river. This done, they made a dash into Béhencourt. There was a stubborn combat in the streets of the village; the French resistance was only overcome when the 2nd Battalion and other units of the 32nd Brigade were brought up.[21]

Colonel Mettler's 70th Regiment had led the advance of the 32nd Brigade, passing through Montigny before taking part in the struggle for Béhencourt. Thereafter, at about 4.00pm, the regiment had moved up the road to Bavelincourt, into which the 5th Company had already forced its way. Behind it, two batteries had opened fire from the height north of Beaucourt; but even when reinforced by the four batteries of the 2nd Field Division they could make little impression on the French gunners, firing from well-chosen positions on the commanding heights.

The capture of these three villages, and their successful defence against French counter attacks, was the most that Barnekow could achieve. Goeben's hope of turning Faidherbe's right had failed, because the French position extended much further north than had been realised. Barnekow had therefore become bogged down in what amounted to a stalemate; the strength of the French position was such that what would have been a frontal assault up the heights towards Franvillers must necessarily have cost very considerable casualties. Nor, it had become clear, would an assault on the wooded hill to the south of Fréchencourt succeed, even with further reinforcement from the 32nd Brigade.

Late in the afternoon Patry's battalion took part in an advance on the right of the French position, recrossing the river and occupying Contay without opposition. He thought that if this movement had been made two hours earlier it would have obliged the Germans to pull back from the villages which they had occupied along the river and the French would have had a real success to record:

> However, during the afternoon the commanding general had come to see what was happening on his right wing. General Derroja had explained the situation to him. Why had we not acted, particularly as we were risking nothing? Faidherbe had passed his whole military life far from the command of troops. An engineering officer and doubtless very intelligent, he was most interested in the study of colonial questions. His republicanism alone had got him appointed to the high post which he occupied. On that day he should have realised, if indeed he was a man able to estimate his own actions impartially, that one cannot improvise a commanding general. For he held in his hand a unique opportunity to inflict a first class lesson on the enemy, but he either did not know how or did not dare to take advantage of it.[22]

This sour comment, published very many years after the war, illustrates only the extent to which officers on the lower rungs of the ladder may fail to grasp the true situation. Although Patry's regiment was not launched in an assault on Barnekow's left, there is little doubt that if it had been it would have met the same fate as the assaults that were made, from Bavelincourt all the way down to Daours; and the Official History records in any case that one such attempt was made from the furthest north of the French positions:

> Shortly after 4.00pm a French column was already pressing forward from Contay upon Beaucourt; it was, however, compelled to turn back owing to the effective fire of the batteries unlimbered to the north of this village. When, subsequently, amid total darkness, the contending artilleries had ceased the struggle, and the German batteries were withdrawn to a position of readiness, the adversary threw himself suddenly into the wood north of Beaucourt and drove the troops of the 3rd Battalion 40th Regiment out of the wood. On being reinforced by the 7th and 8th Companies, the 40th Fusiliers, dislodging the enemy, re-established themselves, however, shortly afterwards in the wood in question.[23]

With the light beginning to fail, it was clear to Goeben and Manteuffel that further attacks would be pointless, as the Official History pointed out:

> As the short December day was already drawing to a close, no further offensive movement on the German side could be contemplated for the moment; the more pressing matter was to maintain the localities in our possession against any possible attempts at recapture by the enemy, for whose batteries excellent targets were offered in the villages on the Hallue, which illuminated the neighbourhood to a considerable distance with their flames.[24]

However, it was beginning to look as if the French might be preparing for a further assault, and Mirus was ordered to bring forward the reserve, which had been augmented by a battalion just arrived from Rouen, to a position close to the headquarters on the windmill hill.

It was a wise precaution. As night fell, Faidherbe judged that the moment had come to recapture the villages along the Hallue. Palat noted that so many houses had caught fire because of their thatched roofs: 'The columns of flames which eddied the whole length of the valley illuminated the positions of the enemy and served as a landmark for our guns.'[25] Faidherbe joined Moulac to watch the latter's assault on the right of the German line; simultaneously Lecointe, with Bessol's division and the Gardes Mobiles Regiment de la Somme et la Marne, was to launch a fresh attack on Pont Noyelles. Wartensleben described the start of the assault:

> About 5.00 pm, when darkness had completely set in, an advance of the enemy took place along the whole line. It was heralded in by the horn signal so well known from former battles, and accompanied by the noise which the French always make when they attack. At first a strong column advanced between Daours and Querrieux, trying to gain the passage over the Hallue and intercept the communication between both villages. It was a critical moment. The Commander in Chief immediately sent forward the 1st Battalion of the 4th Regiment from the reserve to meet the enemy.[26]

The reserve advanced from a position close to the headquarters hill, losing its commander, Captain Grumbrecht, who was killed almost at once. The battalion pressed on, however, and the destructive power of its rifle fire inflicted heavy losses on the French, who reeled back from the river; the battalion lost only six men wounded in this encounter.

On the extreme left of the French line Moulac sent forward Payen's brigade in a fierce attack on Daours. This attack made progress at first, certainly getting as close as 30 yards from the village; Palat says that it got into part of Daours and even into Vecquemont. In the end, however, Payen's men were beaten back with heavy loss by the weary troops of Loë and Lewinski, especially at the hands of the 8th Rifle Battalion, firing from the houses of Daours. Faidherbe had accompanied this attack in person; after it was launched, he withdrew to Corbie, where he met Doctor Testelin who had come to witness the battle, reporting that his troops had achieved complete success.[27]

Further up the river Lecointe had launched another attack on Pont Noyelles. In the first wave came the Gardes Mobiles Regiment de la Somme et la Marne, the most readily available troops of Bessol's division. Although the fire of the 33rd and 65th Regiments had begun to slacken because they were running out of ammunition the gardes mobiles hesitated in their assault in its village. When they got within 50 yards, a volley of rifle fire from the defenders threw them back, and they retreated in disorder, stumbling up the slope and being taken for Germans by the 72nd Regiment du Marche. In spite of the confusion caused by this mistake, Lecointe put together yet another attack on Pont Noyelles with all that he could gather up of the 72nd, the 18th Chasseur Regiment, and

Lecointe's attack on Pont-Noyelles, by Pallandre. (Rousset/*Les Combattants*)

the 101st Gardes Mobiles Regiment. This attack was at first successful, the leading troops entering the village. The Germans, whose ammunition was now all gone, defended themselves with the bayonet, and a bitter struggle ensued.[28] Manteuffel then sent forward two infantry battalions from his reserve and these stabilised the position before driving the French back out of the village again.

By about 7.00 pm the fighting ceased all the way along the line of the Hallue, with the Germans in occupation of all the villages which they had taken and the French still in possession of the line of hills on the east bank of the river. It was evident that there would be no further assaults that night, and Manteuffel ordered that the troops occupying the villages from Beaucourt to Daours should prepare them for defence. Mirus and the reserve went into alarm quarters between Allonville and Cardonette. The intention was that on the following day it should move to a position between St Gratien and Querrieux. The commander of the 3rd Regiment had arrived from Rouen, and he joined those of his troops that had been fighting at Daours and Vecquemont alongside the detachment of Loë and Lewinski; the orders were for those villages to be held until further orders, since they were crucially important for the defence of the line of the Hallue. Wartensleben noted, with some satisfaction, that it was possible in this way to put the troops into quarters for the night 'whereas the enemy, in expectation of our attacking him, was obliged to bivouack with almost the whole of his troops on the heights which formed his position, and on which there was a scarcity of villages.'[29] This was, of course, one point of view. Predictably Faidherbe put it very differently; after referring to his mistaken belief that his troops had taken Daours and Vecquemont:

French Chasseurs and Fusiliers Marines in the streets of Daours, by Pallandre. (Rousset/*Les Combattants*)

Despite these incidents, which were not known until the night, our troops occupied the positions which we had chosen and as a result believed themselves the victors. They were given to understand that in wartime a victory is gained when one bivouacks on the field of battle and that there could be no question of their returning to their billets, several miles to the rear.[30]

His young soldiers suffered dearly for their participation in this morale building exercise; during the night the temperature fell below -10°c, there was no wood for campfires and the only bread they had was frozen. That night Faidherbe shared their discomfort,

Streetfighting in
Pont Noyelles,
by Knötel. (Lindner)

shivering with cold and fever as he lay on a bed of snow among his troops near the village of Lahoussoye.[31]

Tactically, it had been a drawn battle, although events were to show that strategically it had been a German victory. Goeben subsequently took Faidherbe to task over a number of issues arising over the latter's account of the battle, and he was particularly cross about his claim that it was a French victory:

> The claim has no justification, as the following narrative of the facts sufficiently proves. The French may nevertheless have seen in the fact that we did not succeed in inflicting on them the complete defeat we had hoped for, with some justice a result, which even if it was clearly negative, was under the circumstances of that time very important, and permitted them to bewail more lightly the positive advantages won by us. That was enough to proclaim themselves victors.

He pointed to the strength of the French position; to the capture and the defence of the villages along the Hallue; and to the subsequent retreat of the French. He added sardonically that 'we, according to the French assumption the beaten ones, passed the night comfortably under cover, we cooked and we slept quietly, while the poor victorious ones up on the heights, had to stand out in the severe winter cold without fire and without nourishment.'[32] Nor was Goeben particularly impressed by Faidherbe's claim to have saved Le Havre by fighting on the Hallue; he was regretfully 'compelled to dispel this illusion,' pointing out that as early as December 11 he had pursued his march to the Somme, and that Le Havre was never in danger.

8

Retreat

While Faidherbe tried to compose himself for sleep among his shivering troops on the hills above the Hallue valley, Manteuffel and Goeben rode back to Amiens, pondering the conclusions to be drawn from the day's events. It was evident to them that the strength of the Army of the North was such that it was not feasible to get around its right flank, while a direct frontal assault would be altogether too costly. Wartensleben set out the position as it was seen at First Army's headquarters:

> To expose the army to such a loss would have been all the more unjustifiable because, in consequence of their loss from fatigue and fighting, and the vacancies not being always able to be filled up regularly, our battalions did not at that time upon an average number more than about 500 fighting men each. On the other hand, the firmness and brilliant bravery of our troops justified unbounded confidence in their power of endurance and tactical mobility, in both of which qualities they were superior to the enemy.[1]

For December 24, therefore, it was decided that the position currently held should be maintained until the enemy's intentions were discerned. If Faidherbe stayed where he was, the best option would, it was thought, be to attack him across the Somme at Corbie.

Léonce Patry spent the night of December 23/24 with his company on a hillside near Bavelincourt, particularly concerned to maintain a state of alert throughout the fearful cold of the night. He reflected on the position of affairs:

> While going from one man to another, as much to warm myself as to supervise them, I thought of the events of that day and congratulated myself that circumstances had given my men a post of such little danger for their first battle. In this way they were becoming inured to war effortlessly. They had maintained their position very well under a fire to which they could not respond, which nearly always gives rise to great nervous tension followed by profound demoralisation. Their morale was very good, and I was optimistic after their first trial.[2]

Although the German troops had the benefit of quarters, it was not always possible to be comfortable, as Captain Seton found:

> At dark I followed into a peasant's house the Brigade and Regimental Staff, where reports were received and orders issued. There was nothing to eat, but the poor old woman kept a fire for us all night; her husband was taken to show somebody somewhere, and was too frightened to return, so the poor creature sat up in great anxiety.

A French infantry Regiment on the march, by Detaille. (Rousset/*Histoire*)

Myself collected four chairs as a bed, but as each orderly who came in to see the Brigade Adjutant – lying on straw beside me – took one chair from under me, my rest was somewhat broken, and about midnight I had only one left.³

There was little contact during the night, apart from the occasional brush between outposts. As dawn broke beneath a leaden sky a bitter north-east wind blew in the faces of the German troops as they took up their positions along the Hallue. Soon, the French artillery opened up, and skirmishers moved forward between Contay and Beaucourt, but no attack was pressed. At about 10.30am there seemed to be some indication of a movement from the principal French position at Lahoussoye in the direction of Vadencourt, and Goeben ordered Dohna, with his six squadrons, a horse artillery battery and the 9th Hussar Regiment to move towards the French right flank; an infantry detachment covering Contay fell back, and the horse artillery shelled the village for a time.⁴

Around noon Prince Albrecht Junior arrived on the battlefield, having ridden ahead of his brigade to announce its imminent arrival. It was directed to take up a position on the right of the reserve, which had been brought up nearer to Querrieux. As the afternoon wore on there were reports of movements on the French side, especially in the vicinity of Corbie. Whether the columns reported by the Rifle Battalion at Daours were reinforcements or units retreating towards Arras was not at first clear. By 3.00pm however, there were indications that the numbers of French troops in their position on the hills was diminishing, and by 4.00pm it seemed certain to Colonel von Witzendorff,

Goeben's Chief of Staff, that the French were retreating. As darkness was falling by then, final confirmation could not be obtained, and Goeben was reluctant to take a chance on a night attack.[5]

What was now clear was that the possession of Corbie was critical to the French position. If Faidherbe stood his ground, this was an obvious point of attack; if he really was in retreat, he must be followed up. The orders issued for Christmas Day allowed for either eventuality. First, Mirus, with the reserve, the troops at Daours and the corps artillery, was that evening to cross to the left bank of the Somme and move eastwards, in order then to recross the Somme and attack Corbie. Bridging material was provided. The 15th Division would move southwards in the Hallue valley and, leaving a detachment in Daours, follow Mirus, while Barnekow edged to his right to keep in touch. Prince Albrecht's brigade was quartered in Amiens for the night. Orders also went to Senden to march westwards from St Quentin towards Ham.

During the night it became more apparent that the French were pulling back, and Manteuffel gave instructions to Goeben to hold fire on the orders previously issued until the situation was finally clarified. If indeed Faidherbe was falling back, then Goeben was to pursue him, while Mirus, after occupying Corbie, was to march eastwards on the left bank of the Somme to Bray.[6]

By dawn on Christmas Day the Army of the North was in full retreat, and having begun its march during the previous afternoon, and continued it during the night, it had gained a head start on its pursuers. Wartensleben generously observed that for the most part the retreat was conducted in an orderly fashion:

> We need not lay any great stress on the roads having been strewed by the arms which the less disciplined parts of the army had thrown away, nor on the number of stragglers captured during the pursuit. We also fully acknowledge the conduct of the newly organised French army, and the way it was handled in the battle; and we are far from calling the latter a defeat of the enemy, if this expression be understood to denote a catastrophe in which the tactical order of the beaten troops is more or less broken. Nevertheless, for us the battle of the Hallue had the value of an important and decisive victory.[7]

As to casualties, Faidherbe admitted to 141 killed, with 905 wounded, several hundred prisoners and about 1,000 missing. Most of the latter, he claimed, were gardes nationales who left more because of the privations and weariness of the two previous days than out of fear of the enemy. Many soon rejoined their units, and each day several more came in. He put the German loss as several thousand.[8] The actual German losses were 203 killed, 863 (plus one chaplain) wounded and 93 missing. The French losses were certainly much heavier than Faidherbe admitted. 291 of their dead were buried on the battlefield; by nightfall on December 23 19 officers and 953 unwounded prisoners were sent back to Amiens; more prisoners were taken during the following two days. What might be the true figure of the French wounded is unknown.[9] Palat, for his part, merely restated the figures given above, while setting out the wide disparities in the numbers taking part in the battle in the accounts given.

For General Derroja, the closing stages of the battle, and the subsequent retreat, had been somewhat unfortunate as Patry gleefully related:

German hussars skirmishing, by Knötel. (Pflug-Harttung)

General Derroja, in returning on horseback to Contay on the evening of December 23, got entangled in the stacked arms of the sentry post at the entrance to the village, no doubt placed too far in the middle of the road. Man, horse, the orderly who was following, and rifles were all reduced to a jumble which men of the post, who came out on hearing the commotion, had the utmost difficulty in untangling. The general was set on his feet again, all bumps and bruises. The next morning he could not move at all. However, he was bent on marching into combat with his division.[10]

Since mounting a horse was out of the question, Derroja attempted to requisition a carriage from the nearby château of the Countess de Ranchey. In this he was obstructed by the parish priest who only allowed the removal of the carriage, after lengthy negotiation, upon production of a formal written receipt.

On the German side Sir Randal Roberts rode with Goeben's staff as the pursuit began on December 25, heading in the first instance towards Albert:

At Franvillers we heard that Albert was occupied by the French troops: so that it would be necessary, if they intended remaining, to drive them out in order to get quarters for the night. As we rode through Lahoussoye the dead bodies lying about and collected close by the graveyard spoke but too plainly of the carnage of December 23. The severe frost had stiffened them into all sorts of quaint attitudes; and as we passed the churchyard, friend and foe were being buried in the same grave. Arrived at Albert, we found that General Robin with 3,000 men had just left it; so that we were treading on the heels of the retiring enemy pretty quickly.[11]

Faidherbe was clear that he should ask no more of his inexperienced troops for the moment; they had become disorganised after the days of combat and manoeuvre, and needed rest. In addition, it was necessary to resupply them, and Faidherbe selected a position behind the Scarpe, with his left on Douai and his right on Arras, in which to give them time to recuperate. In his account of the campaign, he observed that the enemy did not try to seek out the Army of the North, but merely sent scouts around Arras and as far as the Lens road.[12] In fact, the Germans were a good deal more active than this. On December 27 Goeben pushed forward the Guard Cavalry Brigade on his right as far as

Fins, moving the 29th Brigade to Sailly-Saillisel. The 32nd Brigade occupied Bucquoy. The 31st Brigade was committed to the operations against Péronne, to take the place of the 3rd Brigade, which was to be returned to Rouen, where Bentheim required it.

The cavalry continued to be active in probing the positions occupied by the Army of the North:

> Strong columns scoured the neighbourhood for some distance, but only on rare occasions fell in with hostile parties, and frequently penetrated with patrols to the very walls of Arras; a small detachment of cavalry, among others, rode unopposed into the streets of Cambrai. These enterprises had more particularly for their object the destruction of the railways leading to Arras.[13]

One such expedition, led by Colonel von Wittich, with the 9th Hussar Regiment and some infantry in carts, had as its objective the railway at Lens. Reaching Avesnes le Comte, it advanced on December 29 in a north-easterly direction. At Souchez, about six miles north of Arras, Wittich surprised a battalion of gardes mobiles, taking 8 officers and 173 men prisoners. Pushing on, he encountered very superior forces, and was obliged to fall back without reaching Lens. On December 31 the 4th Squadron of the Guard Hussars advanced from Fins and destroyed the railway north of Cambrai, near Iwuy, returning on the same day to its quarters after a ride of 50 miles.[14]

The return of the 3rd Brigade to Rouen was a response to reports of increased French activity on both banks of the Seine. On December 27 Bentheim reported to Manteuffel that strong columns were advancing on Bourgachard. Continuous skirmishing was now taking place between outposts. By December 29 a French column, said to be 10,000 strong was approaching the line La Bouille-Elbeuf, while on the right bank there were some 8,000 men at St Romain, between Bolbec and Harfleur. During the evening of December 30 there was further news for Manteuffel from Bentheim; the French had begun an attack which his troops were resisting at Grande Couronne, while on the right back patrols had encountered French troops between Bolbec and Yvetot. The threat to Rouen was one which Manteuffel was obliged to take very seriously. All the indications were that the I Corps was likely to be heavily outnumbered by the forces approaching on both banks of the Seine. Bentheim's reports appeared to be confirmed by a despatch from Versailles to the effect that at Bernay General Lauriston had six line battalions, a marine battalion, 12,000 gardes mobiles, 600 cavalry and several batteries, and that he was advancing to support the attack down the right bank from Le Havre.[15]

Manteuffel decided that Rouen was now the point of greatest danger and with part of his staff and a small infantry escort set off by train on the morning of December 31 from Bernieres. The journey of just over 67 miles was accomplished in a little more than two hours. Other units detached from the I Corps for the fighting around Amiens followed him. As his missing troops were returned to him, Bentheim was asked to reinforce his defensive positions on both banks of the river, awaiting the expected French offensive. When this failed to materialise on December 31, Bentheim himself went over to the attack. Falkenstein, advancing in three columns between Grande Couronne and La Roquette, was soon in contact with the enemy. On his left, moving towards Orival, he soon overcame the French troops in that village. His centre column got as far as La Londe before running into very superior forces. On his right the column under

Lieutenant Colonel Von Meerscheidt-Hüllessem advanced through the woods south of the main road against the ruined castle of Robert Le Diable, on a steep conical hill, which was held by some 200 French troops. The 3rd and 4th companies of the 41st Regiment, after driving off some French infantry that had come up in support, stormed the ruin, taking prisoner two officers and 80 men. As night fell, Falkenstein pulled all three columns back to their start line.[16]

Manteuffel, satisfied that Bentheim had matters in hand, returned to Amiens on January 1, having agreed with the latter that as soon as the 44th Regiment had been returned to him from Amiens he should make a brisk attack on the French troops on the left bank of the Seine. Thereafter the I Corps must be prepared once again to give up units that were required for the operations on the Somme. It was Manteuffel's intention, when he got back to Amiens, to make arrangements to bring up the 14th Division, which had been besieging Mézières; the fortress capitulated on New Year's Day. In this, however he was disappointed; with an eye to the developing situation in the south-east of France Moltke had already decided that it should be sent to Châtillon-sur-Seine, where it would in due course form part of the South Army. Back on the Somme, meanwhile, the issue that was occupying much of the attention of Manteuffel's staff was the need to deal with Péronne.

9

The Investment of Péronne

It was becoming apparent at the headquarters of the First Army that the question of Péronne must urgently be dealt with. Wartensleben reviewed the position:

> Ever since the campaign in Picardy began, the influence of this small fortress had been felt, from its disturbing our lines of communication and in every way assisting the operations of the enemy. In the beginning it was only a starting point and support for flying columns and small surprises, but latterly it had served to cover the concentration of the enemy's army and to assist its action, which, to a certain degree, took us unawares. Being situated on the *right* bank of the Somme, it was not, properly speaking, a *tête du pont* for operations directed southwards; but, nevertheless, it favoured any sudden debouché of the enemy, unless it was continually watched and held in check by a body of troops sufficiently strong for the occasion.[1]

All the while the French held Péronne the First Army could not completely control the line of the Somme from La Fère to Amiens, and this, to hold off any attempt by the Army of the North to move south towards Paris, it must be able to do.

Thus far, the commitment to hold Rouen, and the active operations against the Army of the North, had limited the First Army's ability to deal with Péronne. An even greater problem had been the lack of a siege train; it had been resolved not to attack any fortress until this was available. It was a principle that experience before La Fère, and in relation to the fortresses of the Ardennes, had already proved sound. Once the siege train was in place, a couple of days' bombardment had been enough to overcome the resistance of these fortresses. Against this, there was the example of Amiens, where the deployment of a large force of field artillery had been enough to lead to the citadel's surrender; and it was thought possible that Péronne, which did not appear formidable, might go the same way. The Germans were, perhaps, getting a little overconfident.

Péronne, at which several main roads intersected, commanded the swampy river valley, which was more or less impassable for very large bodies of troops. The town lies about 12 miles east of Albert and the same distance south-east of Bapaume. Tiedemann, the historian of the siege operations during the Franco Prussian War, described the fortress as it stood in 1870:

> The fortifications date from different periods, and have therefore a very irregular trace; some of the ramparts are connected with a castle which appears to be very ancient; it is included within the works. The main enceinte is in the form of a long rectangle, in front of it and to the north lies the suburb of La Bretagne, to the south the suburb of Paris, both defended by crownworks. The west side of the fortress

consists of four irregular bastioned fronts with small ravelins; the east, on the other hand, consists of an almost straight line of fortification without a single outwork. On the ramparts of the town are four mediaeval towers, one of which in 1468 served as a prison for Louis XI when he fell into the hands of Charles the Bold, whilst at the foot of another Charles the Simple died.[2]

Tiedemann noted that in spite of its small area the fortress belonged to the first class, and was one of those that were kept in a good state of defence. It was, however, surrounded by flat topped ridges useful for artillery positions at long range. On either side of the Somme the ground rises to a height of about 200 feet above the valley, and it effectively commanded the fortress.[3] The village of Ste Radegonde, close to the west front, also hampered the defence. Ultimately, therefore, the fortress was not capable of a sustained defence. It had been strengthened in the seventeenth century on the basis of Vauban's recommendations, and later on was further extended. The range and power of modern artillery, however, rendered it vulnerable to a determined attack.

Péronne had about 4,000 inhabitants in the old town and the two suburbs. At the end of December 1870 the garrison consisted of some 3,500 men, mostly gardes mobiles. The commandant was the able and energetic Major Garnier, who had been in post since the middle of August. He had a total of 49 guns with which to defend the place, of which 14 were rifled; the garrison was well supplied with ammunition.[4]

At Péronne, the Somme was about ten yards wide, with a depth of five feet. However, the navigable canal which flowed parallel to it was much broader and deeper. The valley could be flooded to a considerable distance by a system of dams, and in this way provided protection to the south-east, south-west and part of the north-west front against a *coup de main*, and made difficult an approach to the fortress.

The first contact with the fortress had come on November 23, as von der Groeben's 3rd Cavalry Division had been marching towards Amiens, ahead of the main body of the First Army. Patrols approaching Péronne from the south had at that time encountered no French outposts at all, and von der Groeben's troopers had gone on their way without incident. It seems that at that time the fortress had not yet been provided with ammunition.[5] During the following days, and after the battle of Amiens, it continued to be von der Groeben's responsibility to keep an eye on Péronne. Although at the beginning of December there were still no outposts in front of the place, by December 6 patrols reported that the French had now occupied the village of Biaches, to the west of the fortress. When the 3rd Cavalry Division moved to the left prior to the battle of the Hallue, von der Groeben pushed the 3rd and 4th Squadrons of the 14th Uhlan Regiment to watch Péronne.

Faidherbe, concerned at the speedy surrender of so many French fortresses, had written to Garnier on December 15 to stiffen his resolve, urging him not to follow these examples of weakness, and promising that while the Army of the North was in the field he could count on its support. In his account of the campaign Faidherbe describes two incidents involving parties of von der Groeben's cavalry at Péronne.

> The Prussians approached. Their insolence revealed itself in an audacious attempt: a young lieutenant presented himself as a parlementaire and summoned the fortress to surrender in the name of an imaginary general. From considerations of respect

he was allowed to leave. It was attempting the impossible: 'I had 12 troopers,' he said laughingly in the inns of the neighbouring villages, 'if I had had 24 the place would have been mine.' The demand was presented again some days later by a captain from the same regiment (7th Lancers of the Rhine) who was accompanied by a lieutenant and the trumpeter prescribed by custom. He left outside our lines 20 troopers, who scattered around the fortress in order to reconnoitre our position, map in hand. He also summoned the town to surrender. However, these officers were less fortunate than their predecessors; they were held prisoner in Péronne because they had none of the regulation characteristics of a parlementaire. Later it was known with certainty that their approval had been equally a bluff.[6]

It should be borne in mind, however, that Faidherbe's comments on the siege of Péronne may not be entirely reliable; they were based, as he acknowledged, on the account provided by the Sub Prefect, M. Blondin, who remained within the town until its capitulation.

Following the battle of the Hallue, Manteuffel gave orders for the investments to be completed by December 27. This was to be undertaken by the army reserve under Mirus, which was to cross to the right back of the Somme at Bray and march to the north front of the fortress, and by Senden's force advancing from Ham to take up a position on the south and east. In case the *coup de main* should fail, the First Army staff had looked about for siege guns, and found these among the captured French materiel at Amiens and La Fère, so far as they could be spared from the defences of these places. The officer in command of the artillery at Amiens, Lieutenant Schmidt, had already advised that ten siege guns, with 200 rounds of ammunition per gun, could be released from the citadel. If not as powerful a siege train as would be desirable, it would certainly strengthen the chances of success, and Schmidt was ordered on December 25 to prepare it for action under his command. It would consist of six rifled 12-pounders, with two mortars and two howitzers. Its movement would require 257 horses and 53 wagons. 6 mortars were also procured from La Fère. Since Schmidt could not be ready to move before December 28, the attempt on Péronne was to begin with a brief bombardment by field artillery.[7]

Goeben and Wartensleben were very sensitive to and much annoyed by the criticisms made of the Germans in relation to their siege operations by Faidherbe and others, and were at pains to point out that the policy adopted was no different from that of the French. Watensleben wrote of these French critics:

> They attempt to stigmatise our treatment of the hostile fortresses as inhuman, because the form of attack we employed against the smaller places was that of bombardment, which produces the quickest result. Setting aside the fact that their mode of attack is perfectly justified by the usages of war, we find the conduct of the French themselves inconsistent with this opinion. In point of humanity there can be no difference between the inhabitants of a town or those of a village. If, therefore, from good military reasons, the *French* General Faidherbe bombarded and burnt the *French* village of Pont Noyelles, the *German* general was surely justified in bombarding a *hostile* town defended by fortifications and troops, the possession of which was of military importance to him.[8]

Goeben was, for his part, sharply critical of Faidherbe for the observations which the latter made; after remarking that his opponent had merely reproduced extracts from the article by M. Blondin, and that it was 'not to be wondered that the appreciation of the military relation of things to each other is very weak', he went on:

> It is certainly in the highest degree surprising that even a man like General Faidherbe, in his reflections on the capitulation of Péronne, allowed himself to be moved to similar and still stronger invectives.[9]

The Germans certainly intended to waste no time in dealing with Péronne. On the morning of December 27 Mirus crossed the Somme with his main body at Bray and moved to a position south of Combles without meeting any opposition. From there he sent forward patrols which reported that the villages between him and Péronne were occupied; when he formed up his advanced guard to attack, however, he found that the French had fallen back to Péronne. His force went into quarters that night at Cléry, some four and a half miles south of Combles, while his cavalry rode further east to the road to Le Catelet in order to make contact with Senden's force. Meanwhile south of the Somme Colonel Tietzen had reached Villers-Carbonnel. Senden, advancing from Ham, found the villages of Bruntel and Doingt to be held by French troops, but a brisk attack by his advanced guard soon drove the defenders back into Péronne, their retreat being covered by the guns of the fortress. Senden took up a position to the south of the town, as far as the Somme, going into quarters in Bruntel, Doingt, Cartigny and the villages around Tincourt. Major General von Strantz, with the 3rd Reserve Cavalry Brigade, had ridden to Tincourt to establish communication with the Guard Cavalry Brigade at Sailly, completing the ring of German units around Péronne. Away to the south, Lippe had arrived at Roye with two cavalry regiments, a rifle battalion and a battery of horse artillery, and during the day he moved forward to Nesle, about eight miles west of Ham.

During the day Manteuffel rode to Combles, establishing his headquarters there about noon. Before setting off, he had issued orders putting Senden in command of all the troops facing Péronne, and instructing Lippe to continue his march eastwards to St Quentin to cover the east flank of the investment, and also to reconnoitre towards Cambrai. Later he sent orders to Senden to establish his field batteries on December 28 in the positions selected for a bombardment of Péronne. These were a little over a mile from the centre of the town, one to the southwest of the Péronne-Cléry road and one on a hill west of Doingt. Péronne was to be summoned to surrender at once: if it did not, the bombardment by the field artillery was to be commenced, although to conserve ammunition for subsequent field operations, it was not to be prolonged.

Covering the north of the investment, Goeben remained in position close to Bapaume. Probing forward towards Arras, his patrols had found that the nearest villages to the west of that fortress were unoccupied, suggesting that there was no immediate advance contemplated by the Army of the North, which appeared to have retreated to Douai. Kummer's 15th Division, with 11 battalions, 4 squadrons and 24 guns, moved towards Arras; on the left at Bucquoy von der Groeben had one battalion, with 12 squadrons and 6 guns, while Prince Albrecht was at Fins with three battalions, 12 squadrons and 18 guns.

By midday on December 28 Senden had his batteries in place, and at that time he sent in a parlementaire with a summons to surrender. According to Faidherbe's account, borrowed from M. Blondin, (and followed by Palat), the summons read as follows:

> The Army of the North has retreated to behind Arras, my troops have surrounded the fortress of Péronne on all sides. I summon you to surrender, declaring that I have the means to compel you to do so and will hold you responsible for all the misfortunes which a bombardment will inflict on the civilian population.

To this Garnier replied:

> I have but one reply to make to your summons: the government of my country has placed the fortress of Péronne under my command and I will defend it to the last gasp. I throw back on you the responsibility for all the misfortunes which, by your account and and contrary to the practices of war between civilised nations, you will inflict on a peaceful population.[10]

This account is at odds with that of Wartensleben, who records that the first response by Garnier to the summons was to say that he would send a flag of truce but that when none arrived, the batteries opened fire in spite of a thick mist at 3.00 pm.[11] The Official History puts the time of opening fire at 2.30 pm. 58 guns were in position. Three heavy batteries were located east of Hallue, south of the Péronne–Cléry road; two light batteries between Mont St Quentin and a windmill to the east on the road to Fins; two heavy batteries and a light battery on the height west of Doingt; a light battery to the west of Biaches; and a horse artillery battery on the height north of La Maisonette.[12]

The batteries had been located with particular care:

> It appeared that the place could be bombarded best from the heights on the north, west, and east, from which position there were good objects for the batteries to aim at, so as to meet the artillery of the place on favourable terms, without danger of suffering from its fire on account of the nature of the ground. The guns on the north front were very well placed for successful practice, as they faced the long side of the fortress. There being no intention of constructing regular batteries with approaches, the guns were placed so as to take advantage of natural cover, or they were protected by epaulments.[13]

The need to avoid damage to the field artillery was paramount; it was highly likely that it would soon be required for mobile operations against the Army of the North. The bombardment was at first not intense, but the volume of the fire was gradually stepped up. The fortress artillery replied, concentrating particularly on the heavy batteries near Hallue, where they caused some loss. As the bombardment continued, fires broke out in various parts of the town, whose inhabitants took refuge in their cellars. Apart from the damage to buildings, the bombardment seems to have been relatively ineffective; according to General Palat only a few men were killed or wounded.[14]

Senden's orders having been to be sparing of ammunition, and not to continue the bombardment beyond December 29, the rate of fire was reduced during that day

A scene from the Siege of Péronne, by Pallandre. (Rousset/*Les Combattants*)

and entirely stopped at nightfall. Nonetheless, it was calculated that at its height, the German field artillery was firing at the rate of 600 shells per hour and that when it ceased some 10,000 shells had fallen on the town. Not perhaps surprisingly, the inhabitants on December 29 petitioned Garnier to capitulate, a request which he refused.[15]

At the headquarters of the First Army it soon seemed clear that more would be required to bring about the early fall of Péronne, and Schmidt's siege train was put in motion, to reach Villers Carbonnel on December 30. If by nightfall on December 29 the place had not capitulated Senden was to break off the bombardment, pull back his infantry as well as the artillery, and await Schmidt's arrival. On December 30 Mirus was relieved by Gneisenau's 31st Combined Infantry Brigade, since the troops constituting the army reserve were now urgently needed at Rouen, whence Manteuffel, as has been seen, had gone on December 31.

At Lille the indefatigable Colonel Villenoisy had been working tirelessly in support of the operations of the Army of the North. Under his management astonishing progress had been made to strengthen the army, both in terms of the numbers of infantry units that had been raised and also the even more difficult task of creating new batteries of artillery that were already playing an important part in operations. A stream of proposals came regularly from him to Faidherbe and Farre; his distance from army headquarters meant that he was frequently obliged, in order to avoid delay, to take critical decisions himself. Paying tribute to the energy with which he discharged his functions, the French Official History later listed the kind of problems which Villenoisy had to overcome:

> To the lack of arms, the exhaustion of resources, the impossibility of forming new units were added many other difficulties which might cause him to despair. Among

German prisoners are brought into Péronne, by Tiret-Bognet. (Deschaumes)

these were the inventors who besieged him with their obsessions; a former prefect who claimed to have established a camp of mobiles at Helfaut, near Saint Omer; the senior officer at Givet, one Major Voluet, who announced that he was going to sell all his provisions and disperse his garrison in small groups.[16]

Evidently the prefect referred to had been making trouble with the War Ministry, for on December 31 we find Villenoisy writing an impassioned letter to Tours on the subject:

> Neither the Commander in Chief, nor his staff, have any intention of hampering the organisation of the camp at Helfaut, so long as the army is not deprived of the men, the arms and the materiel, without which everything becomes impossible. We are snowed under with the day to day work; we are trying to provide for the army without weakening the garrisons; we are doing all we can and implore you not to render our efforts fruitless. It is very difficult to appreciate these things at a great distance, but particularly to be convinced that there is no bad intent.

Villenoisy went on to a subject on which he felt especially deeply:

> General Faidherbe spends ten hours on horseback each day, exhausting himself and, in the opinion of everyone, does far too much; but who could replace him? General Farre is, like him, under enormous pressure.[17]

10

Bapaume

The energy with which the German forces were setting about the task of reducing Péronne made it evident to Faidherbe that he must do something very quickly if the town was to be saved. His troops had had several days to recover from their exertions on the Hallue, and he determined once again to advance out of the protection of his fortresses against Goeben's troops which barred his way. Patry, writing of these days 'sheltered behind the almost impassable line of the Scarpe' recorded that his battalion, in its billet at Athies, 'had a very pleasant existence.'[1] Not all of the Army of the North had been enjoying such a peaceful relaxation, since German cavalry patrols had been actively reconnoitring the positions of the French, giving various detached bodies of French troops a very hard time.

On the western flank of the VIII Corps Lieutenant Colonel von Pestel had been particularly active. His flying column consisted of the 7th Uhlan Regiment and the Fusilier Battalion of the 70th Regiment. This force had been assembled at Picquigny on December 25, and had marched via Molliens Vidame through Airaine. On December 28 he swung to his right on Longpré and surprised a detachment consisting of three battalions of gardes mobiles. After an engagement of two hours he routed this force, suffering casualties of only five wounded. The French lost 50 men killed and wounded, and 252 prisoners. Pestel continued his march through Domart to Abbeville. On December 30 he attempted, without success, to induce the commandant of the place to surrender. Abbeville was no longer a regular fortress, but it was partly protected by a formidable wall as well as earthworks, and provided an assembly point for the gardes mobiles.[2]

A French advance with the object of relieving Péronne was always seen by Manteuffel and Goeben as being very much on the cards, and the cavalry activity was intended to give as much warning as possible of such a move. The troops available to Kummer to resist a southerly advance by Faidherbe were so weak that they offered in any case a tempting target, and it was no surprise when the cavalry reported that the Army of the North had begun to move south. Faidherbe had concentrated his army to the south of Arras, and on December 31 advanced with the 22nd Corps towards Bucquoy and Achiet le Grand, and the 23rd Corps down the road to Bapaume.

Faidherbe issued an Order of the Day on December 31 from Arras, over the signature of his Chief of Staff:

> We are about to manoeuvre in the presence of the enemy. We must march and guard ourselves in a military fashion; not a single man must leave the ranks. Unit Commanders will take care to ensure this; during our advances and our battles, cavalry will be placed in the rear to prevent stragglers from abandoning their posts.

Unit Commanders will take care to evacuate their sick and those unable to march, to Arras.

At Pont Noyelles we were unable to complete our victory because the enemy was close to a fortified city. Today, that advantage is in our favour.

I am therefore counting on you, when the order is given, to charge the enemy vigorously, in the French way, until he is put to flight.

The eyes of France are upon you; let each of you swear to conquer or die, and victory is certain.[3]

On the following day, on the other side of the hill, Manteuffel was issuing a New Year's Day order:

I wish a happy New Year to the First Army. I feel pride in being at the head of this army. It has gained the victory single handed in four battles: before Metz, at Noisseville, Amiens and the Hallue; in three other battles, Saarbrücken, Vionville, and Gravelotte, it has taken a decisive part and helped to achieve the victory ... It has always been the lot of the First Army to fight against superior numbers of the enemy, because its manifold and extensive labours seldom allowed it to be concentrated. The fatigues the army has undergone and the difficulties it has surmounted were of no common kind, and even now it has still been fighting and bivouacking amidst ice and snow ... May God's blessing rest on our shoulders in the new year also, and grant them new victories. That is my prayer.[4]

In maintaining the siege of Péronne while the enemy was moving forward, Goeben was taking a considerable risk, since the covering force was so weak as to be extremely vulnerable. He was under no illusion as to the hazardous nature of his situation. He could of course have raised the siege of Péronne, leaving a small covering force to watch the fortress, while concentrating the rest of his army to deal with the Army of the North, but he was determined to take out Péronne as quickly as possible. He reported candidly to Manteuffel on the dangers of the situation on December 31:

I am sorry to say that matters in front of Péronne have in no way changed, or rather, had not done so up to yesterday evening; but I hope that we shall succeed today in opening fire with the small siege train from Amiens. With regard to the enemy's army, a change has in so far taken place, as it now occupies the villages in the immediate neighbourhood of the fortresses, and displays, on the whole, a greater degree of activity. It is said that considerable transports of troops from Douai to Cambrai took place yesterday, and that up to yesterday evening 15,000 men were assembled there. Our patrols have observed a great many trains passing from Douai. It seems, therefore, that an advance will be made for the purpose of relieving Péronne, and I do not deceive myself as to the fact that, if such an attempt should be made on a large scale, I shall – as two infantry brigades must be left at Péronne – not remain strong enough to resist it with the prospect of success.[5]

Goeben added that the covering force would be only 16 battalions strong. He was anxious about the situation of Pestel's flying column; its ambitious commander had reported his intention of going with his force first to Crécy and then to Nouvion which, he thought, was 'very venturesome as regards the infantry.' Goeben demonstrated his determination to maintain the siege of Péronne by moving his headquarters to Combles in order to be nearer to the operations against the fortress.

Randal Roberts did not like Combles; it was, he thought, 'not an engaging town – it is straggling, ill-built, dirty and comfortless.' However, he went on to record that it was not to be despised:

> In the best house of the town we found the ever-provident and truly wonderful Baron von Lilien had metamorphosed a dreadfully cold and uncomfortable room into a cheery-looking dining *Saal*. 16 plates were laid upon a table which, of course, as an article of furniture, would hardly bear inspection; but then a long white tablecloth covers a multitude of sins.[6]

The first of Goeben's units to make significant contact with the enemy was the 1st Battalion of the 28th Regiment, which he had pushed forward to Béhagnies as a result of reports from the cavalry that French units were advancing down the Arras road. At about noon on January 2 a strong force began an enveloping attack on the village. This was the leading brigade of Payen's division, commanded by Lieutenant Colonel Michelet, who had taken over the brigade when naval Captain Payen was made divisional commander in succession to Admiral Moulac. It consisted of the 19th Chasseurs de Marche, a regiment of Marine Fusiliers and the 48th Garde Mobile Regiment, amounting to seven battalions in all. In the face of an advance by what was obviously a considerable force, the 1st Battalion retreated from Béhagnies, and took up a position at Sapignies, alongside the 2nd Battalion, and the 2nd and 3rd Squadrons of the 7th Hussars. Behind these units, the 2nd Heavy and 2nd Light Batteries of the VIII Corps artillery had come up from Bapaume. The position extended on the right about one and a half miles to Favreuil, and was about two miles north of the centre of Bapaume. To its left, it was supported by two fusilier companies and two guns, which had moved from Achiet le Grand towards the high road. Kummer, with Strubberg, the 30th Brigade commander, was on the high road as the French attack developed.[7]

Derroja's division, of which Patry's regiment remained part, was advancing to the right of the advance on Béhaguies and Sapignies. Marching out of Bucquoy at midday Patry could hear the gunfire:

> So had the battle already begun? We must get going at once if we were to take part in it. We were ordered to hurry. We crossed the Arras-Amiens railway line at Achiet le Grand station. We halted for a few moments. It seemed that the struggle hereabouts had been hot. The station was almost completely demolished. As we could make out the smoke of battle in the distance, I climbed to the first floor for a better look. A shell had burst right in the middle of the stationmaster's living room and had left all the furniture in a pitiful state. The appearance of this room was truly grotesque. You could no longer recognise the shape of any object, so greatly had the shell splintered and the flame from its charge disfigured, mangled, pulverised and consumed everything.[8]

The combat at Béhagnies, January 2, by Pallandre. (Rousset/*Les Combattants*)

Marine Hamel carries a wounded officer to safety during the Battle of Bapaume, by Bombled. (Grenest)

Derroja's division had driven back von der Groeben's outposts south-east of Bienvillers aux Bois and was advancing to the support of Bessol's division. Night fell before it could take part in the fighting, and the division went into quarters for the night, Patry's regiment being billeted at Achiet le Petit.

Meanwhile at Sapignies the action was hotting up. Several French batteries deployed around Béhagnies and opened fire, under cover of which a large body of infantry advanced against Sapignies, forcing back the 8th Company of the 28th Regiment. At this point Major Mertens, the commander of the 15th Division artillery, countermanded an order to the artillery to retire, and responded vigorously to the French bombardment. A half squadron of the 7th Hussar Regiment was close to hand; Mertens ordered its commander, Lieutenant von Pourtalès, to charge the advancing French infantry. This he did, at once driving back the French skirmish line. Kummer now ordered a general advance, and by 2.00pm the 28th Regiment had driven the French out of Béhagnies, taking 250 prisoners in the process. The regiment then halted and prepared the village for defence.[9]

On the left of Payen's division, that of General Robin had been advancing further to the east by way of St Léger. This advance obviously threatened the units in the Sapignies position, and Kummer ordered Major von Olszewski to take the Fusilier Battalion of the 68th Regiment to a position east of Sapignies to cover the right flank. His 11th Company, which pushed forward to Mory, soon encountered large bodies of enemy infantry, and was obliged to fall back, Olszewski taking up an extensive position on the hills north of Favreuil and Beugnâtre. The activity shown by the fusiliers entirely

An episode of the action at Sapignies, by Leclercq. (Rousset/*Histoire*)

deceived Robin as to the strength of the enemy opposing him, and in spite of a good deal of manoeuvring on his part, night fell with his division still at Mory and Vaux. It was a missed opportunity; had he pressed forward he could certainly have driven Olszewski back and turned the right of the Sapignies position. Faidherbe certainly thought so, commenting that Robin's arrival would have changed the outcome if he had moved as swiftly as he had been ordered.[10]

Bessol's division had, after a combat of about an hour and a half, taken Achiet le Grand and advanced as far as Bihucourt. The two companies of the 28th Regiment, which had opposed them, had fallen back through Biefvillers to Avesnes les Bapaume, where it was undisturbed for the rest of the day. Night fell with the Germans being reinforced by Bock's 29th Brigade, two battalions of which went to the right of the line, occupying Beugnâtre and Frémicourt, while a third battalion reinforced the Biefvillers-Avesnes position. The remainder of Kummer's 15th Division was concentrated in and around Bapaume, while von der Groeben was south-west of the town on the Albert road.

Faidherbe's plan for January 3 was to attack Bapaume, advancing from a half circle around the town from the west to the north-east. Derroja was to move on Grévillers, Bessol on Biefvillers, Payen down the high road and Robin to the east of Favreuil. Faidherbe enjoyed a very substantial numerical superiority; the strength of the German battalions had been generally reduced to some 600 men, and several had no more than 350-400. Squadrons had from 100 to 120 men. Goeben calculated Kummer's strength as being no more than 5,500 men, with 24 guns.[11] The forces available to resist Faidherbe's advance consisted of Kummer's 15th Division (Bock's 29th Brigade had five battalions, a squadron of the 7th Hussars and two batteries, while Strubberg's 30th Brigade amounted to four battalions, three squadrons and two batteries); von der Groeben's 3rd Cavalry Division (Mirus's detachment of one battalion and two and a half squadrons, and Dohna's 7th Cavalry Brigade of two regiments and a horse artillery battery); Colonel

Looking towards Bihucourt in the direction of the French advance. (Duncan Rogers)

von Hertzberg's 32nd Brigade of four battalions, one cavalry regiment and two batteries; and finally Prince Albrecht's Combined Guard Cavalry Brigade, with two cavalry regiments, a fusilier battalion and a horse artillery battery. Goeben's reserve consisted of the 8th Rifle Battalion and two horse artillery batteries. All told, he had no more than 10,000 men available to meet the attack of the Army of the North, which was four times as strong.[12]

In the first instance Kummer was going to have to face the whole strength of the Army of the North. Such as it was, Bapaume itself must be where he based his resistance to the French advance. During the night his engineers began the task of putting the town in a state of defence. It was not a very effective strongpoint:

> This little town, of about 3,000 inhabitants, once a stronghold, had been déclassée in 1846; its enceinte served only as a reminder of its past history. Part of it still existed to the south and southwest; the ditches were intact at these points. Elsewhere a boulevard planted with trees had replaced the ancient ramparts. The Prussians had thus every facility for organising the defence. During the night of January 2 and the following morning they crenellated several houses at the northern end of the town and close to the market. Barricades closed the main street and also those leading from the square. These works, which went on throughout the following day, greatly assisted the task of the 15th Division.[13]

Kummer placed the 30th Brigade and the 7th Hussars in front of Bapaume. Five companies of the 68th Regiment were in a somewhat advanced position at Favreuil. The 2nd Battalion of the 65th Regiment was at Frémicourt, the 1st Battalion at Beugnâtre, and the 2nd Battalion of the 33rd Regiment was distributed between Avesnes, Biefvillers and Grévillers. The other two battalions of the 29th Brigade were held back behind Bapaume, with two batteries. Prince Albrecht was ordered to march to Bertincourt, well to the east, to await further orders; Goeben hoped to use his force to turn Faidherbe's left flank. On the other end of the line, von der Groeben was to be ready to turn the enemy's right flank. In these positions the Germans settled down to await the French attack. Goeben, painfully conscious of the weakness of his force, ordered Barnekow to have three battalions (the 2nd and Fusilier Battalions of the 19th Regiment and the Fusilier Battalion of the 69th Regiment) together with the 2nd Field Division, at Sailly Saillisel, half way between Bapaume and Péronne, as an additional reserve.

At 7.30am on January 3 Goeben, satisfied that his dispositions for the coming battle were as complete as could be in all the circumstances, sent from Combles a telegram to Manteuffel reporting their position:

> Yesterday at midday enemy assumed offensive with considerable forces. General Kummer repulsed all the enemy's attacks until evening with General Strubberg's Brigade, with slight loss to himself and great loss to enemy. Grape shot effectively used; successful charge made by 1st Squadron of 7th Hussars; 250 unwounded prisoners, many sailors. Whole division now in position at Bapaume. I am on the point of riding to Le Transloy; shall assemble reserves there and at Bertincourt. Lieut-Col Pestel destroyed railway and telegraph between Abbeville and Boulogne.[14]

Faidherbe claimed that the Germans had suffered 'serious losses, including 50 prisioners', while the French had 100 killed or wounded. Schell suggested that Faidherbe had conceded that Payen had suffered severe losses on January 2, although this does not appear in his account. At all events, the German loss as recorded by Schell was not great, amounting to 11 killed 76 wounded and 21 missing, a total of 108; the Official History put the total at 125.[15]

The rolling country around Bapaume provided a number of favourable positions for infantry. The villages lay close together and were strongly built, while as has been seen, Bapaume itself was partially surrounded by old fortifications which although defective in places still offered useful positions for the defence.

January 3 dawned bitterly cold. Under a sullen overcast sky the French moved forward. Faidherbe, who had spent the night at Achiet le Grand, accompanied Bessol's division as it headed for Biefvillers; on its right Derroja's division advanced on Grévillers. Patry's regiment was on the left of Derroja's division, and had marched through Achiet-le-Grand and Bihucourt before ascending the Biefvillers plateau. From there it moved to the right, suffering casualties as it passed in front of Biefvillers, before Patry's own company took up a position in support of the divisional artillery in position either side of the railway track, firing on the German positions north of Bapaume. Patry was hugely impressed by the conduct of the gunners:

> The enemy projectiles were raining down on the battery or, to be more precise, around the battery, which responded pluckily. It was an infernal hubbub. The enemy shells bursting very close to us, our guns firing very briskly, the distant noise of the enemy batteries; amidst the uproar made by all this I was astonished that our artillerists did not lose their senses. I had never witnessed such a spectacle. So it was with great curiosity mixed with admiration that I gazed on these soldiers, so calm in the midst of this tempest of fire and iron, manoeuvring their guns with as much precision as if they were on the practice range; the NCOs directing the movements with perfect regularity, correcting the aim, supervising the bringing up of ammunition; the officers, telescope in hand, never taking their eyes off the enemy except to see if everything was going properly around them, and above all that their instructions concerning distances and allowance for wind were being observed.[16]

Bessol's advance against Biefvillers soon bore fruit. Foerster's brigade, advancing on the village at about 9.00am, encountered only the 5th Company of the 33rd Regiment, which was soon driven out, falling back on Avesnes les Bapaume, where the 1st Battalion of the regiment had moved up in support. Kummer regarded the loss of Biefvillers as crucial (although if that was what he thought it is surprising that he did not more strongly defend it) and ordered its immediate recapture. Led by Captain von Fischern, the 1st Battalion forced its way with a rush into Biefvillers, supported by the fire of the 1st Light Battery from a position at the windmills to the west of the town. Once in the village, however, the great French numerical superiority became more apparent, and in the fierce hand to hand fighting that ensued the 1st Battalion lost all but three of its officers. After half an hour of this the Germans were obliged to retreat; the battalion had in this savage engagement been reduced to a strength of 345 men.[17]

Prussian infantry in action in Biefvillers, by Knötel. (Lindner)

The Prussians defend Biefvillers, by Tiret-Bognet. (Deschaumes)

During this struggle, Aynès' brigade of Derroja's division had been drawn into the fighting, while Pittié's brigade continued its advance on Grévillers, where the 6th Company of the 33rd Regiment was driven back in spite of artillery support from the guns at the windmills. With these two villages in their possession, the French continued their advance on Bapaume itself, but were checked at Avesnes les Bapaume largely due to the fire of the German artillery. Thereafter the French remained where they were. They did, however, begin to extend their skirmish line to the south as far as the Albert road.

The loss of Biefvillers exposed the left wing of the 30th Brigade. The 1st Battalion of Rosenzweig's 28th Regiment, which had been facing north in a position to the west of Favreuil, was formed to face Biefvillers; in contrast with the defenders of Avesnes les Bapaume, it prevented Bessol from exploiting his success. Strubberg's artillery had been early in action from the high ground to the west of Favreuil, successfully halting the attempt by Payen's division to advance south of Sapignies with two batteries. As the artillery exchange went on, Payen brought up three more batteries to the ridge west of Sapignies. On the German side the 4-pounder battery by the windmills west of Bapaume joined in to provide support.

Robin's division had advanced through Mory, its objective being to outflank Kummer's right. Kummer had reinforced the 1st Battalion at Beugnâtre with the Fusilier Battalion of the 65th Regiment, together with two more artillery batteries arriving from Le Transloy. Never the steadiest of units, the move of Robin's division broke up under the fire of the two horse artillery batteries, which had been stationed east of Favreuil; the division retreated back to Mory. This enabled Kummer by 10.30am to pull the artillery back to Bapaume, as well as the Fusilier Battalion of the 65th Regiment, that he had sent there to check Robin's advance.[18]

It was still, however, the threat from Lecointe's 22nd Corps at Biefvillers that particularly concerned Kummer. The move south towards the Albert Road by the right of Derroja's division and the continuing pressure down the Arras road obliged Kummer to concentrate his forces in and either side of Bapaume. At this stage of the game he had been hoping for some relief from the operations of von der Groeben on his left and Prince Albrecht on his right. The latter, who had been marching north in the direction of Velu, was ordered by Goeben to move to Bancourt and Frémicourt. His leading troops, the 2nd Guard Uhlans and the 1st Horse Artillery Battery, had already passed the turning when the orders arrived at 11.30am, so it was the next section of the column that headed for Bancourt. This was Hertzberg's detachment, consisting of two battalions, two squadrons and a battery, which was accompanied by Wittich's detachment of one battalion and three squadrons. Prince Albrecht's right flank was covered by his leading units south of Velu.

Hertzberg reached the Bapaume-Frémicourt road at noon; one battalion went to Frémicourt, while the rest of the detachment moved on to Favreuil and Beugnâtre. The latter village was found to be unoccupied, following Robin's hurried retreat; but at Favreuil Payen's advance had led to the abandonment of the village. Further strong French columns were moving up in support from Sapignies. The 6th Light battery came into action against Payen's troops to the south of Favreuil, with the 6th Heavy Battery behind it. The two batteries of the 40th Regiment which had led Hertzberg's advance pressed forward, retaking Favreuil, driving back Payen's 2nd Brigade (de la Grange) and a voltigeur battalion from Robin's division.[19]

The pressure of the French advance could not, however, be resisted; by 2.30pm Albrecht felt obliged to pull Hertzberg's troops back from Favreuil to a position to the east of Bapaume, one battalion being moved to the cover the right flank of the artillery. By 4.00pm he had concentrated his force on the Bapaume-Frémicourt road. He had sent the Guard Hussar Regiment towards Cambrai to make sure that there was no enemy pressure from that direction; during the morning the hussars turned back a body of French infantry.

On the opposite flank von der Groeben had sent Dohna's cavalry brigade north from Courcelette to threaten Faidherbe's right. Dohna was soon held up by substantial detachments of French infantry and was unable to get beyond the line Ablainzeville – Achiet le Grand. Von der Groeben held the rest of his force at Miraumont under Mirus; it consisted of three companies, two and a half squadrons and four guns. Finding no enemy in front of him, and increasingly aware of the sound of heavy gunfire from the direction of Bapaume, Mirus put his small force in motion towards the east. Between 4.00 and 5.00pm he had arrived at Ligny, in time to reinforce the garrison there.[20]

Meanwhile in and around Bapaume Kummer had been bracing himself for a further French attack. The two batteries which had been in action at St Aubin had been forced to retire under the heavy gunfire of the French artillery, and Kummer relocated them behind the town by the windmills to the south-east, where they were joined by the two batteries that had been firing from positions west of the Arras road. The last battery to retreat, the 1st Heavy Battery under Captain Busse, had lost two officers, 17 men and 36

A scene from the battle of Bapaume, by Pallandre. (Rousset/*Les Combattants*)

horses, and could not have got their guns away without the help of the infantry. Kummer now had his whole force in and to the south of Bapaume, apart from the Fusilier Battalion of the 68th Regiment in and to the west of St Aubin. The 29th Brigade, making use of what was left of the old city wall, prepared for a stubborn defence. To the south of the town Strubberg was assembling his 30th Brigade on the Péronne road.

The fighting was beginning to have a considerable effect inside Bapaume itself, as Roberts observed:

> Meantime confusion was supreme in the streets of that town. The inhabitants were rushing off pell-mell in this direction and in that; the shells came hurtling into the houses, the bullets smashed the windows, whilst the town began in some few places to burn. As we stood on the road outside Bapaume which leads towards Beaulencourt, we could distinguish the sound of the heavy guns playing upon Péronne; and I reflected how anxious must have been the commander of that fortress for news of those who were trying to relieve him, and whose fire he could, as we were afterwards told, distinctly recognise.[21]

As the Germans fell back, Derroja's division advanced into Avesnes les Bapaume. Patry had been experiencing a good deal of difficulty in getting his company to advance in the face of the German artillery's 'infernal cannonade':

Mobiles from Lille during the Battle of Bapaume, by Bombled. (Grenest)

I rejoined them and walked up and down the line exhorting them, swearing at them, threatening them, without much result ... It was necessary for the lieutenant, the NCOs and me virtually to apply ourselves to each individual in turn and, partly by reasoning and partly by more or less rough handling, we got them on their feet and started them forward. Once the line was shaken out and in motion, the advance on Avesnes was very soundly executed and the village fell into our hands in a very short time. Upon my word I had never been so hot in my life. Yet there were 15 degrees of frost that day, but despite that I was soaked in sweat.[22]

As the afternoon wore on Patry found it hard to understand why the French were not pushing on into Bapaume itself. By 2.00pm the front line of Bock's 29th Brigade was along the edge of the town, with the 65th Regiment facing north and the 33rd Regiment in what remained of the old fortifications on the western side of the town. In spite of a heavy French bombardment Bock held on, and Lecointe did not launch the infantry assault which Patry felt he should.

Lecointe's attention had been focused on the events on the right of his advance, where Derroja had been preparing an attack on Tilloy. At about 2.00pm he opened an artillery barrage on both Tilloy and Ligny, in each of which was posted one company, supported by two batteries and the two remaining companies of the 8th Rifle Battalion under Major Bronikowsky. These had marched from Le Transloy through Beaulencourt to the two villages, Goeben having decided that he must commit his precious reserves to this critical point. It was as well that he did so. Derroja, in the teeth of heavy fire from the German artillery, launched a series of attacks from 3.00pm which ultimately succeeded in taking Tilloy at 4.00pm. The two companies which had been holding the village retreated to Ligny, the closely adjoining village, and succeeded in repelling an attempt to advance out of Tilloy. There, at about 5.00pm, they were joined by the detachment of Mirus.

At about this time the 3rd Battalion of the 33rd Regiment arrived on the scene. Goeben was determined that Tilloy should be recaptured, and as darkness fell the troops in Ligny advanced from the south and the 3rd Battalion from the east under cover of a heavy bombardment form the German artillery. At this point Strubberg took a hand. Part of his brigade was now south of Bapaume and he led forward the Fusilier Battalion of the 28th Regiment and the 1st Battalion of the 68th Regiment to support the attack on Tilloy. Under the pressure of this combined assault Derroja pulled his troops back. Night had fallen, and this engagement brought the battle to a close with the exception of some desultory firing by French artillery on the northern front of Bapaume.

On the right flank, the fighting had been intense around the hamlet of St Aubin, outside Bapaume to the northeast of the town, on the road to Beugnâtre. The Fusilier Battalion of the 68th Regiment had fallen back there from Favreuuil, as Strubberg retreated to the north and east of Bapaume, and had been reinforced by the 2nd Battalion of the 40th Regiment. Part of Wittich's detachment, this unit had moved forward from Bancourt at about 1.00pm. When the retreat into Bapaume by Hertzberg's detachment got under way, it was followed up closely by troops from Payen's division and part of Bessol's division. These forced their way into St Aubin, only to be ejected by the 2nd Battalion of the 40th Regiment and the Fusilier Battalion of the 68th Regiment, which launched a counter attack at 2.45pm. By 3.30pm St Aubin was once more entirely in German

The Prussian 8th Jäger Battalion, supported by the 33rd Fusilier 69th Infantry Regiments repel the French from Tilloy during the Battle of Bapaume, by Amling. (Fehleisen)

Looking away from Ligny facing the French advance. (Duncan Rogers)

The French Fusilier Marines at Béhagnies, by Tiret-Bognet. (Deschaumes)

hands; as the French fell back they left behind 122 prisoners. It had been a savage hand to hand combat, the advancing Germans taking the place by a house-to-house advance. No further assaults were made on St Aubin.[23]

Payen's attack was not yet over, however. Although no further infantry assaults were launched against Kummer or Prince Albrecht, a French battery opened fire from a position south of Sapignies, only to be silenced by the three batteries on the Frémicourt road. Another heavy battery suffered the same fate. At about 4.15pm four guns then appeared between Favreuil and Beugnâtre but were forced back by the German gunfire before they could take part in the aaction, and a body of infantry that showed itself in the same area was also driven back. The rest of the afternoon passed with only artillery exchanges and these came to an end at about 6.00pm.

During the day Dohna's cavalry brigade had continued to operate against the right flank of the Army of the North, albeit rather ineffectually. With the 5th and 14th Uhlan Regiments and two guns, Dohna had found Puisieux occupied, and moved around it to the left on Hannescamps. From there the brigade moved south-east to Bucquoy, where it encountered hostile infantry. Bypassing Bucquoy to the north, it pushed on past Ablainzevelle before, as night began to fall, returning westwards to Jébuterne and then to Sailly aux Bois.

After being driven out of Tilloy, Derroja retreated to Grévillers, closely pursued and losing a substantial number of prisoners in the process. Bessol, abandoning his attack on Bock's positions, fell back from Avesnes les Bapaume and the Arras Faubourg to Bihucourt and Achiet le Grand. Payen remained where he was, at Favreuil and Béhagnies, while Robin, whose part in the battle had been feeble in the extreme, was echelonned back from Beugnâtre to Vaux.

According to the Official History, total German losses in the two days' fighting amounted to 750, of whom 124 were killed, with 558 wounded and 68 missing. Schell puts the total somewhat higher, at 870. He accepts Faidherbe's figures for the French casualties; 192 killed, 1,177 wounded and 800 missing, a total of 2,172. Faidherbe claimed that the Army of the North lost no prisoners during the battle of January 3, a claim which Schell refutes, pointing out that a total of 303 prisoners were taken during the day.[24]

Patry's regiment had fallen back through Biefvillers to Achiet le Grand:

> So we passed back over that undulating ground which had witnessed our day's struggle and was strewn with corpses; as many of ours as the enemy's. The cold was so intense that most of them were already stiff and hard. Most, not to say all, were barefoot. Well indeed, it is at such moments that shoes are at a premium![25]

That night, as he sat in his headquarters in Le Transloy receiving the reports of his subordinate commanders, Goeben felt very uncomfortable about his position. Certainly he had been able to hold a line from Ligny through Tilloy to Bapaume and thence to St Aubin, and he could feel reasonably sure that there was no threat coming down the road from Cambrai. His troops were, however exhausted, and the stocks of ammunition were running extremely low. Wartensleben summed up the considerations in Goeben's mind:

> Under such circumstances the immediate continuation of the struggle against such superior forces of the enemy who had maintained a firm and steady demeanour up to the last moment, might, if unsuccessful, cause a serious defeat. In correct appreciation of the general political and military situation, General Goeben, however, wished to avoid a battle in which the advantage of victory would have borne no comparison with the disadvantage of defeat.[26]

Accordingly, Goeben ordered Kummer to retreat southwards at 8.00 am on the following day, while Prince Albrecht was to fall back in the direction of Roisel, to the east of Péronne. Von der Groeben, taking with him the infantry that had been engaged on the left of the German position, was to retreat to Albert, taking up a position on the flank of any French advance to Péronne.

While Goeben had been reaching this decision, Faidherbe was reviewing his own situation. He was no happier than Goeben. The French troops, like their adversaries were exhausted. They had suffered much heavier casualties, and were much affected by the extreme cold. Faidherbe decided on retreat; at 4.00am on January 4 the Army of the North began its march back to the billets it had previously occupied. In his account of the campaign, Faidherbe wrote that he would have remained where he was, but the villages occupied by his troops were choked with dead and wounded. He felt at risk of further attacks from the Germans 'since the battlefield was so close to Amiens, where the enemy had more forces.' Additionally, his information (incorrect as it turned out) was that the bombardment of Péronne had been suspended and that the siege artillery had been withdrawn.[27]

The events on January 2 and 3 prompted subsequently a considerable war of words. As usual, Faidherbe claimed that he had won a splendid victory, having convinced himself that the Germans had suffered 'several thousand killed and wounded' and that some of their units had 'fallen apart.' General Palat commented, not unreasonably, that Faidherbe's decision to retreat had rendered pointless the sacrifice of the 1,400 men who had fallen on January 2 and 3. As they fell back along the now familiar road to Arras, many of his men thought Faidherbe had passed up the opportunity of a great success, 'the last that fortune would offer him in this gloomy campaign.'[28]

The 20th Chasseurs are cheered by fellow soldiers due to their actions at Bihucourt, by Bombled. (Grenest)

Faidherbe at Bapaume, by Armand-Dumaresq. (Private collection)

Wilhelm Bigge, reviewing the battle of Bapaume from an entirely different perspective, was in no doubt as to how the outcome should be considered:

> General Faidherbe had to renounce his plan of compelling the Germans to raise the siege of Péronne. After a two days' battle his troops on the 3rd of January were in such a state as to forbid the thought of renewing the attack on the 4th; the position of the Germans also was far from favourable; their ammunition was well-nigh spent, there were no reserves worth mentioning, and the troops were thoroughly exhausted. Only a staff like that of the German Army would ever have ventured to offer resistance to an enemy three times as numerous as themselves and at the same time to continue the siege of Péronne. The hazardous venture succeeded, because the whole military mechanism worked to perfection in every detail, and because the Commander in Chief was confident that under any circumstances the troops would do all that could in any way be expected of soldiers.[29]

Wartensleben took a similar view, noting that the French suffered casualties twice as great as the Germans. Had Faidherbe really won a victory, he would have gone on to raise the siege of Péronne instead of retreating:

> The reasons which he gives as his motives, viz, want of shelter for his troops in the villages full of dead and wounded, a report that the bombardment of Peronne had been discontinued, the severe cold and fatigue of his troops, etc., etc., are all more adapted to veil a defeat than to illustrate a victory. The fault is, perhaps, that the

Faidherbe's headquarters at Boisleux. (*The Graphic*)

The Battle of Bapaume - Looking north from the Bapaume monument, towards the French advance. (Duncan Rogers)

tactical victory remained undecided, because *neither side* was disposed to renew the struggle immediately; both felt themselves little capable of doing so, and therefore each wished some distance to intervene between him and his adversary. The *strategical* victory, however, consisted in the attempt to raise the siege of Péronne having been frustrated, and was therefore decidedly on the side of the Prussians.[30]

When Goeben came to review Faidherbe's account of the battle, he was particularly cross about a number of misstatements, not least a suggestion that the following appeared in a report from him on the battle:

He states that too few troops came into action, from the overslow marches of the forces; and also that the new regiments appeared to be weaker. He demands from the commanders of regiments a list of the officers who fled, that they may be instantly cashiered.[31]

Faidherbe was pleased to use this as proof that Goeben knew he had been defeated; in fact, as the text clearly indicates, the author was General Robin. What annoyed Goeben was that when this flagrant error was pointed out to Faidherbe, he simply omitted the reference from a subsequent German edition of his work 'without all the same honour having been paid to truth, and the actual author having been named'.[32]

List of Maps

Map 1 – The Theatre of War.
Map 2 – The Battle of Amiens.
Map 3 – The Battle of the Hallue.
Map 4 – The Battle of Bapaume.
Map 5 – The Battle of St. Quentin.
Map 6 – Siege of Péronne.
Map 7 – Siege of La Fère.

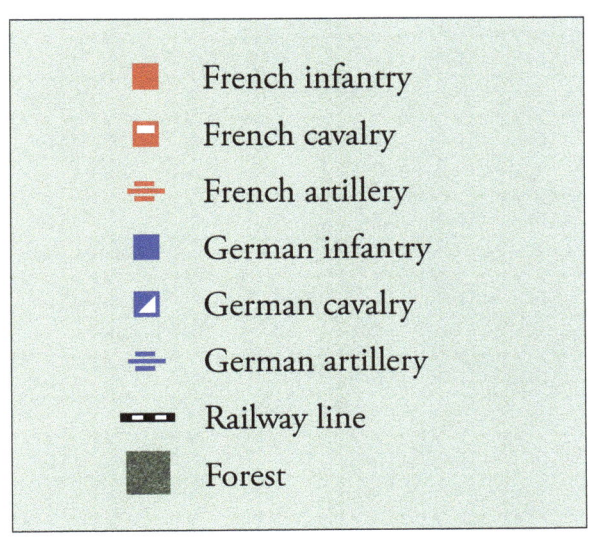

■ French infantry
▫ French cavalry
⚌ French artillery
■ German infantry
◪ German cavalry
⚌ German artillery
▬ Railway line
■ Forest

Key

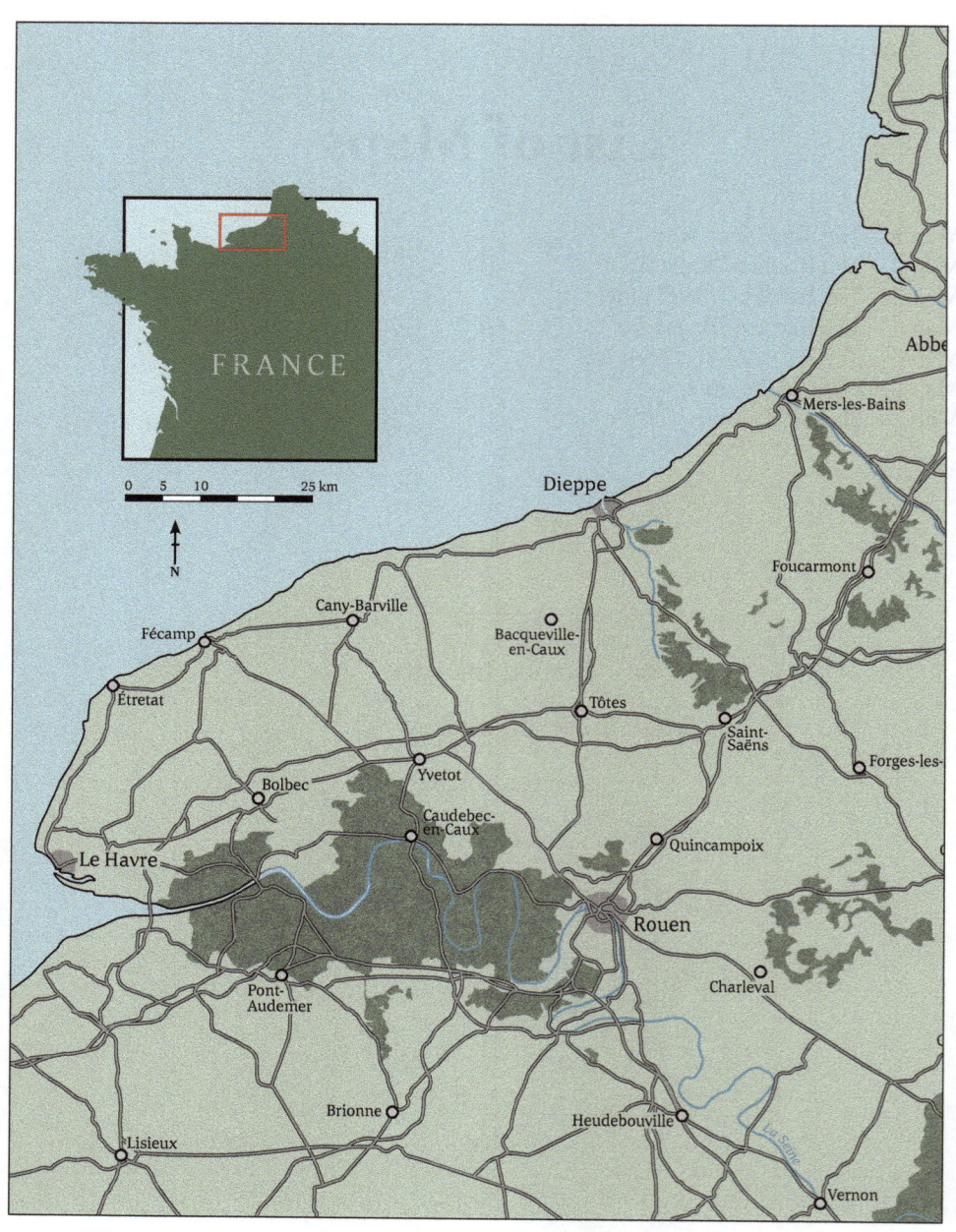

Map 1 – The Theatre of War.

C

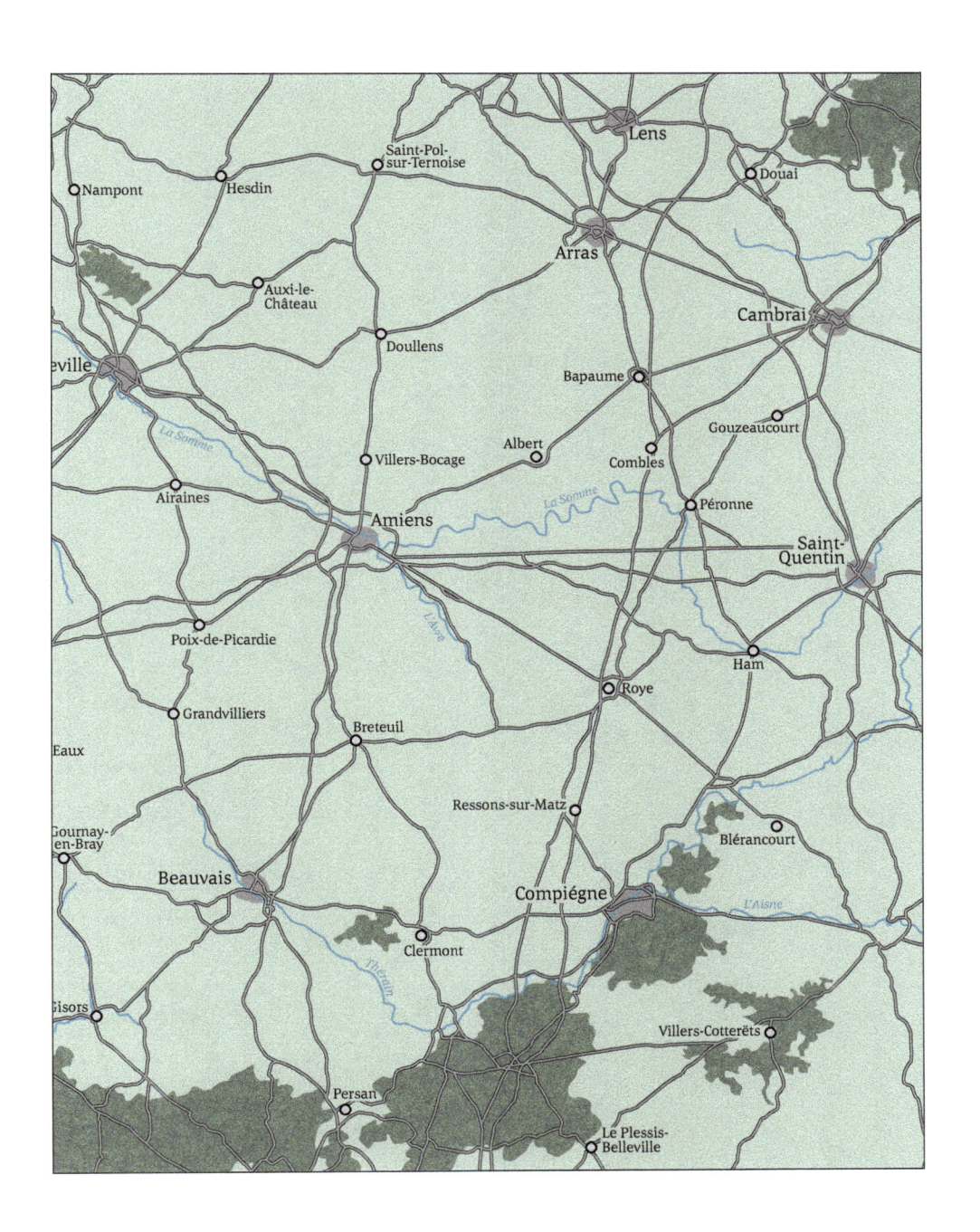

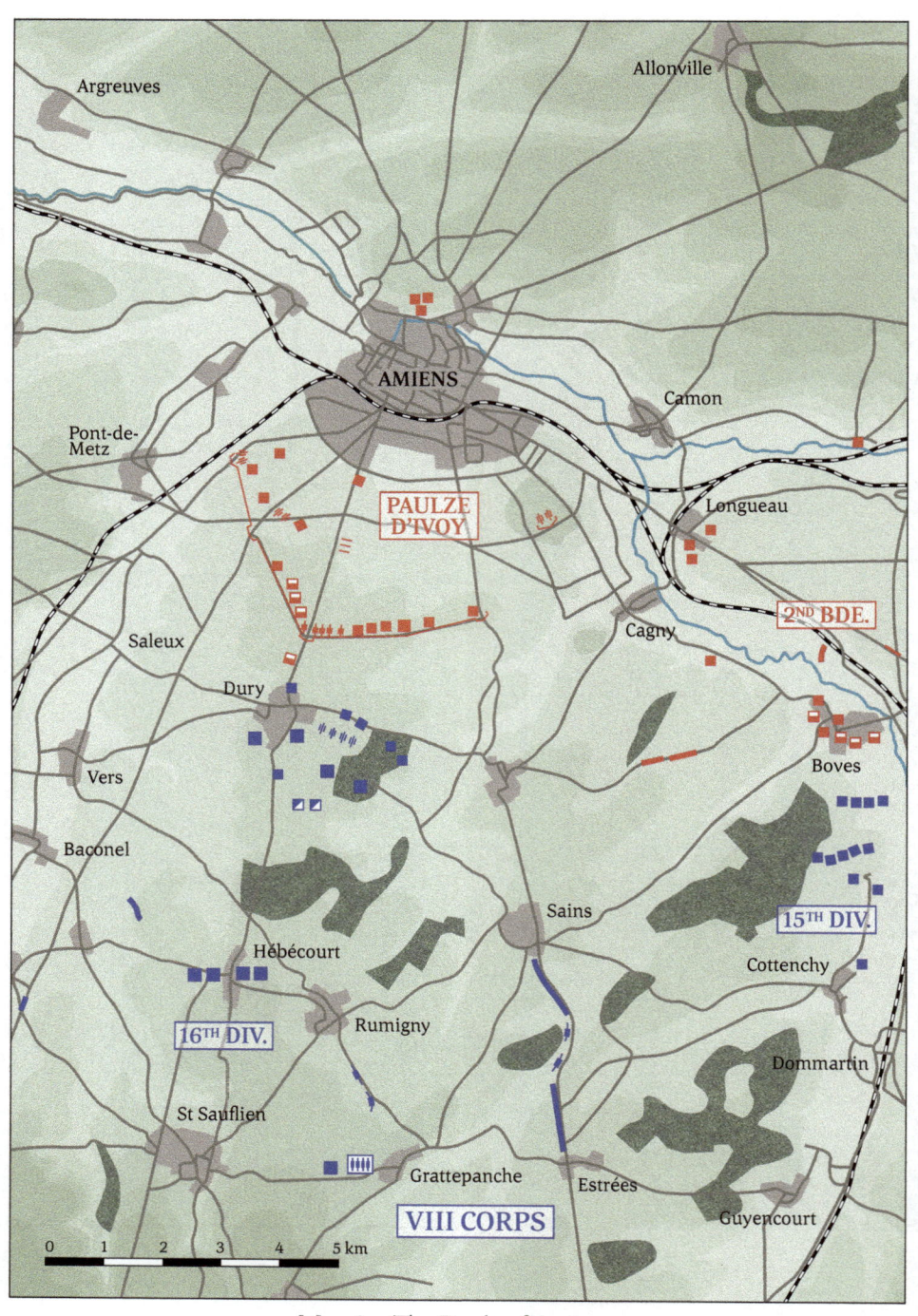

Map 2 – The Battle of Amiens.

E

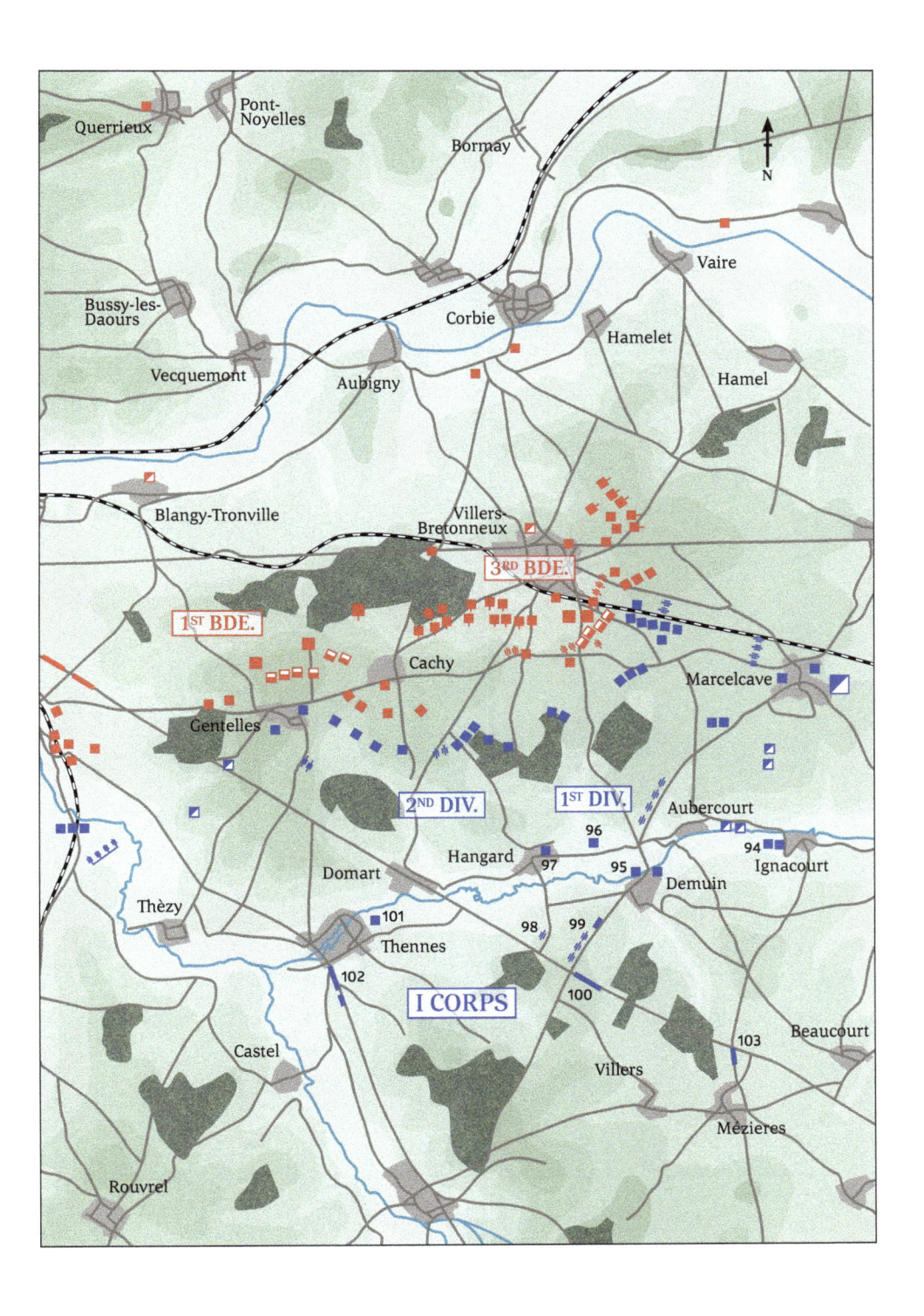

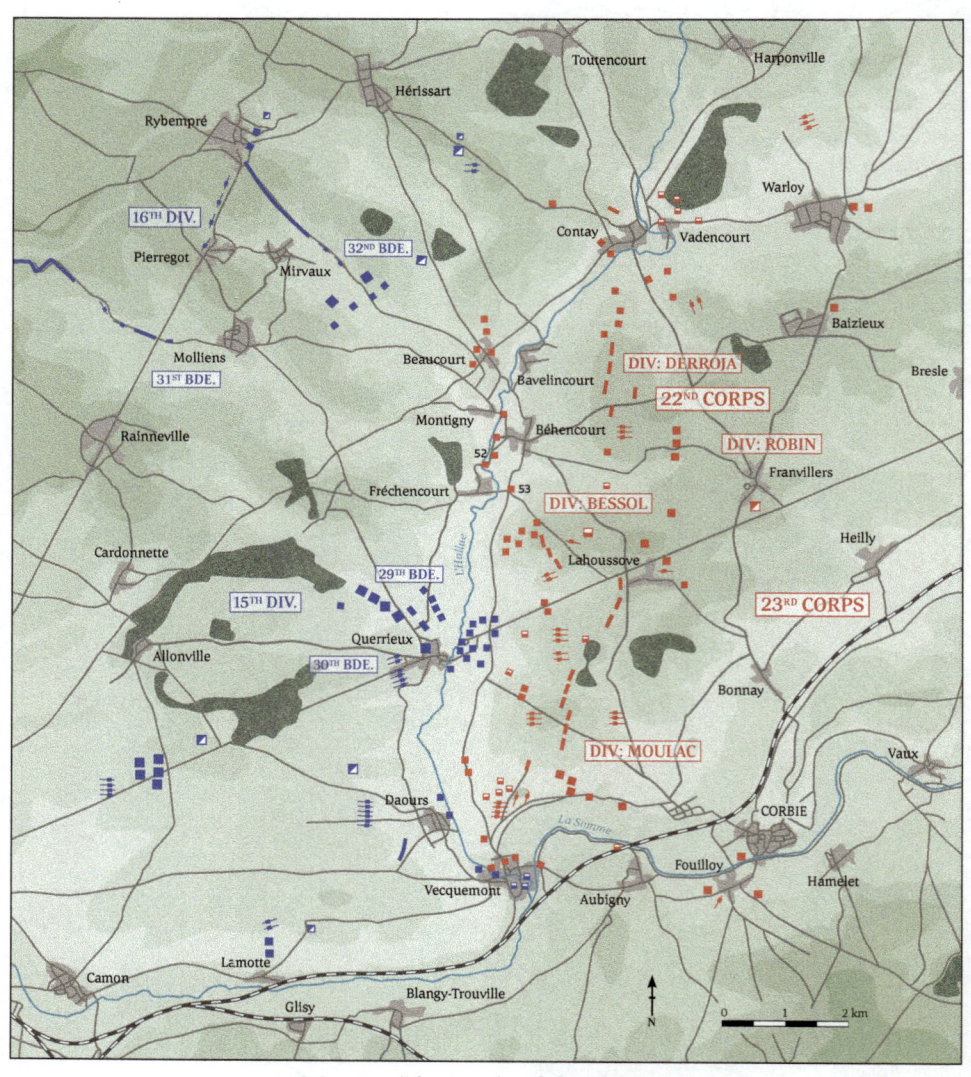

Map 3 – The Battle of the Hallue.

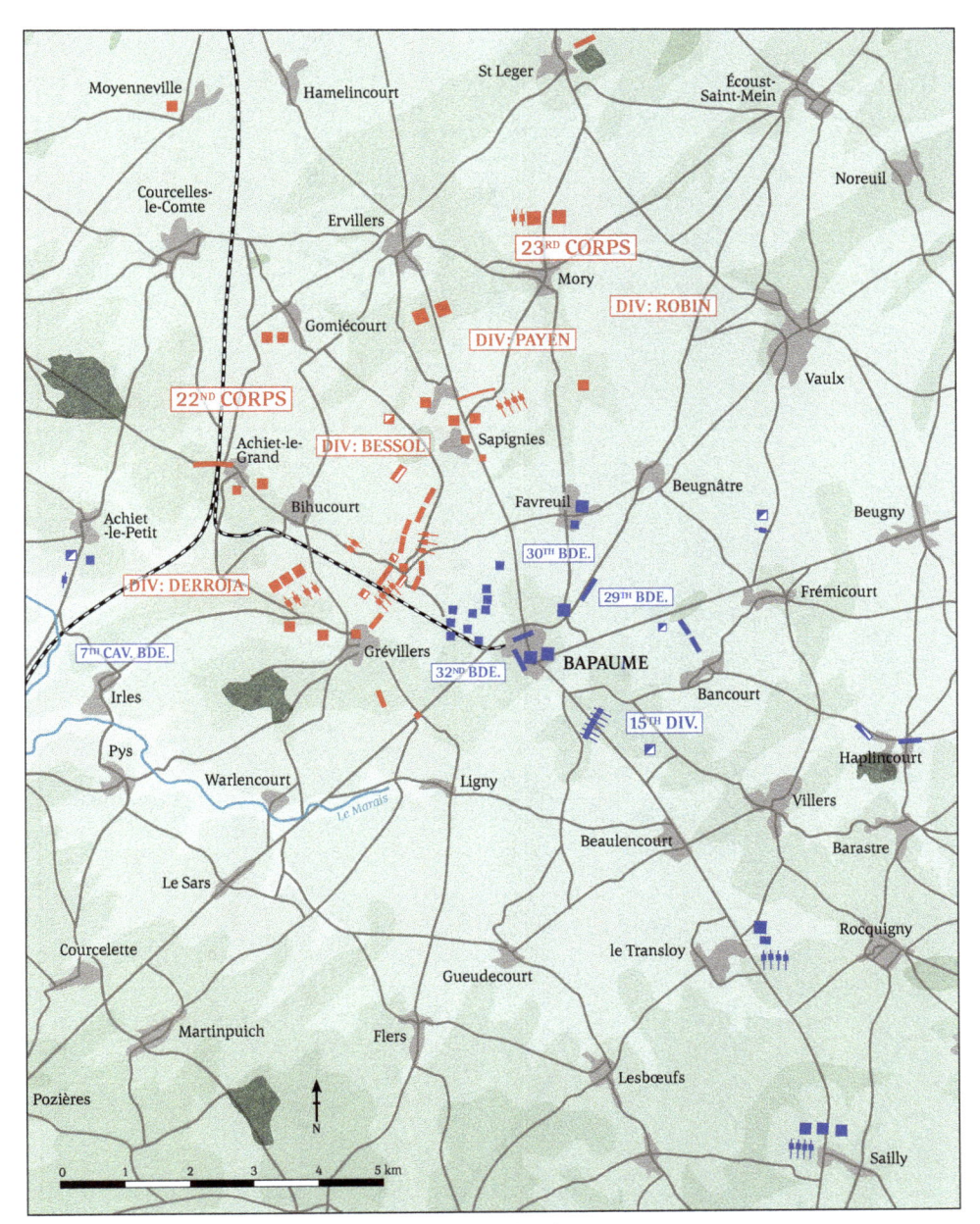

Map 4 – The Battle of Bapaume.

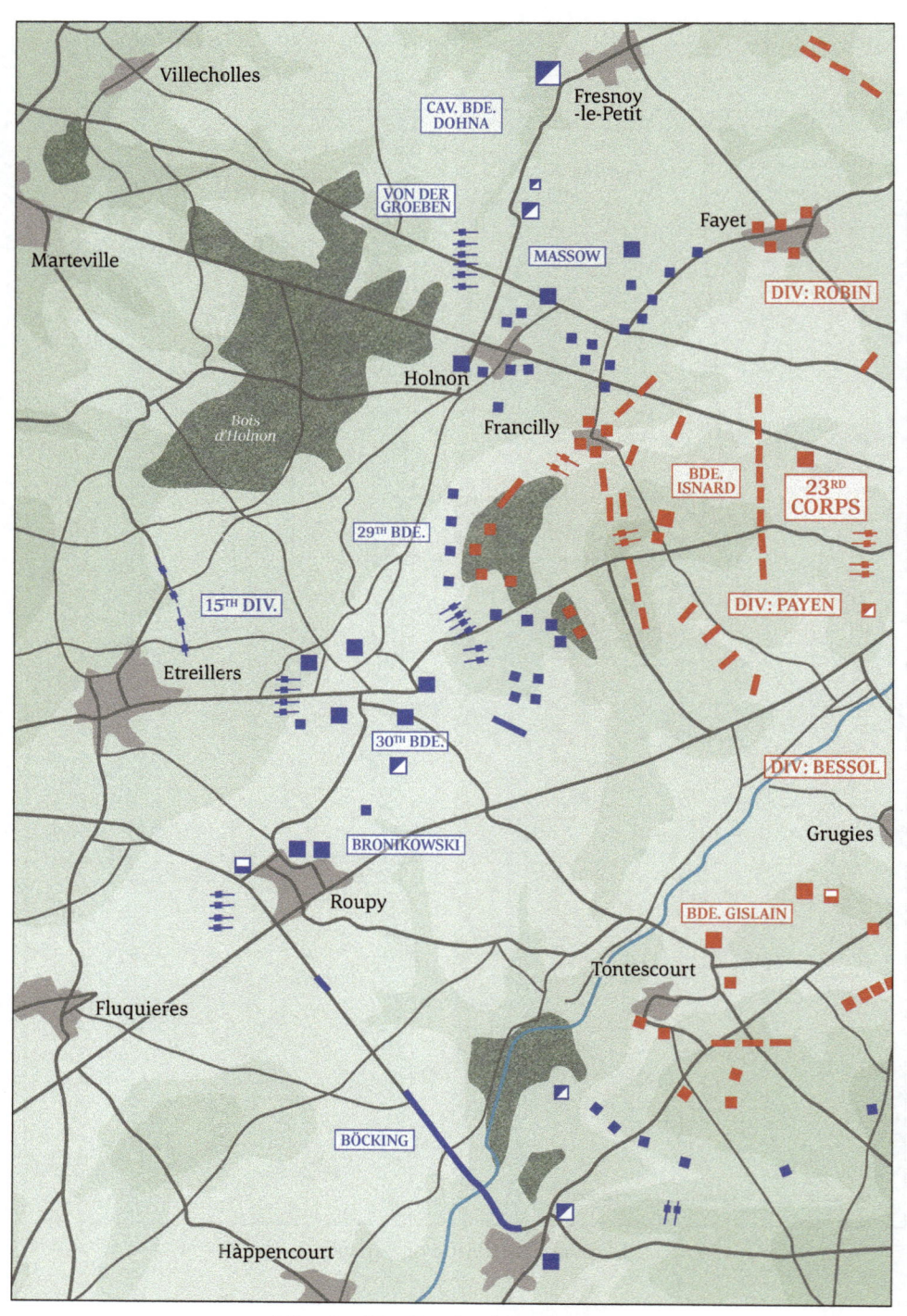

Map 5 – The Battle of St. Quentin.

H

I

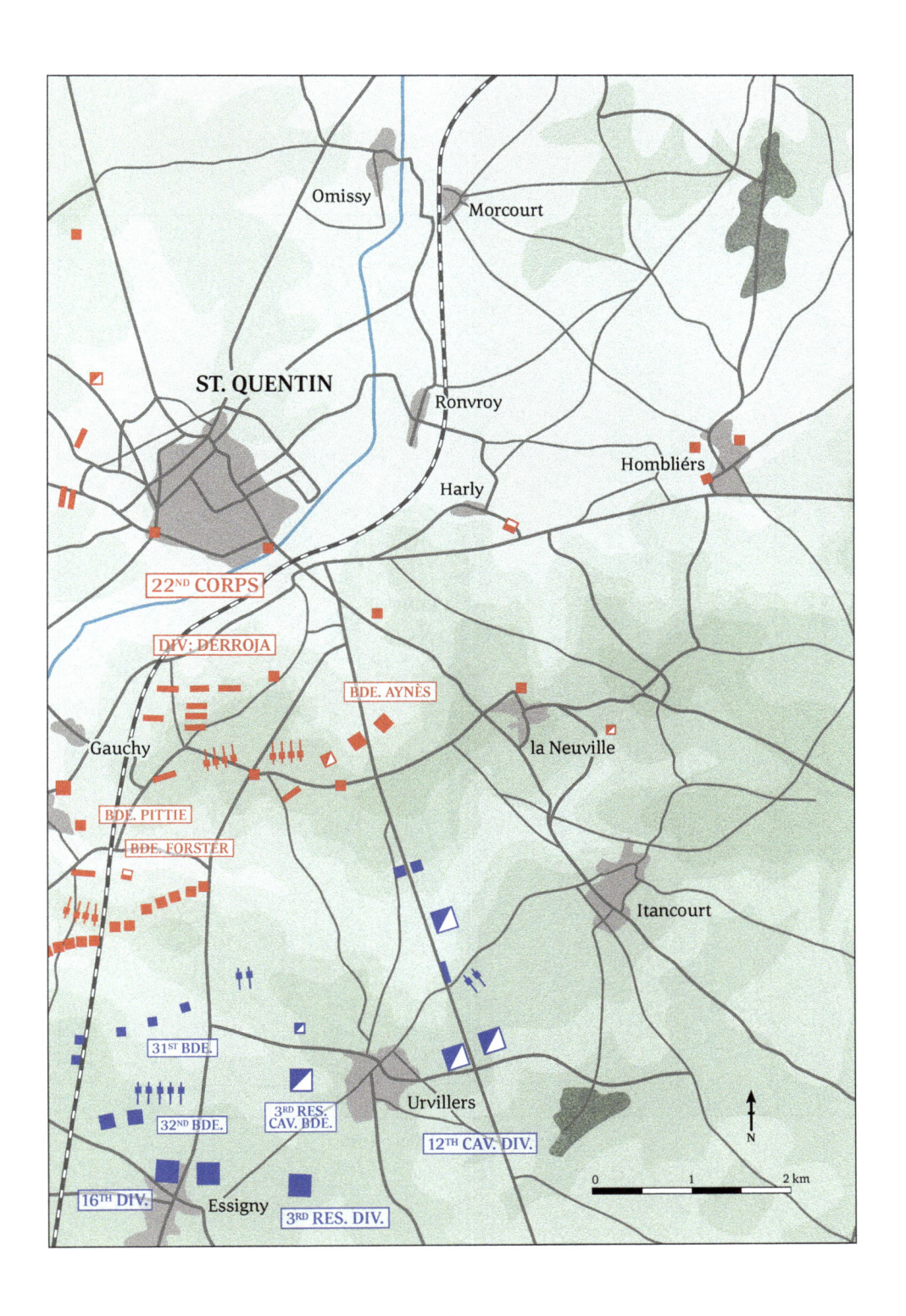

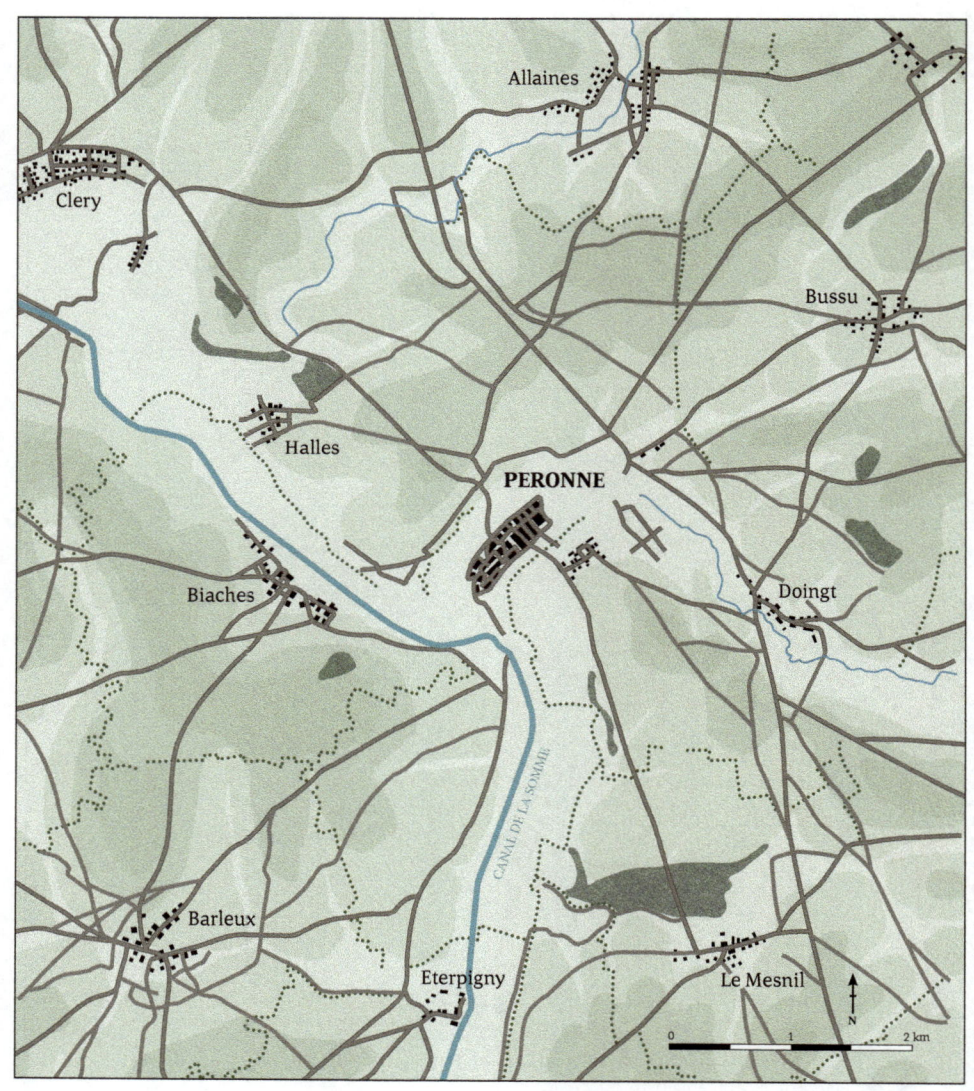

Map 6 – Siege of Péronne.

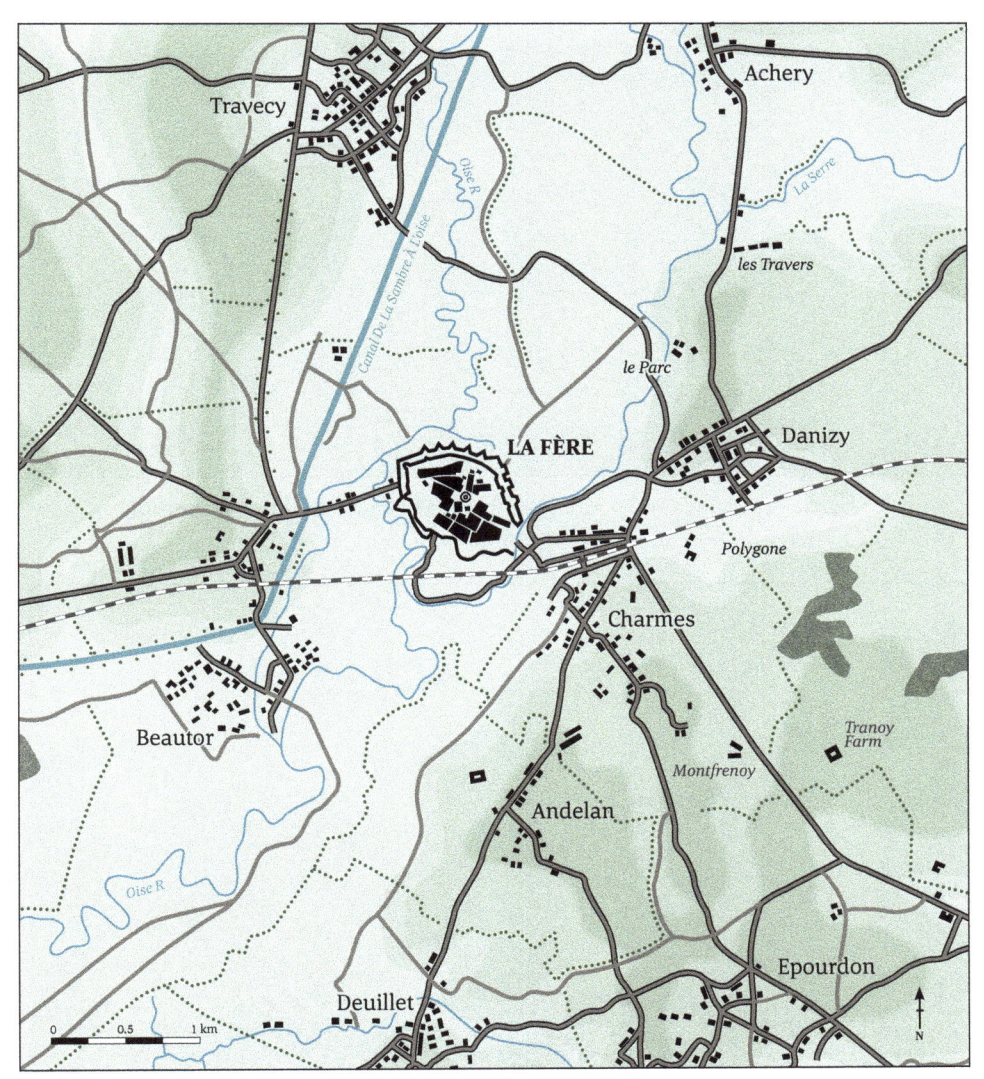

Map 7 – Siege of La Fère.

The Battle of Amiens – the village of Hangard from the French positions.
(Duncan Rogers)

The Battle of Amiens – the railway cutting at Villers-Bretonneux. (Duncan Rogers)

The Battle of Amiens – the monument to the Prussian 70th Infantry Regiment at Dury. (Duncan Rogers)

The Battle of the Hallue – the southern side of Querrieux. (Duncan Rogers)

The Battle of the Hallue – looking from the French positions towards the German lines, near the Faidherbe monument above Pont-Noyelles. (Duncan Rogers)

The Battle of Bapaume – looking towards Bihucourt in the direction of the French advance. (Duncan Rogers)

The Battle of Bapaume – the Bapaume monument. (Duncan Rogers)

The Battle of St Quentin – the Canal de St Quentin at Lehaucourt. (Duncan Rogers)

The Battle of St Quentin – looking at Castres from the road to St Quentin. (Duncan Rogers)

The Battle of St Quentin – the sugar refinery today. (Duncan Rogers)

11

Goeben takes Command

While Goeben had been locked in combat with Faidherbe at Bapaume, the German cavalry had been ranging far afield. Lippe's 12th Saxon Cavalry Division had been co-operating with the First Army by its activity to the east of the principal battleground. On January 2 Lippe had marched from Le Catelet eastwards towards Bohain. His ultimate intention was to probe as far as Vervins. A flank detachment on his left had a brush with the enemy at Maretz, and was soon reporting the presence of superior forces between Premont and Becquigny. The wooded country favoured the enemy infantry, and Lippe concentrated his division with a view to advancing on Busigny. From the west he could hear the roar of artillery around Bapaume. Next day he found that the French had gone, apparently retreating to Cambrai, and Lippe resumed his eastwards march towards Guise. There he encountered a force of gardes mobiles which were, apparently, in the process of retreating. The Saxon cavalry chased them out of Guise towards Vervins, while the Uhlan Regiment moved north to Iron, where it found about 1,000 gardes mobiles in position behind the little River Iron.[1]

Next day Lippe pushed patrols both north towards Landrecies, and east towards Vervins; the detached French units which had been encountered had all now disappeared, presumably to join the Army of the North, and Lippe accordingly concentrated his division and on January 6 marched back to St Quentin. The value to the First Army of Lippe's division had been considerable, and Manteuffel wished to hang on to it.

On Goeben's western flank, he ordered Pestel's uhlans to move closer to the left wing, and these marched to Villers Bocage on January 7 and on the following day to Acheux. This movement encouraged the French detachment at Abbeville, which was said to have received substantial reinforcements, to move rather cautiously, along the right bank of the Somme in the direction of Amiens. Rumours also were heard that as many as 20,000 men had been moved by sea to Boulogne to reinforce the Army of the North. If true, this would very substantially increase Faidherbe's numerical superiority. By the time the First Army headquarters heard of this, Pestel was already on his way to Villers Bocage, so an order to him, sent on the assumption that he was still at Picquigny, to reconnoitre Abbeville was of no effect. All that Pestel could report was that he had found Pont Remy, south-east of Abbeville, to have been occupied by the enemy on January 5.

Manteuffel was feeling decidedly anxious about Goeben's position, and he asked for daily situation reports so that if and when necessary he might bring up reinforcements from Rouen. In response to this, Goeben sat down to write an appreciation of his position, which he regarded as critical. The ongoing siege of Péronne occupied a substantial part of his strength, and limited his freedom of movement. It was Goeben's view that Faidherbe had blundered by showing his hand at Bapaume as early as he did; it enabled him to concentrate just enough troops for a successful resistance there. The Army of the

Von Goeben on the march, by Speyer. (Bleibtreu)

North, secured by its line of fortresses, was dangerously close, and was no more than one day's march from a position from which it could launch an attack. Goeben's solution to this difficult problem was to take up a flank position. When Kummer's 15th Division had had two days' rest, he moved it to Albert-Miraumont, along the Arras railway. Prince Albrecht's 3rd Reserve Division was concentrated at Combles, leaving the 3rd Cavalry Division with two battalions of the 19th Regiment at Bapaume. Barnekow, in conducting the siege of Péronne, must make his own arrangements to cover any French movement from the direction of Cambrai. If Faidherbe did advance south, Goeben would not directly stand in his path, but, leaving the Bapaume road open, would fall on the flank and rear of the Army of the North. For this, he had only 18 very attenuated battalions available, being 13 of Kummer's division and five of Prince Albrecht's division. It was a bold plan but did seem to offer a reasonable prospect of success. If it failed, Goeben would fall back to the left bank of the Somme.[2]

Manteuffel, who approved the plan, did what he could, ordering Bentheim in Rouen to dispatch three battalions and two batteries to Amiens on January 7, telling Goeben that in addition three more battalions would follow next day. Before he had news of this, however, Goeben sent at 10.15am on January 7 a profoundly disturbing telegram from Dompierre-Becquincourt:

Reports have come in changing the whole situation. Faidherbe's army, reinforced by 20,000 men, assembled in great force at Hamélincourt yesterday; Faidherbe has himself arrived with three army corps. Being confronted by such overwhelming forces, I withdraw Prince Albrecht and the corps artillery behind the Somme, where I shall assemble all available troops. Division Kummer is at Albert and Bray-sur-Somme today. If the enemy presses on Count Groeben he will retreat to Flers, Maricourt. Cavalry is continually in close contact with the enemy. If the enemy marches on Péronne, the siege will be raised. Headquarters remain here.[3]

By 2.30pm Goeben was reporting a more encouraging situation; the French appeared not to be moving south yet, and had apparently pulled out of Hamélincourt. It was not now clear what Faidherbe was up to. By 5.00pm the immediate danger appeared to have receded, and Goeben reported that the French outposts were on the line Douchy – Ervillers – Croisilles, and that as a result he would on the following day leave his troops where they were. The reinforcements from Rouen, however, were arriving much more gradually than had been hoped; there was sufficient rolling stock available to transport only one of the six battalions on January 7, and another early on January 8.

At the Royal Headquarters at Versailles, of the various theatres of war with which Moltke was concerned, and which he followed with minute attention, it was the situation in the south-east that was for the moment causing the most concern. He reached the conclusion that it would be necessary to reinforce the troops there, principally the XIV Corps under General August von Werder, and to place them under the command of a new army, to be designated the South Army. In addition to Werder's corps, he assigned the II Corps (von Fransecky) and the VII Corps (von Zastrow) to the new force. On January 7 he decided that its commander should be Manteuffel, and at 12.30pm he sent a telegram informing the latter of his new assignment. Manteuffel was to proceed as quickly as possible to Versailles to receive detailed instructions. Command of the First Army was to be transferred to Goeben. While some members of the army staff were to be assigned to reinforce the staff of the VIII Corps, the majority were, to ensure continuity, to accompany Manteuffel. Wartensleben was among these; he would serve as Manteuffel's Chief of Staff. Sperling, the First Army Chief of Staff, was to remain in that position with Goeben.[4]

The news arrived at the headquarters of the First Army at a particularly anxious time, following the concerns earlier in the day about Faidherbe's intentions. The intelligence about the substantial reinforcement apparently received by or en route to the Army of the North caused Moltke a good deal of concern. Perhaps fearing that the staff of the First Army had, while contemplating their pending move, taken their eye off the ball, Moltke telegraphed to Manteuffel at 6.00pm: 'Have orders been given for troops from Rouen to reinforce General von Goeben?' Receiving no reply, he sent a further telegram at 11.39pm:

> We have not yet received any response as to whether General von Goeben has been reinforced on the Somme. Early tomorrow morning a brigade of the Army of the Meuse will hold itself ready to leave by train from Gonesse for Amiens. Rolling stock must however be sent from there to Gonesse, unless it is being used between Rouen and Amiens. Communicate directly with the Army of the Meuse.[5]

At the same time Moltke sent the necessary orders to the Army of the Meuse.

Manteuffel, before receiving Moltke's second telegram, had reported that three battalions and two batteries of the I Corps were at Amiens, and that six more battalions and two batteries had been ordered up, adding by way of reassurance that the enemy had advanced no further during the day. Moltke was not, however, much reassured. At 11.30am on January 8 he telegraphed Manteuffel to confirm the intelligence that Faidherbe would be receiving reinforcements from Cherbourg, adding: 'If, to hold the line of the Somme you need more troops than can be brought up from Rouen and Amiens, send your rolling stock to Gonesse and let the commander in chief of the Army of the Meuse know immediately.'[6]

Moltke continued to watch the situation closely. He was disturbed by the information that was reaching him as to French claims as well as by the inadequate reports from Amiens, and at 6.30pm on January 8 sent off another, rather irritable, telegram to the headquarters of the First Army:

> French telegrams claim that we have evacuated Bapaume. What is the position of the troops of the First Army and what news do you have of the movements of the enemy? It is absolutely necessary to send to the General Staff an appreciation of the situation, which we lack completely. Has a brigade from the Army of the Meuse been requested? Are other reinforcements necessary?[7]

Soon after this was received at the headquarters of the First Army Goeben was able to report that 'the enemy undertook nothing today, and even seems to have drawn somewhat further off.'

Manteuffel set off to Versailles by train at 10.0am on January 9, accompanied by Sperling, no doubt to provide Moltke with an opportunity to impress on the latter his own ideas as to the future operations of the First Army. Manteuffel had, on the previous evening, taken an emotional leave of many of his senior colleagues at a dinner at his headquarters in a luxurious house in Amiens. Randal Roberts was in attendance:

> At 6.00pm in the gorgeous drawing room were assembled the officers of his exellency's staff, the prefect of Amiens, Count Lehndorf, well known in England as a breeder of horses, and some few other officers of rank connected with the I Corps …. The officers stood about in groups and spoke in whispers; some of them were still to follow the fortunes of their old commander, whilst others were to remain or rejoin their regiments. Presently the door opened, and the general entered. Dressed in the uniform of the dragoon regiment he commanded, with the aiguillettes of an aide-de-camp of the King of Prussia hanging from his shoulder, and without an order upon his breast, the old soldier of Germany advanced into the room with that courtly polished grace of which no man is a greater master.

After dinner Lieutenant General von Schwartz, the commander of the First Army's artillery, proposed Manteuffel's health. Manteuffel, in replying, thanked all those who had supported him, and added, in a voice trembling with emotion: 'I exist in the First Army; and, although I leave for another command, I shall never forget it. But it is the will of his Majesty.' There were, Roberts noted, 'many moist eyes around the table.'[8]

A French bivouac, by Tiret-Bognet. (Deschaumes)

Goeben took up his command on January 9, reporting to Versailles that he had now done so. He retained for the time being the command of the VIII Corps. Michael Howard has noted that the change in the command of the First Army meant that Faidherbe now had a more formidable opponent than Manteuffel to deal with, justly describing Goeben as 'a masterly commander, as cool and clear headed as Moltke himself.'[9] Practically speaking, however, the change may not have made a great deal of difference. It had largely been the VIII Corps with which Faidherbe had been engaged, and Manteuffel had almost invariably endorsed Goeben's operational proposals. On the other hand, the correspondent of the *Daily News* accompanying the First Army recorded a different view:

> I must state that very many officers of this army attribute to Manteuffel's slowness the fact of Faidherbe not having been beaten in a more decided manner on previous occasions. On the march through snow and mud, from morning till evening, you can often hear these tired fellows say. 'Well, von Goeben knows that all this is necessary,' and continue as jolly as ever.[10]

On the ground the situation was not much changed. The reinforcements from Rouen were still on their way to Amiens. On January 10 Goeben moved an infantry regiment and one battery, from Memerty's 3rd Infantry Brigade, from Amiens to Daours, Corbie and La Neuville, in order to secure the crossings over the Somme at these places. For the present he considered that he need not call for more help, reporting to Moltke that 'assistance from the Army of the Meuse seems for the moment not necessary.'[11] His immediate anxiety, was of course to see the siege of Péronne brought to an end without delay. Once he commanded the line of the Somme, he would be in position to await there any move which Faidherbe might make. General Palat summed up the strength of the position:

> In the circumstances of the supposed arrival of important reinforcements for Faidherbe, the Somme was going to play a critical role. By a strange twist of fate, the river that Louis XIV chose at the most harrowing moments of his reign as the last line of defence of his capital and his monarchy, would now effectively cover the siege of that same capital and thus contribute to our ruin. In January 1871, in spite of the cold, it still constituted a strong line of defence; its marshy valley, the canal which ran along beside it for a large part of its course, were frozen and would allow the passage of small troops, but the river itself could not be crossed. Goeben had arranged the destruction of all the bridges not useful to the First Army; the others were organised for defence.[12]

With all this in mind, Goeben could now with some confidence pull back the bulk of his forces behind the river, leaving sufficient on the right bank to watch the movements of the Army of the North. The 15th Division went into quarters south of the Somme, around Bray; the 3rd Reserve Division remained to the west of Péronne. The 16th Division, with Strantz's cavalry brigade, covered the eastern flank as far as Roisel, while Lippe's 12th Cavalry Division marked the extreme right of the Army at St Quentin. The 3rd Cavalry Division remained as hitherto at Bapaume. There was no intention to hold that town in the face of any determined advance by Faidherbe; and on January 10 the Army of the North began just such an advance.

12

The Fall of Péronne

While Goeben had been making the most of his depleted resources at Bapaume, the siege of Péronne had continued. Although the bombardment of the town had continued during the fighting around Bapaume, it had been affected by the battle to the extent that, as a precaution, orders were sent that the ammunition wagons of the batteries in action at Péronne should go into the field to meet any possible contingencies arriving from a scarcity. Once Faidherbe had retreated the bombardment continued with renewed vigour.[1]

The fall of Mézières on January 1 released the siege batteries which had been engaged there, and 28 heavy garrison guns, which had formed part of the artillery park assembled for the siege of that place, were ordered up to Péronne. It seemed evident that the artillery engaged in the siege operations there was in need of reinforcement. However, the heavy traffic on the railway leading to Péronne blocked their passage and only two companies of garrison artillery arrived in time to take part in the siege of Péronne.[2]

On January 1 Senden was appointed to the command of the 14th Division, the responsibility for the siege of Péronne having been entrusted to the reliable Barnekow, commander of the 16th Division. Senden's command had been that of the 3rd Reserve Division, and following the battle of Bapaume Prince Albrecht took command of it. On December 31, at about noon, the French garrison launched a sortie with five companies from the north-west front of the fortress, moving against the line Halle – Mont St Quentin. This assault was only able to get as far as the Quinconce height, where it met the outposts of the Fusilier Battalion of the 29th Regiment. After a brief exchange of fire, the attackers retreated in disorder to Péronne.

In developing the artillery attack on the fortress, it had been found that the south-western front was likely to prove the most effective target. With the least breadth, it enabled the fortifications to be shelled in their greatest length from commanding positions, and had the added advantage of allowing the batteries to be located on the left bank of the Somme. Work on these batteries began on January 1 and continued during the following night; by 10am on the next day 12 siege guns and 12 field guns were in position and able to open fire. The French fortress artillery responded vigorously, but during the afternoon fell silent for about an hour. During this time a parlementaire came forward and, arriving at Barnekow's headquarters, asked for permission for part of the civilian population of the town to leave. The request was refused, and the bombardment continued, although only by the siege guns.[3]

The positions occupied by the troops besieging the fortress fell into three groups, the river Somme and the Péronne – Roisel road marking their boundaries. On the right bank of the river, north of the Roisel road, the positions were along the line Halle – Mont St Quentin – Bois des Bacquets and the ground behind it. The force here comprised the 1st Battalion of the 29th Regiment, the 2nd and Fusilier Battalions of the 69th Regiment, two squadrons of the 1st Reserve Dragoon Regiment and five batteries, being the 5th 6-pounder battery and the Field Division of the corps artillery. To the south of the Roisel road there were four battalions, four squadrons and three batteries, which carried the line of outposts up to the river, passing over Doingt. This force comprised the 2nd and Fusilier Battalions of the 19th Regiment, the 1st and Fusilier Battalions of the 81st Regiment, the 3rd Reserve Regiment of Hussars and the three reserve batteries of the 3rd Reserve Division. Finally, the left bank of the Somme was held by three battalions, two squadrons and one battery, being the 1st Battalion of the 19th Regiment, the 2nd and Fusilier Battalions of the 29th Regiment, two squadrons of the 1st Reserve Regiment of Dragoons and the 5th 4-pounder battery of the VIII Corps. Barnekow thus had ten battalions, eight squadrons, and nine batteries with which to conduct operations. There were also two pioneer companies. Command of the engineering operations was in the hands of Captain Kluge; Colonel von Kameke directed the artillery attack.[4]

Easy communication between the besieging units was essential, and the pioneer companies were immediately put to work to restore the bridges over the Somme canal at Brie; they also threw two bridges over the river at Ham below the fortress. There were passages over the Cologne stream at Doingt, Cartigny and Tincourt. The key villages around the fortress were fortified, including Cartigny, Le Mesnil and Brie.[5] Since the garrison had, after the unsuccessful sortie on December 31, not displayed a great deal of activity, the German outpost line moved forward to between 600 and 2,000 yards of the glacis of the fortress.

During January 2 and 3 Barnekow kept up the bombardment as best he could, although obliged to use the field artillery to a very limited extent in order to husband both guns and ammunition against the likely contingency of their being required to participate in the fighting around Bapaume. He had, of course, been ordered to detach three battalions and four batteries to Sailly-Sailisel to reinforce Kummer on January 3; these units were the 2nd and Fusilier Battalions of the 19th Regiment, the Fusilier Battalion of the 69th Regiment, and the 2nd Field Division. In addition Barnekow despatched two squadrons to Villers Bretonneux and Nesle to protect the line of communications. The Germans were thus getting very stretched; these detachments left Barnekow for the moment with only seven battalions, six squadrons and five batteries with which to carry on the siege.[6] As a precaution against a possible sortie by the garrison against the northern section, Barnekow moved the Fusilier Battalion of the 29th Regiment and the 1st Reserve 6-pounder battery to reinforce this part of the front.

While the battle of Bapaume raged, and the roar of the artillery there could be plainly heard at Péronne, the besieging troops watched anxiously for signs of activity on the part of the garrison. There was, apparently, a plan for a sortie during the night of January 2/3, but nothing came of it. All the same, the outcome of the fighting at Bapaume was very much in doubt, and Barnekow was obliged to prepare plans to move the whole of his force to the left bank of the river, in order to cover the withdrawal of the siege artillery if this became necessary. With the fighting little more than 11 miles away from Péronne, Goeben had to be ready to lift the siege at very short notice indeed.

At 2.00pm on January 3, with the pressure on Kummer at its height, Goeben ordered Barnekow to make preparatory arrangements to lift the siege. The trains and baggage of the troops on the right bank of the river were moved to the left bank, and the troops themselves were told to be in readiness to move at a moment's notice. As the day wore on,

Barnekow reduced the bombardment to the fire of three guns; preparations were made for the movement of the rest of the siege artillery to Nesle and La Fère early next day, if this should prove necessary.[7] Goeben had already been obliged, at about midday, to order the ammunition wagons serving the batteries in front of Péronne to Le Transloy, in order to provide the gunners in action around Bapaume with a reserve of ammunition.

Goeben's decision during the night of January 3 to retreat from Bapaume meant, he realised, that it might still be necessary to lift the siege of Péronne, at least for a short while. His orders to Barnekow, however, were to keep up the bombardment as energetically as possible, and at 5.30pm Barnekow reported to Manteuffel's headquarters at Amiens on the present position:

> I have just established a telegraph station at Cartigny. The bombardment of Péronne continues. The garrison is inactive. To judge from the fire, the battle seems to be moving further away from Bapaume. Much ammunition has been expended, the completion of which seems to be desirable.[8]

On the following day, with the French in retreat and Goeben's troops moving back to the left bank of the Somme, Barnekow was able to report from Cartigny: 'Blockade of Péronne has not been disturbed; our fire still continues'[9]. During January 4 and 5 the bombardment of the fortress continued, but only slowly, due to the shortage of ammunition. The French artillery still kept up a lively fire in return, but there was no sign of activity on the part of the garrison. On the evening of January 5 a fresh supply of ammunition for the siege artillery arrived from Amiens.

Within the fortress, the sound of the guns of the Army of the North had raised hopes of an imminent relief; the disappointment of these hopes severely sapped the morale of both the civilian population and the defenders. The situation was evidently deteriorating:

> The temporary Mayor, M. Fournier, who was conscious of the support of the inhabitants, did not hesitate to test the patience of the commandant. As early as January 5, he addressed a fresh note, in outspoken terms, to the council of defence itself. This *démarche* had no more success than its predecessors, but it contributed to the highly excited atmosphere. In it he reproached certain officers, all too truthfully, for not playing their part in facing the common danger; the most absurd rumours struck a chord in these sour hearts.[10]

So serious was the disaffection of some of these men that threats were made against Garnier by a mob around one casemate; the incident only ended when an officer of the Garde Mobile, who had gone to collect shells from a magazine, threatened to use them to blow up the mutineers.

At the headquarters of the First Army, however, there was considerable anxiety as to the progress of the siege. It was entirely possible that Faidherbe might make another attempt to relieve the fortress, particularly since the French might be expected to co-ordinate such an attempt with their efforts to restore the position around Paris, where the crisis of the investment was evidently approaching. The Army of the North had, in the battles it had fought, demonstrated increasing solidarity, and continued to enjoy substantial numerical superiority. Schell described the significance of the siege of Péronne:

The fortress of Péronne was an important object to the French army, because if it were in the undisputed possession of the latter it would – like Arras now did – enable it to advance unexpectedly across the Somme; whereas, if the fortress ultimately fell into the hands of the First Army, this army would obtain the undisputed command of the line of the Somme, upon which Abbeville would be the sole remaining obstacle. In this case, in spite of its weakness, the First Army would be able calmly to await the sequel.[11]

Schell went on to observe that 'a high moral value attached to the continuation of the siege.' As so often was the case when a war was apparently coming to an end, it was important to the parties to be in as strong an apparent position as possible.

The need, therefore, to reduce Péronne without delay, had led Manteuffel to cast about for reinforcements for the siege. On January 3 he asked Versailles for ammunition supplies to be sent forward from Soissons. He set about bringing more guns and ammunition from La Fère; and in particular, as has been seen, efforts were made to bring siege guns and gunners from the units that had taken Mézières. These had not yet been able to move. Even with them, the artillery commander of the First Army, Lieutenant General Schwartz, was not optimistic as to the chances of capturing Péronne quickly. It was his view that to be sure of this, an additional 20 rifled 24-pounders would be necessary.

Captain von Schell. (Priesdorff)

The guns from La Fère, 11 captured French guns, had been sent off at once by rail to Péronne; but Barnekow, in view of the uncertain situation and as yet unaware of the French retreat to Arras, sent them back again. Manteuffel left it to Goeben to decide when they should again be brought forward. On January 5 Manteuffel notified Goeben that ammunition for the French guns already in place in front of Péronne had left Amiens, and added (over optimistically, as it turned out) that the Mézières contingent would arrive in the next few days. In the meantime, he went on, field artillery ammunition must be used very sparingly.[12]

On January 6 Barnekow reorganised his forces for the continuing siege. The 3rd Reserve Division was cantoned north-east of the fortress, with the Combined Guard Cavalry Brigade at Roisel. From there a detachment of the 3rd Pioneer Company, with a squadron of Guard Hussars, had broken up the Cambrai – St Quentin railway during the night of January 6/7. Next day they destroyed the viaduct at Essigny. Two battalions of the 19th Regiment, which had for the past two days been attached to the 3rd Cavalry Division, had reoccupied Bapaume. Of the 16th Division, the 70th Regiment was for the moment in Amiens, and the 3rd Battalion of the 40th Regiment was at Ham. The rest of the division, together with Strantz's Reserve Cavalry Brigade, continued the investment of Péronne. Directly in front of the fortress there were eight battalions, five squadrons and four batteries. Three squadrons of Strantz's brigade covered the south-east of the investing forces, while the 9th Hussar Regiment was at Nurlu – Liéremont.[13]

The pressure from the First Army headquarters to get an early result led Barnekow to commission a report on the possibility of carrying Péronne by storm. Four engineer officers, Captains Kluge and Pagenstecher and Lieutenants Wagner and Gerhardt reconnoitred the fortifications, in places penetrating as far forward as the glacis. Their unanimous view was that the garrison was properly carrying out its outpost duties, and that the suburbs were strongly occupied; the defences of these had recently been much improved, especially at Flamicourt, which lay in front of the weak south-east front of the fortress. It was the engineers' opinion, though, that this was still the most promising point of attack, since the wet ditches were partly frozen, although in some places clear of ice. Overall, their report was firmly against the advisability of attempting an assault at once. There was no hope of achieving surprise; and the hoped for arrival of the additional siege guns should enable the imperfectly covered walls of the east front to be breached. The heavy frost should render the crossing of the ditches easy enough. Barnekow had no difficulty in accepting this emphatic advice, and gave up on the idea of an attempt to storm the fortress.[14]

Inside the fortress the dispute between the civilian and military leadership continued. On January 7 the town council renewed its attempt to obtain a surrender. A copy of its deliberations, claiming the support of the 'unanimous wish' of the inhabitants, was addressed to Garnier, who again convened a meeting of the defence council, which once again decided on a continuation of the resistance.[15] And, indeed, the defenders of the fortress were still capable of military effort. During January 6 the German outposts had reported very much more activity, and during the following night fire balls were thrown towards the German lines, and electric searchlights illuminated the glacis. All the while, however, the German batteries continued a slow bombardment of the fortifications; the arrival of reinforcements to enable the shelling to be stepped up was hourly awaited. That night the 11 French guns from La Fère arrived, together with a siege artillery company, and this encouraged Barnekow to hope that he might soon be able to batter down the defences. The expected arrival of no less than 28 Prussian siege guns from Mézières should certainly make this possible.[16]

Goeben had ordered that all the newly arrived siege guns should be posted on the left bank of the Somme, his object being first to ensure that no matériel should fall into French hands if the investment had to be raised, and secondly to be able to continue the bombardment even if he was obliged to evacuate the right bank. It was the arrival of the siege train from Mezierès that would signal the start of regular siege operations; but as the hours passed very many difficulties arose to impede this progress. The problem was the amount of rail transport required for the transfer of the 14th Division from Mézières to Paris, which completely absorbed all the rolling stock available, and in the event the siege train never reached Péronne.

This left Goeben with the continuing task of facing any further movements by Faidherbe towards the relief of the fortress. Barnekow continued a deliberate fire on Péronne throughout January 7 and 8; two companies were moved from the right to the left bank of the river in order to strengthen the protection of the siege artillery, and at the same time the rifle pits opposite the fortress were moved forward to within about 400 yards of the glacis. Meanwhile the German railway authorities continued to block the movement of the Mézières siege train, on the basis that they had been ordered to give priority to the transfer of the 14th Division. Seriously annoyed by all this, Manteuffel had appealed to Moltke for help; but the latter, preoccupied with the situation in the south-east, had no help to give. And by January 7, Manteuffel's future employment had been determined; Moltke's telegram conferring upon him the command of the Südarmee was despatched to Amiens at 12.30pm on that day. At the same time, as has been seen, Moltke addressed the question of reinforcements for Goeben, who took command of the First Army.

Monument to the defence of Péronne. (Rousset/*Histoire*)

On the evening of January 8, there arrived at last from La Fère a fresh supply of ammunition for the captured French guns to be employed in the siege, which meant that, without waiting for the siege train from Mézières, Barnekow could increase the intensity of the bombardment.

Before he did so, he thought it worthwhile making another attempt to persuade Garnier to give up the struggle. On the morning of January 9 he wrote again to the commandant pointing out the uselessness of continuing the resistance, and calling on him to surrender. He was not optimistic, but he accompanied this message with a persuasive gesture, stopping the fire of his batteries until 12 noon. Schell explained Barnekow's thinking:

> Considering the stubborn energy hitherto shown by the Commandant Garnier, General Barnekow did not reckon for certain upon this renewal of the summons to surrender proving successful; but nevertheless there was a chance that the commandant's scruples might perhaps be overcome by referring to General Faidherbe's fruitless attempts to raise the siege, and by offering favourable and honourable terms to the garrison and the town.[17]

Barnekow was prepared to go a long way to meet any demands that Garnier might make, even to the extent of allowing the garrison to depart freely; the vulnerable situation of the First Army ensured that Goeben would assent to such a provision.

Negotiations continued; on Garnier's part a request was made that the French should be enabled 'to obtain ocular proof' of the superiority of the German siege artillery, a demand which was refused. However, Barnekow extended his ceasefire until 7.30pm to give Garnier time to make up his mind. The council of defence had resolved, before considering Barnekow's summons, to demand the evacuation of non-combatants from the fortress. Not surprisingly, this was firmly rejected. Going on to discuss the possibility of capitulation, the council had a number of grave considerations to take into account:

> The state of the inhabitants, crammed into damp cellars in the bitter cold, a prey to the ravages of smallpox and typhus, was to several members a powerful argument for their succour. Moreover, they added, Péronne had no news at all from Faidherbe. After the attempted relief during which the cannon fire could be heard, this silence surely announced his retreat.[18]

Those arguing against a surrender were energetically led by the chief engineer, Commandant Peyre. He pointed out that the fortifications were still intact and that Péronne was of crucial importance to the Army of the North. It was at least necessary for the sake of the heavy sacrifices of the town to wait and see the effect on the enemy of the defence that had been made. Sous-préfet Blondin, naval Lieutenant Poitevin, (the commander of the marines), and the commander of the garde mobile artillery Captain Dehaussy, all vigorously supported Peyre. However, their passionate arguments failed to carry the day. Garnier had reached the conclusion that the further defence of the fortress had no chance of success.

As Palat pointed out, his position was extremely difficult, and the suffering of the population was all too real; nonetheless, his first duty was clear:

Péronne had acquired so great an importance that the need for defending it outweighed all other considerations. Commandant Garnier should have had in mind Faidherbe's pressing advice. In any case, the advice of the council of defence should have carried little weight in his deliberations. One recalls the words of Villars to Marsin: 'A council of war! They are no good unless one wants an excuse to do nothing.'[19]

While these negotiations were proceeding, Goeben anxiously awaited news. There were indications that Faidherbe might again be on the move southwards from Cambrai. All that Goeben knew was that at 5.00pm the guns were silent at Péronne and that negotiations were imminent. An hour later he sent another enquiry as to the situation, but it was not until 11.15pm that Barnekow was able to offer some qualified hope of success; it was clearly a matter that was touch and go:

Capitulation signed by deputy, but not yet ratified. Officers liberated on parole. Terms advantageous for enemy. Garrison to start for Eterpigny at 1.00pm on the 10th. I beg that all troops of the 15th Division, quartered in the neighbourhood, be placed at my disposal. I fear capitulation will not be carried out, because Wittich has fallen back from Fins to Nurlu. I shall weaken the north line of the blockade to support him, and shall send a battalion and as much of the Reserve Cavalry Brigade as I can collect to his assistance.[20]

At 3.00am on January 10 Barnekow reported again:

Capitulation of Péronne concluded. The garrison marches out at 12.00 noon. Officers free on parole. Favourable terms granted to the town. Relief by Army of the North has become less probable. Enemy withdrew from Bouzeaucourt in the direction of Bonavy at 9.00pm.[21]

All was still not plain sailing, however; at 7.45am Barnekow was reporting that 'considerable forces of the enemy' were advancing from Bapaume, and that Sailly had been evacuated. Goeben replied at once; there was nothing that he could do that day that would slow up any French advance southwards; if Barnekow could not hold this off until he had occupied Péronne, he was to carry out his previous orders and take up a position behind the Somme.

This put Barnekow in a distinctly odd position. On the one hand, the capitulation had been signed, yet on the other he must try to oppose the advance of the Army of the North while at the same time making arrangements for taking charge and disarming the garrison of Péronne; and his overriding instruction was, if necessary, to retreat to the south bank of the Somme. Barnekow instructed the battalion on the north face of the fortress to fall back through Ham and cross the river there, if the anticipated French advance materialised; otherwise it was to march into Péronne at noon. The troops to the east of the fortress were to enter at the same time, and the garrison was to be received and disarmed by the troops on the left bank.[22]

If there really had been a French advance as feared, Barnekow would have been in a terrible mess, and Goeben was right to conclude that in that case there was no option but to cut his loss and fall back. Fortunately, however, the news of the movement southwards of the Army of the North turned out to be a false alarm, and the surrender of Péronne was completed without further incident, the garrison marching out with drums beating in good order to Eterpigny, where it was disarmed.

Sir Randal Roberts, riding along the Villers road, met the French garrison marching out of the fortress:

> I was particularly struck with the appearance of the garde mobile. Fine, tall, soldierly looking young fellows they were, who, if they had been only as good as they looked, were just as well on the other bank of the Rhine. The town itself was nothing but a heap of ruins. There was not a house, not a corner, on which a shell had not inflicted more or less injury. Of the beautiful old church, the two lofty Norman-built towers reared themselves alone above the desolation which surrounded them. It is easy to imagine the completeness of the destruction, when I say that the houses of Péronne were no exception to the thin unsolid architecture which characterises most French habitations.[23]

47 garrison guns were captured in Péronne. The garrison consisted of a total of 75 officers (25 of whom preferred captivity to parole) and 2950 men. A large quantity of war matériel of all kinds was captured as well. It had been a near run thing; the victors at once embarked on repairs to the fortifications, since it was seen as entirely possible that the fortress might have to resist an attempt by Faidherbe to retake the place.[24] Within the town, some 80 houses were in ruins. Both the church and the hospital had burned down. Most other buildings in the town had been damaged to some extent. Captain Kluge was appointed Fort Engineer, and was entrusted with carrying out the work necessary to put the place as quickly as possible in a state of defence. The ground round the fortress was cleared by the 3rd Field Company, assisted by working parties of infantry. Ice was cleared from the ditches, which were kept clear, and the sallyports in the glacis were barricaded. The drawbridges and gates which had been demolished were restored. Blindages were constructed and wire entanglements were spread along the glacis using the stumps of trees that had been left standing.[25]

Casualties during the siege had been very low; the Germans lost ten killed and 50 wounded. Nor had the garrison suffered heavily, with 13 killed and 50 wounded; in addition five civilians had been killed and between 30 and 40 wounded. There had also, however, been a considerable number of civilian deaths from disease. Set against the volume of the bombardment, these figures are remarkable; the siege guns had fired 6,800 shells, and the field artillery a further 10,000.[26]

Faidherbe, when he got the news of the capitulation, was understandably furious. The importance of Péronne was well understood by both sides; in Faidherbe's view, Garnier had no business to take into account the sufferings of the population while the fortifications and the garrison remained intact. He grimly repeated the provisions of article 218 of the French regulations for troops in the field:

> Military law sentences to death any commandant who delivers up his fortress without having forced the besieger to carry on the siege by slow and continuing works and at least having repulsed one assault of his force in practicable breaches.[27]

To Testelin he wrote on January 12 to express his amazement at the fall of the fortress:

> On my arrival at Arras I found to my astonishment that Péronne was in the hands of the Prussians, although I had been clearly informed that on January 3, in consequence of the battle of Bapaume, the siege had been raised, and the besieging artillery withdrawn from before the fortress. Since then I had manoeuvred in front of the Prussian army, on the faith of the daily accounts which announced that the bombardment had not recommenced. What has then occurred? If you learn, let me know. It is certain that during the bombardment the artillery of Péronne had silenced the siege guns, and that the defences of the fortress remained uninjured.[28]

The unfortunate Garnier on January 11 wrote an account of the circumstances which, when it reached him, can have done little to moderate Faidherbe's fury. (See Appendix VI)

13

Robert Le Diable

The ruined castle of Robert Le Diable had already been the scene of a sharp engagement on December 31. Situated on a steep hill some ten miles south-west of the centre of Rouen, it is a dominant feature of the landscape, lying about a mile from a sweeping bend of the River Seine, on the edge of the Forêt de la Londe, and overlooking the village of Moulineaux. Although the castle takes its name from Duke Robert of Normandy, the father of William the Conqueror, there appears to be no evidence that he built it. It was constructed originally in the eleventh century and was subsequently remodelled. During the struggle between King John of England and King Philip II of France the castle was destroyed, but subsequently rebuilt. Later, during the Hundred Years War, the inhabitants of Rouen destroyed the towers to prevent their use by the English. By 1870 it was in ruins; the moats had been filled in in 1855. Notwithstanding this, it was still a position of key strategic importance, at the base of the peninsula formed by the Seine as it swings first towards Rouen and then away from it. It remains, in its ruined state, immensely impressive.

Bentheim, aiming to carry out Manteuffel's orders to take the offensive south of the Seine, had been strengthened by the return to Rouen of the 44th Regiment, which arrived on January 1. Nothing much seemed to be going on on the right bank of the river, so Bentheim assembled on January 3 at Grand Couronne and La Roquette a force of 12½ battalions, 2 squadrons, 4 batteries and a pioneer company. Before dawn on January 4 Lieutenant Colonel von Hüllessem, commanding the advance guard, moved out of Grand Couronne with six companies of the 1st Grenadier Regiment along the high road towards Moulineaux. To the south of the road two battalions of the 41st Regiment, with two companies of the 1st Rifle Battalion and half a pioneer company, moved across the thickly wooded heights towards Robert le Diable. Behind these, on the high road, followed the main body under Colonel von Legat, with the 2nd and Fusilier Battalions of the 3rd Grenadier Regiment, the 1st Squadron of the 1st Dragoons, and two batteries. In reserve, some way behind, came Colonel von Busse with the Fusilier Battalion of the 43rd Regiment, the whole of the 44th Regiment, the 2nd Squadron of the 1st Dragoons, two batteries and the rest of the pioneers. The force was placed under the command of Major General Bergmann, the corps artillery commander, who had taken command of the 1st Division, Falkenstein having been taken ill. Bentheim retained two and a half battalions under Colonel von Massow in the position at Grand Couronne.[1]

Across the neck of the peninsula, on the line La Bouille – Elbeuf, the French had about 10,000 men, with 16 guns, under General Roy, consisting of gardes mobiles and gardes nationales. Because of the densely wooded heights which lay in the centre of the French position, Roy was obliged to divide his force into two groups; to the north, at Moulineaux, La Bouille and in the rear, there were four battalions and six guns, while to

The Château at Robert Le Diable. (Rousset/*Histoire*)

the south at Elbeuf and Orival there were five battalions and four guns. Communication between these separated forces could not have been easy. The rest of Roy's force constituted a reserve, standing in part at Bourgachard and part at Bourgtheroulde.[2]

Bentheim counted on surprise, and to ensure this the orders for the attack were only issued during the night of January 3/4. It was bitterly cold, the temperature having fallen to -10°C, as the assaulting troops moved silently forward towards the unsuspecting French.

It was still moonlight when Hüllessem leading troops advancing through the woods reached the French outposts, which were taken entirely by surprise and driven back to the heights of Robert Le Diable, where they were supported by other troops which occupied shelter trenches there. The three leading companies of the 41st Regiment were now reinforced by two more companies and together they stormed the conical hills from several sides. Most of the French troops retreated through the forest to the west; some tried to put up a resistance in the ruins of the castle, but were soon taken prisoner by further Prussian troops coming up in support; others who took refuge in a little church, were also made captive.

The column on the high road had encountered an enemy detachment on the heights to the west of Moulineaux, but this soon retreated as Hüllessem's troops advanced from Robert Le Diable. A little further down the road, at Maison Brûlée, further resistance was met with, before Legat's leading troops turned the position. During this engagement two guns were captured.[3] With Moulineaux and Robert le Diable in German hands, the cork was out of the bottle, and Bergmann gave orders for the development of the advance, directing Legat on Bourgachard, while Hüllessem turned southwards towards La Londe. Busse, advancing between the two of them, was to make for Bourgtheroulde. In the foggy weather, and due to the intricacy of the country, the advancing Germans were not at all clear as to the strength of the opposition. The French troops in their immediate front appeared to have divided into three groups; at least 14,000 were at Bourgachard, with 1,500 at La Londe and rather more than 2,500 at Bourgtheroulde.[4]

Legat's advance on Bourgachard was held up at St Ouen, where he encountered considerable resistance, supported by eight guns. On his left he was hard pressed by a French column which attempted to turn his position. Shortly after this, however, the Prussian artillery came up, which checked the Fernch advance. A battery commanded by Captain Hoffbauer galloped forward, and debouching from St Ouen delivered a withering blast of grapeshot at the French infantry which had got to within 300 yards of Legat's troops. With the collapse of this assault, the French fell back before Legat's advance, and by nightfall he had taken Bourgachard. The French retreat continued; Bentheim ordered their pursuit by a small detachment under Major Preinitzer consisting of one squadron, two guns and a company of infantry in carts; a large number of bandsmen were added to the force. A little under six miles west of Bourgachard they caught up with the enemy at Rougemontier. Preinitzer wasted no time, and launched an immediate attack, led by First Lieutenants Luetken and Oehlmann in the face of which the French broke and retreated in disorder towards Pont Audemer. Cutting down the artillerymen, the attackers captured two rifled 12-pounders at the entrance to the village, together with an ammunition wagon.[5]

Meanwhile Busse's column, advancing towards Bourgtheroulde, encountered a French detachment in front of the south-west edge of the forest of La Londe. After an exchange of rifle fire the French were dispersed, and Busse occupied Bourgtheroulde. Quite where the French had gone was not clear to him; they disappeared in the fog, apparently partly taking the direction of Bourgachard and partly towards Brionne.

The left column, which had marched on La Londe, met with opposition near this straggling village; it was only after a lengthy engagement during the afternoon that

Francs-Tireurs during the assault on Robert Le Diable, by Pallandre.
(Rousset/*Les Combattants*)

Hüllessem's men succeeded in occupying the place, with the exception of one large isolated farmhouse. During the day two other small detachments had been sent forward, one from Grande Couronne and one from Tourville. The first of these got as far as Orival, where it exchanged fire with a French force in position there; the second advanced to Elbeuf during the afternoon but as evening fell went back to Tourville.[6]

Next day the Tourville detachment again marched to Elbeuf, where it met Busse's column, which had advanced in that direction from Bourgtheroulde. Patrols sent forward in all directions failed to find any collected bodies of French troops, which had abandoned the country as far as the Rille. During the fighting on January 4 the Germans had lost a total of 172 killed and wounded; the French casualties were probably about the same, but in addition about 300 unwounded prisoners, with four guns, fell into German hands. Bergmann, whose mission had thus been successfully completed, left detachments to hold Bourgachard, Bourgtheroulde and Elbeuf. A reserve of three battalions was posted in the Grand Couronne position, and the rest of the force returned to Rouen.

This, for the foreseeable future, disposed of any threat to Rouen on the left bank of the Seine. On the opposite back General Peletingeas, with some 12,000 men and three batteries, had cautiously emerged from his positions at Le Havre, advancing on January 2 beyond Bolbec. On January 4 he became alarmed by the movement of German patrols at Fauville, which he was convinced was a prelude to an attempt to outflank him, and he hastily withdrew. That night he heard of the defeat of Roy's force south of the Seine, and he fell back further towards Le Havre. By the night of January 5 Peletingeas was once more in his entrenchments around Le Havre on the line Octeville – Montivilliers – Harfleur, and showed no further intention of coming out again. Roy had also removed himself from any danger of attack by Bentheim, taking up a position behind the Rille from Pont Audemer to Brionne.[7]

Quite how much coordination had been attempted between the French forces either side of the Seine, or indeed with Faidherbe's army, is far from clear. As it was Bentheim could now feel that there was little to be feared from either Roy or Peletingeas, which meant that the reinforcements so urgently needed by Goeben could easily be spared.

The retreat by Peletingeas without having achieved anything at all, and the comprehensive defeat of Roy on the other side of the Seine, did generate a good deal of indignation on the part of the population of Le Havre. Roy was superseded by General Saussier; Peletingeas was replaced by General Loysel, although he continued to serve under the latter. Loysel did his best to restore discipline to the disheartened gardes mobiles, and ostentatiously began to collect materials for a further advance. In the days following the fighting around Rouen there were a number of very minor skirmishes, principally arising from the probing of German cavalry patrols. The French warships in the harbour of Le Havre, which might have been expected to support the military operations, appear to have done little or nothing. Bentheim sent a report to Goeben on January 12, which summarised the recent activity:

> The enemy on the left bank has the bulk of his forces behind the line of the Rille; weak advanced posts are pushed forward in the direction of Bourgachard and Bourgtheroulde; they are confronted on our part by eight battalions, four squadrons and four batteries. Two men-of-war have come up the Seine as far as Caudebec:

one lies at anchor at Guerbaville. Principal force of the enemy on the right bank is at Le Havre; advanced posts were pushed forward to Gainneville, but a flying column (one battalion, one squadron, and two guns) drove them back into the entrenchments at Harfleur on January 10. Our loss, five men wounded. Fécamp was visited by a flying column on January 10, Dieppe on January 11, and found to be unoccupied.[8]

Goeben had, that same day, issued an order to all the units of the First Army in which, so far as Bentheim's command was concerned, he had indicated that if attacked by superior forces, it should 'in case of extreme need, evacuate Rouen, and retreat straight towards Paris, in order to oppose the enemy's further advance in a suitable position.' In such a case, Bentheim should look to the armies investing Paris for support. Before receiving this order Bentheim had already warned Goeben that if he had to give up three more battalions for the Somme, he would not be strong enough to resist an energetic attack on Rouen and must think of evacuating the city. Goeben was unmoved; the events unfolding required Memerty, who commanded the I Corps units already on the Somme, to be raised to divisional strength, and he ordered Bentheim to send a further infantry regiment and two batteries for this purpose.[9]

On January 15 Bentheim reported that there was no movement of the enemy on the left bank of the Seine, but that there had been an advance by an enemy force on January 14 to Bolbec which had occupied the place briefly before being driven out again. He went on to reassure Goeben that his orders relating to the transfer of troops were being carried out. Goeben, meanwhile, had reported his intentions regarding Rouen to Moltke in a letter of January 15, explaining that his instructions to Bentheim had been given to ensure that any French advance on Paris could be checked. He did, however, consider that 13 battalions, with 16 squadrons and eight batteries were enough to hold Rouen, the military and political importance of which he recognised. That being so, the rest of the I Corps could be moved to the Somme.[10]

Bentheim's force had been, nonetheless, stretched very thin. His responsibility for holding the rail junction at Vernon, and watching Evreux was now transferred to the 5th Cavalry Division, which had been sent up from Paris for this purpose. On January 14 Bentheim had on the right bank of the Seine four battalions, ten squadrons and four batteries under Pritzelwitz on the line Duclair – Barrentim – Pavilly – Clères, from which he could watch both Le Havre and Dieppe. Since it was reported that some 15,000 men had recently arrived by sea at Le Havre, it would mean that the French army there was some 30,000 strong; if it moved forward, Pritzelwitz would have his hands full. As it was, however, the French remained passively behind their entrenchments at Montivilliers – Harfleur.

On the left bank Bentheim had Gayl in a position to cover Rouen with seven battalions, four squadrons and three batteries. His outposts remained at Bourgachard, Bourgtherolde and La Londe. Gayl's patrols were active in the direction of Pont Audemer and Brionne. So far as they could tell the French had about 12,000 behind the line of the Rille. Bentheim's report of his position, which reached Goeben on January 16, had ended with his conclusion that his orders meant, if he had to evacuate Rouen, he could retreat on either the left or the right bank of the Seine, or even on both. Goeben did not much like the sound of this, which suggested that Bentheim had not understood at all

Major General von Gayl. (Rousset/*Histoire*)

what was intended, and on January 17 he replied to Bentheim to spell out clearly what were his responsibilities:

> The instructions given to the First Army fix the Seine as the west boundary of the district it has to protect; if detachments of the I Corps are pushed forward on to the left bank, this is only to be considered as a measure taken to protect the position at Rouen; and, if in any case this town has to be abandoned, the march of the enemy on Paris must be checked on the *right* bank of the river. Only quite exceptional circumstances would justify the corps in crossing to the *left* bank of the Seine.[11]

In fact the problem of defending Rouen was already on the point of solution. By January 15 the process of mopping up Chanzy's Second Army of the Loire, following its defeat by the Second Army at Le Mans, was virtually complete. As a result of this it was possible for Moltke to assign the Grand Duke of Mecklenburg – Schwerin's XIII Corps to move from Alençon to the Lower Seine, where it could assist in the defence of Rouen in the event of the French making an attempt on the city.

14

Faidherbe Advances Again

Goeben could breathe much more easily now that Péronne was in his hands. He no longer needed to hold Bapaume or indeed to have any substantial forces north of the Somme, apart from the garrison of Péronne. All that was required was to leave advanced guards to watch Faidherbe's movements, while the remainder of the army could enjoy a brief rest south of the river. While waiting for their next move Goeben speculated as to the options open to the French. One might be to take the direct route towards Paris; this would involve tackling the Somme crossings in the face of the First Army. Another option for Faidherbe was to move to his right, on Amiens; but here he would have to get past the heavily armed citadel, and would still have to cross the Somme, with his flanks and rear exposed to the First Army. Finally, there was the possibility of advancing on St Quentin, aiming for Laon and Reims. This would involve a move eastwards; but while Faidherbe was marching in that direction, Goeben could match him, moving in safety behind the Somme as he headed for La Fère.[1]

Since the function of the First Army was to screen the investment of Paris, it was unnecessary for Goeben to try to seize the initiative, and in his orders for the First Army of January 10 he was quite content to wait and see what Faidherbe would do. On the left, covering Amiens, he posted Memerty's detachment made up of nine battalions transferred from the I Corps, with four batteries and two squadrons. Kummer's 5th Division remained at Bray-sur-Somme and Prince Albrecht's 3rd Reserve Division at Chaulnes. Barnekow, with the 16th Division, was at Péronne, from where he could watch for movements by the Army of the North. Also north of the Somme was von der Groeben's 3rd Cavalry Division, with one cavalry regiment at Bapaume, and the rest of the division to the west of the Amiens – Arras road, north of Albert. Covering the opposite flank, at St Quentin, was Lippe's 12th Cavalry Division.

The movement which Goeben was expecting was not long in coming. While he was making these defensive dispositions, Faidherbe had decided to advance, apparently in another attempt to relieve Péronne, the fate of which at that time was still unknown to him. On January 10 the Army of the North was around Ervillers; that night, in a series of surprise attacks, French troops captured German outposts at Béhagnies and Sapignies. On the following day Derroja's division entered Bapaume at 3.00pm, which the Germans, aware of the French advance, had immediately evacuated. News of this from Colonel von Witzendorff, the VIII Corps Chief of Staff, reached Goeben on January 12 at Amiens at 9.00am, with confirmation that von der Groeben was retreating. At this stage it seemed to Goeben entirely possible that Faidherbe's intention was to lunge at Amiens, and the orders he issued at noon on January 12 reflected this. He did not, of course, appreciate that Faidherbe was still unaware of the fall of Péronne.

That information only reached the headquarters of the Army of the North on January 12, by which time the army was established between Bucquoy and Bapaume, with the exception of Robin's division which was in the second line. Faidherbe himself was in Bapaume, where he was thunderstruck by the news about Péronne. It meant that he must at once reconsider the steps open to him:

> This sad event took the commander in chief entirely by surprise. He had been without news of the garrison, which is barely credible considering the short distance involved and the weakness of the investing troops. The instructions which he had given on December 9 to the Commandant of the fortress were such that an early surrender was not to be expected. Perhaps the example of most of our fortresses, reduced one after another by the semblance of a bombardment, had given him little confidence.
>
> The conditions in which it was possible to continue his [Faidherbe's] movement were altogether changed. Whatever remained of his plans, it was clear that the possession by the Germans of Péronne would cause us the greatest difficulty, if not real danger. It was this that would soon lead to the movement on St Quentin.[2]

For a while after the fall of Péronne Faidherbe was uncertain as to what he should do. At first, he contemplated making an attempt to retake the fortress, believing that

Troops from the Army of the North on the march, by Pallandre.
(Rousset/*Les Combattants*)

he could take the new garrison by surprise. The ditches, which constituted the principal strength of the fortifications, were covered with a layer of ice, and an attempt at a *coup de main* might succeed. The danger posed by the freezing of the ditches, and the possible freezing of the canalised Somme, had been clear to the Germans as well; but an attempt to prevent this by systematically opening and closing the sluices had proved unsuccessful.[3] Faidherbe began to make preparations for such an attack, identifying the units to carry it out; but he was soon obliged to give up the idea as impractical. Reports showed that the garrison was very much on its guard, and the work of restoring the fortifications was being carried on night and day. Barnekow had been able to report:

> Péronne is in a good state of defence, and storm free. High masonry work well preserved. Wet ditches. Platforms well protected by traverses. Many casemates. Work of arming fortress progressing. The guns used in the bombardment will be brought in today with their ammunition.[4]

The Army of the North spent the day of January 13 in its quarters to the west of Bapaume. During the day, having given up the plan for a descent on Péronne, Faidherbe gave orders for a movement towards Amiens on the following day. Derroja took up his quarters in Albert; Bessol was around Pozières; Payen was in and around Martinpuich, and Robin in the hills around Bapaume. As the French advanced, the Germans fell back from Albert to the Hallue. Faidherbe's original movement had seemed to Goeben to presage an attack on Amiens; a report that large numbers of French troops were advancing on Albert had led to the abandonment of that town on January 12, but when this proved a false alarm it was reoccupied on January 13 by Memerty with three battalions, one and a half squadrons and a battery. His left was covered by the 3rd Cavalry Division at Hédanville and Warloy.[5]

When, on the following day, the French really did begin to move, Memerty's troops pulled back again to Querrieux on the Hallue, and the cavalry went to Beaucourt and Fréchencourt. The strength of the enemy advances made it clear to Goeben that Memerty must be further reinforced, and he ordered Bentheim to send a further infantry regiment and two batteries from Rouen to Amiens by rail. Three trains per day should, it was reckoned, enable this force to be assembled by January 18.[6]

Before news reached him of the French advance on Albert, Goeben had taken the step of placing all the troops at Amiens under von der Groeben, who would report direct to him. The 3rd Cavalry Division, or, rather, the few units remaining to it, was reconstituted as a cavalry brigade under Count Dohna and formed part of von der Groeben's command; it consisted of the 5th and 14th Uhlans and the 8th Cuirassiers. The 7th Uhlan Regiment was assigned to Memerty. A flying column consisting of a squadron of the Guard Hussars, with two companies of the 1st Battalion of the 1st Regiment, was detailed to watch both banks of the Somme in the direction of Abbeville. The First Army headquarters had always been anxious about the possibility of a serious advance from Abbeville, but it never materialised.

Memerty's advance guard had estimated, correctly, that the strength of the French troops in Albert was about one division. On its own, that should not prove too much of a threat, but there were clearly other elements of the Army of the North close behind it. In order to check what these might be, and the direction they were taking, Goeben ordered Barnekow to reconnoitre in the direction of Bapaume early on January 15. Before undertaking this task, Barnekow reported during the night of January 14/15 that a substantial force appeared to be building up south and southwest of Cambrai. He proposed pushing forward columns from Rancourt towards Longueval, Martinpuich and Bapaume, unless the troops to the south of Cambrai threatened him. It appeared to Goeben that Barnekow was getting a bit carried away, embarking on rather too ambitious a movement, and he promptly replied:

> 15th Division has certainly occupied Bray, but only pushes forward weak reconnoitring patrols in the direction of Albert. I remark that it is not my intention to bring on an engagement on the 15th, but only to ascertain whether any considerable force of the enemy is between Albert and Bapaume, especially at the latter place, in order in that case to arrange a combined attack for the 16th; you will therefore not make a forcible reconnaissance tomorrow, but will only observe with small detachments, and then report by wire.[7]

At the headquarters of the First Army not a great deal was known about the composition of the Army of the North, although it was obviously increasing in strength. The body of troops in the Cambrai area, which had alarmed Barnekow, was in fact the independent brigade of Colonel Isnard, which did not form part of either the 22nd or the 23rd Corps. It had been intended that this brigade should operate against the troops besieging Mézières, but before it could take any action that fortress had capitulated, leaving the brigade to march back again to the Cambrai area, which it reached in an exhausted state.

Faidherbe, meanwhile, was pondering his options. He had begun his advance with the idea of relieving Péronne; when he found that he was too late, he contemplated the idea of a stroke to retake the fortress; but having given up on that, he must take some alternative step. Being in possession of the most effective military asset of the Government of National Defence, he was determined to do something with it, and there was nothing to be gained by hesitating. It was of course obvious to both Faidherbe and his staff that any offensive move must be a high-risk option; but in the existing situation that had to be faced.

15

The Plan to Move East

The genesis of the plan for the Army of the North to set out on the eastward march which would take it to St Quentin, and the final showdown with the First Army, is a matter of some doubt. On January 14 Faidherbe was with his headquarters at Pozières when he received from Freycinet, on behalf of Gambetta, the news that the garrison in Paris was preparing a major attempt at a breakout. According to Faidherbe, Freycinet's despatch from Bordeaux informed him that 'the moment for action had come; he especially requested us to draw on us from Paris as many forces as possible'.[1] This telegram has been regarded by a number of historians as the direct origin of the march on St Quentin. General Palat, for example, pointed out that the 2nd Army of the Loire was effectively off the board following its defeat at Le Mans; the 1st Army of the Loire, while engaged in an operation of which the Delegation entertained high hopes, would not immediately be able to have any effect on the Paris situation. This only left the Army of the North to answer the call. Palat noted that Freycinet's message arrived at the moment that Faidherbe was considering the extreme difficulty of advancing against the defensive line that Goeben had taken up along the Hallue, or indeed against the German position on the Somme:

> Faidherbe was thus compelled to give up the war of manoeuvre, which he had so far succeeded in prolonging without serious damage to his four divisions. He must now attempt to strike a great blow. Which direction should he take? It would be extremely dangerous to continue the move on Amiens. Beyond the Hallue we would run into the side of the city protected by the citadel; the German troops in and around Bray could attack us in our flank and rear, while Memerty was in our front. To try to cross the Somme below Amiens exposed the army to the risk of being driven into the sea. It was no less difficult to cross the river between Péronne and Amiens, where the enemy could rapidly concentrate his forces.[2]

There was only one other direction which Faidherbe could take, and that was to march rapidly in an easterly direction. He would try to get away from the enemy by a series of forced marches, which would put him south of St Quentin, from where he could threaten the railway lines on which the First Army depended for supplies. Of course the Germans would bring large forces against him, but he would have drawn them off from Paris, and he could hurry back to the safety of the northern fortresses. It would be a desperate throw. The numerous German cavalry would soon pick up his trail, and only if he was actually able to threaten the enemy lines of communication would Moltke detach troops from the investing army. If he was caught before he could reach the railways, he would have to fight with exhausted troops in a situation worse than if he had advanced

Charles-Louis de Freycinet. (Rousset/*Histoire*)

directly on the Hallue. Moreover, the location of the various units on each side meant that he could not move more quickly to his destination than his adversary. As a result of the loss of Péronne he must march on local roads which the winter, and the lack of maintenance, had left in a dreadful state, in some cases impassable by wheeled traffic and, as Palat observed, the French must cover a distance of between 35 and 45 miles from their camps to St Quentin while the Germans, except for Memerty, and Dohna's cavalry, were only between 20 and 32 miles from that city.[3]

Not least of the advantages which Goeben possessed was the use of the long straight Roman road between Vermand and Amiens, which was immediately accessible to most of the troops which he would employ against Faidherbe. And these battle hardened veterans were, in any case, much better organised to undertake rapid marches than the French, whose armies had been assembled in such haste and which lacked the infrastructure to allow them to move swiftly. Goeben could therefore await Faidherbe's movements in the positions he presently occupied.

The possibility that the Army of the North might make for St Quentin was one of the options of which Goeben had taken account in the two long letters which he sent to Moltke on January 15. In these, he explained that he intended to hold the line of the Somme firmly in the position Amiens – Péronne – Ham, behind which he could give his exhausted troops a rest. He would watch Faidherbe and at the right moment launch an attack with all his forces. He thought it likely that the French would attempt a move on Paris by way of Ham and St Quentin; this would give a good opportunity to

THE PLAN TO MOVE EAST 165

strike at their flanks. In this case he would move with the bulk of his forces, if necessary occupying only the citadel at Amiens and the fortress of Péronne, to give him the maximum strength with which to encounter Faidherbe. He had two other points to make. First, he would like more locomotives assigned to the First Army. Secondly, he asked how long he was to remain in command of the army, since he reckoned that simultaneously commanding both an army and a corps was more than was reasonably to be expected.[4]

Other historians, such as Howard and Fermer, have echoed Palat's view as to the significance of Freycinet's intervention; but not the French Official History:

> The precise date of a communication that gave no indication of the direction to be taken by any offensive, and the extent to which it more or less encouraged General Faidherbe to act is of little importance. The documents irrefutably confirm this; on January 16 he telegraphed the government without giving any indication of his plans; later, Gambetta commented to the commissary general: 'The movement of which you have told me shows General Faidherbe to be a man who thinks, who anticipates and who acts on his own initiative.'[5]

In reality, Faidherbe had already, before hearing from Freycinet, begun to work on a plan which was in any case the subject of discussion among his staff. From Lille, for instance, the indefatigable Villenoisy sent a telegram to Farre. Observing that the population was glad to see the back of the enemy, he added that it was 'nevertheless necessary to profit from his departure.' The best way to achieve this, he added, was to move towards St Quentin.[6] He repeated the suggestion on the following day: 'Is it not possible for us to cut the German lines of communication? It would be an operation to be attempted with strong forces.' That evening Farre replied from Avesnes-les-Bapaume:

> I have pursued the idea of cutting the railway lines for a long time, but I am not the master. Send me the precise requirements of the works needed to destroy the line from Paris to Epernay and Paris to Soissons.[7]

Farre's comment would seem to confirm that Faidherbe was keeping his cards very close to his chest, and keeping the plan from his staff until the moment came to carry it out, as he later claimed. The French Official History is somewhat sceptical about this, pointing out, as has been seen, that the possibility of a move eastwards was something in contemplation by Moltke at Versailles and Goeben at Amiens. Goeben himself later emphasised the extent to which an eastward move was probable:

> The eye of the Commander in Chief was, to be sure, constantly fixed on St Quentin as the point by which, as well as could be foreseen, General Faidherbe would attempt the movement on Paris, which had been announced indeed long before by the French newspapers, and also by himself in presence of a Prussian officer sent to parley.[8]

The latter suggestion particularly enraged Faidherbe, who wrote in his indignant 'Réponse a la Relation du General von Goeben' published in 1873:

> As to this, we do not know if we are expected to believe our eyes. Is it complete stupidity, or treachery, of which the commander in chief of the Army of the North is accused? General Faidherbe had not seen at this time any Prussian officer; and as for his plans, he only made them known, even to his Chief of Staff, at the very last moment. The movements of the Army of the North were always kept completely secret and carried out without advance warning.[9]

Quite where Goeben got the story of the Prussian officer at Faidherbe's headquarters he does not say; and, indeed, it does seem highly improbable.

At all events, whether or not Faidherbe had fully shared his intentions with Farre, or indeed made up his mind entirely, the project was taking shape during the evening of January 14, when Faidherbe cryptically telegraphed Villenoisy: 'For reasons known to me, it is necessary to enlarge immediately the inundations around the entrenched camps behind the Scarpe and the Escaut.' Farre followed this up with a telegram of his own: 'Reply as soon as possible to my request for advice on the structures to the east of Paris.'[10]

By the afternoon of the following day, Faidherbe's mind was made up, when he tersely ordered Villenoisy: 'Drive the Saxons out of St Quentin.' This instruction was passed on to Isnard, who had set off from his camp around Cambrai that day in a southward direction. In the course of his march Isnard encountered in front of Le Catelet a force consisting of a company of Jägers, two squadrons of Uhlans and two guns. To this Isnard, with six battalions and eight guns, was decidedly superior and he brushed it aside, reporting that the brief engagement which lasted an hour and a half had not halted the march of his column. He pressed on and, after a further brief engagement in the suburbs of St Quentin, entered the town with the whole of his brigade.[11]

Faidherbe formally communicated his intentions to Villenoisy in a note sent from Albert on January 15, which included the plan for a daring commando operation:

> The army will march eastwards tomorrow and will be between Sailly Sallisel and Nurlu by nightfall. On January 17 it will move towards Saint Quentin, tending a little to the right. It is necessary that at the same time the mobilisés of the Aisne and Isnard's column to the north and east of that town, are able to cut off the retreat of the enemy troops that will be there and which will be attached on the following day.
>
> On January 19 the march will be continued. En route a bridge on the railway line from Compiègne will be destroyed to prevent any traffic from Laon to Paris by this route. At the same time the army will move on Laon. A *coup de main* will be attempted against this town, into which will be sent 60 brave men, carefully chosen, whose leader will be the bearer of this note. These men are to be sent to Lille to be dressed as civilians and armed only with daggers. As early as January 16 they are to be directed towards the department of the Aisne to make their plans in concert with the prefect, and to act on the order which you will send when you are ready to support them. One reliable man will be detached to the army's headquarters, near to Saint Quentin, by this force, to carry the order to act at the right moment. The subsequent march will be in accordance with circumstances.
>
> The railway will cease all movements to Albert which, as early as 10.00am will be without protection. A telegram will warn M. d'Arcangues to stop the service at

Achiet tomorrow. The following day it will not go beyond Boisieux and then on January 21 will end at Arras. This station, and the line from Arras to Douai, must be carefully guarded by the garrison of Arras, which will be reinforced accordingly. It is important that the rail service there is not suspended.

The mobilisés will be echeloned, in large groups, for the protection of Saint Quentin, of Cambrai, and the railway lines which will be prepared to be put in service to Tergnier; but this must be kept secret until January 18.[12]

It is evident from this that Faidherbe intended an extremely ambitious stroke aimed at drawing on his own army as many of the enemy as possible. He set this out in his own account of the campaign:

General Faidherbe, strongly convinced of this necessity, believed that he would attain this end in freeing himself from the army in front of him by forced marches towards the east and southeast in order to speedily arrive south of Saint Quentin, where he would threaten the railway line from La Fère through Chauny, Noyan and Compiègne.[13]

He was, however, under no illusions as to the difficulties he would face, as he grimly observed; he was certain to encounter considerable forces before he had got very far; however, if he was entirely overmatched, he could hope to retire northwards and await the enemy under the protection of his fortresses. Reviewing his plan, the French Official History concluded that it stood little chance of success, and that the individual objectives it was aimed at were misconceived. In any case it was essential that he should reach St Quentin before giving battle. From there, the breaking of the railway link La Fère – Chauny – Noyan – Compiègne could be carried out by a small unit, well led, much as had occurred at Fontenoy in another theatre. At the same time the proposed commando operation attracted particular censure: 'As for the expedition to Laon, it displayed a romantic side which baffles discussion.'[14]

16

The March Begins

Whether he had any choice in what he must do, Faidherbe at least moved as swiftly as he could. He pushed out reconnaissances in force along the whole of his front, the object being to deceive Goeben as to his intentions. Bessol's division moved towards Hédauville and the upper Hallue, before retreating through Albert. Following this it made a demonstration in the direction of Querrieux. Derroja, advancing towards Bray, reconnoitred the German positions, on the south side of the Somme. The 23rd Corps similarly made gestures towards the south, but in all these movements Faidherbe intended that his troops should avoid engagement with the enemy. Their purpose was merely to be seen. These movements having been carried out without incident, Faidherbe issued his orders for the eastward march to begin on January 16 at 7.30am. It did not get off to a good start:

> This march began in regrettable circumstances. The disorder was so great among the troops that almost without exception they left their quarters after the scheduled time. Furthermore, it began to rain, and a thick layer of black ice covered the roads hardened by the frost of previous days. The march was thus very slow; at several points the infantry had to pull the artillery and their trains.[1]

Many of the troops did not reach the quarters assigned to them, or arrived late in the evening. The 22nd Corps, intending to reach the line Guyencourt – Hendicourt, got no further than Combles and Sailly. For the following day Faidherbe prescribed shorter marches of about a dozen miles; but his troops would now be close to the enemy and the movement was becoming more and more difficult.

Goeben did not long remain in ignorance of Faidherbe's intentions. Isnard's advance on St Quentin, which he may have begun sooner than Faidherbe intended, was a clear indication of what the French were up to, and the ubiquitous German cavalry patrols were soon sending back reports of the movement. On the other hand, Dohna's cavalry were reporting strong forces as appearing north of the Hallue, and Goeben, to check whether this was merely a demonstration, ordered a concentric advance from Querrieux and Bray on Albert for January 17. St Quentin had been held by Lippe's 12th Cavalry Division; as Isnard advanced, the Saxon cavalry quietly left the town after a slight engagement, retreating to Ham.

In a thoroughly mendacious despatch, said to have been published in Bordeaux on January 18, and apparently emanating from Faidherbe, there appeared a very different spin on the reoccupation of St Quentin:

> Having learnt that the Prussians at St Quentin demanded of the inhabitants a sum of 548,000 francs, he had resolved to put an end to their exactions, and sent a flying

column for that purpose under the orders of Colonel Isnard. That officer encountered the enemy at Catelet Bellicourt, and pursued him, killing and wounding 30 men. Colonel Isnard subsequently entered St Quentin on the 16th, the enemy flying in great disorder, and abandoning 130 prisoners, as well as a considerable store of provisions. The inhabitants of the town received the troops with great enthusiasm.[2]

It is perhaps just possible that Faidherbe issued this report in order to obscure the real reason for the advance on St Quentin, although in his account of the campaign he does not suggest this. He describes Isnard's advance somewhat differently from the account given above, and seriously annoyed Goeben by suggesting that the latter's move on St Quentin was occasioned by Isnard's capture of the city rather than as a result of prompt appreciation of Faidherbe's intentions.[3] Goeben pointed out, in his rejoinder to Faidherbe's account, that it was on the contrary quite clear that Isnard's force was not strong, and that the movement was merely a demonstration. On the other hand, as we have seen, St Quentin was well in Goeben's mind as the point at which Faidherbe must aim if he was to carry out the movement on Paris, which had been so loudly touted in the French newspapers. The occupation of St Quentin, wrote Goeben, had no influence on the subsequent operations; 'it was much rather merely the extraordinary power of marching possessed by the Prussian troops which secured the result of them.'[4]

Meanwhile Barnekow, who had already sent the 2nd Battalion of the 29th Regiment to Vermand, reinforced it with the 3rd Battalion of the 40th Regiment and half of the 6th Light Battery of the Corps Artillery, the detachment being under the command of Major Holleben. There was also a detachment under Lieutenant Colonel Reinecke at Tincourt.

Goeben's intended attack on Albert did not take place. By the afternoon of January 16, he was already receiving reports of the eastward move of strong columns of the Army of the North. During the night of January 16/17 von der Groeben came to Goeben at his headquarters with the news that as early as noon a patrol had found Albert to be unoccupied; the information had been delayed first by the slippery black ice on the roads, and then by the anxiety of a cavalry commander to make sure of his facts. Meanwhile on January 16, a French battery commander, Captain Dupuich, had been captured at Fins:

> Lance-Corporal Kraemer of the 9th Hussars, as he saw near Fins troops marching on the high road, with one hussar rode along a side road close up to them in order to be able to report positively what was on the march there. An officer separated himself from the column on its march and asked the lance corporal, quietly halted, the way to Sorel; the latter, meanwhile, caught hold of the Frenchman's bridle and galloped off with him towards Péronne, followed by the hussars.[5]

From this prisoner it was gathered that three battalions and two batteries had been marching eastwards with the object of reaching Sorel by nightfall.

Lippe's report of his retreat from St Quentin, and its occupation by Isnard's brigade, did not reach Goeben until early on January 17. By then it seemed very likely that Faidherbe was heading east with his whole army. Goeben had already put Barnekow on notice that the French were on the move:

This will in all probability afford General Barnekow an opportunity which must not be neglected, of dealing a blow on the enemy's flank with his whole available force, or, if it should be an isolated corps which is advancing, of attacking its rear, thereby cutting it off from the army, and as far as possible destroying it, with General Lippe's co-operation.[6]

It might, of course, have been a complex feint on the part of the Army of the North, designed to draw large forces of the First Army in an easterly direction with the intention of turning back and descending on Amiens, and although Goeben thought this very improbable, it had been a little while before he set his forces in motion to march parallel with Faidherbe. It was tempting to consider getting behind him, and forcing him away from the security of his northern fortresses; but the security of the German lines of communication, and the prevention of any interference with the investment of Paris, must be Goeben's first priority, and the orders he gave to his army for January 17 reflected this. All his troops were to move eastward. South of the Somme, Lippe's 12th Cavalry Division was pushed forward to Flavy le Martel, the 3rd Reserve Division marched southeast behind the Somme Canal to Nesle, and the 15th Division moved eastwards along the Roman road as far as Villers – Carbonnel and Licourt. One battalion crossed the canal at Brie. On the north bank of the Somme, the 16th Division left Péronne, and moved southeast on the east bank of the canal to Ham. Finally von der Groeben marched due east on the right bank of the river, his destination being Cléry sur Somme. Behind all these movements came Goeben's only reserve on the Roman road, which consisted of the units most recently arrived from Amiens, the 41st Regiment and the 3rd Heavy and 3rd Light Batteries of the I Corps artillery. Goeben himself took his headquarters to Nesle.[7]

The detachments of Reinecke at Tincourt, and Holleben at Vermand, were in a fearfully exposed position as the whole of the Army of the North rolled eastward. Goeben had suggested to Barnekow that there might be an opportunity of dealing a blow 'with the whole of his available force.' Naturally he expected Barnekow's patrols to be in constant contact with the enemy; but the two detachments, while much more substantial than was required to monitor Faidherbe's progressive, were not strong enough to cope with what was coming down on them. Barnekow had notified Goeben at 11.15pm on January 16 of his intention that Reinecke 'should fall upon the enemy's marching columns, which seem to be moving eastwards,' and also reported on the detachment at Vermand. Barnekow's idea was that Reinecke would 'disturb the enemy's flank march;' as soon as he got his orders to move on Ham, he endeavoured to recall Reinecke.

By then, however, the detachment was already heavily engaged with the leading brigade of Derroja's division and it was not until 10.30am that Reinecke succeeded in breaking off the action and falling back towards the main body of the division. This also left Holleben in the path of Derroja as he pressed on, and this detachment was also ordered back to Ham. By then the French were in Poeuilly, and Holleben made his way round by Caulaincourt.[8] Losses on either side were not substantial; the total of German casualties was 16 of which 6 were killed.

Meanwhile, Randal Roberts had been on a visit to Rouen, which he found much quieter than Amiens. Some of the factories there had reopened, and the population seemed more contented. He cut short his stay when news arrived of Faidherbe's move, and caught the next train to Amiens:

As my train steamed into the station, the platform presented an unusually bustling appearance. Evidently something was afloat; for as I searched among the crowd, I saw many staff officers, who could be there but for one purpose. As we alighted, I was told I had just come in time – for the general would be on his way to Nesle by the next train; that my horses and baggage had been sent on, and that we were going to meet the advancing army of Faidherbe. How I wished that really hard working soldier-like Frenchman at the bottom of the sea, and deplored not having eaten a good breakfast before I left Rouen![9]

As was usual with foreign observers, however, Roberts was well looked after; breakfast was served to him, with a flask of good Bordeaux, which soon cheered him up.

Faidherbe's march on January 16 had, by nightfall, got no further than Combles (for the 22nd Corps) and Sailly – Saillisel (for the 23rd Corps), with the newly constituted brigade of Colonel Pauly in rear at Bapaume. The condition of the roads continued to slow up his progress on January 17, and the various divisions were now more strung out. Derroja's division of the 22nd Corps was by the end of the day between Trefcon and Vermand, following his engagement with Reinecke's detachment at Tincourt. Bessol was to his north between Bernes and Poeuilly. The detachments which Barnekow had sent to Roisel and Vermand prudently withdrew before the advancing French, falling back on the rest of the division at Ham. Of the 23rd Corps, Payen was quartered between Roisel and Vendelles, while Robin was somewhat detached at Epehy. Further behind, Pauly had reached Bertincourt.

French troops suffering in the cold weather, by Knötel. (Pflug-Harttung)

During the day Patry's battalion had been marching as part of Derroja's division towards Vermand, but somewhat behind its leading units. He was becoming concerned about the morale of his men:

> All along our route the cannon had thundered to our right, but quite distant from us. This could not but make us anxious, and you could guess from the men's preoccupied air that grave worry was besetting their minds. I sought to raise their morale, but without great success; and then, it has to be said, they were beginning to have had enough of it. If to that you add intense fatigue and a diet which had become deficient and very irregular, you can understand how little faith we were entitled to place in their resistance or their spirit in case of an encounter which appeared imminent.[10]

Before he left Amiens, Goeben had taken the precaution of instructing that for his men there should at least be the relief of not having to carry their packs; carts were to be requisitioned for this purpose. The army's reserve, under Colonel Böcking, was of particular concern; the carts were to be used not only for the packs, but also for those troops particularly fatigued. Böcking was ordered to arrange his march at his own discretion, but to aim to get to Ham by the afternoon of January 18. Including the reserve, Goeben would have a total of 38 battalions available for the coming encounter.

Goeben had reported the situation to Moltke on the morning of January 17, before he set off to Nesle. The rail system let him down; he hoped to reach that place by 5.00pm but in the event he did not get there until 8.00pm. There he received a series of reports which gave him a good deal of information about the position of the enemy, although it was still not certain that Faidherbe intended to make a stand at St Quentin. As Schell explained, however, the First Army was well placed whatever Faidherbe decided to do:

> It was still possible that General Faidherbe was continuing his march from St Quentin on Reims, and care must be taken to avoid giving the enemy the advantage of a day's march by making a false move. General Goeben's measures, therefore, made it equally possible to wheel round the right wing of the army on the enemy, if he held his ground at St Quentin, or, if he did not do so, to continue moving parallel to the enemy's line of march. Thus the position of the First Army was by no means an unfavourable one; on the contrary, it was one which admitted of making a concentric attack on the enemy whenever the moment came.[11]

Particularly for the soldiers of the Army of the North, the weather made marching conditions extremely difficult. The snow and ice which had so hampered operations previously had given way to a sharp thaw, and the deep mud meant that progress was much slower than Faidherbe had hoped. The historian of the 19th Chasseurs wrote of this march:

> Never had soldiers found themselves in such bad conditions in which to fight. Most of their shoes were in holes, and many were abandoned in the mud, the men wearing clogs or going barefoot.[12]

French Gardes Mobiles on the march, January 16 1871, by Knötel. (Pflug-Harttung)

At Versailles, Moltke was keeping a watchful eye on Goeben's progress, and at 2.30pm, having decided to take a hand, he sent a telegram with news of reinforcements:

> Today and tomorrow a brigade of infantry of the Army of the Meuse will be conveyed from Gonesse to Tergnier, and will be at your disposal. Fix its point of disembarkation. XIII Corps will march tomorrow from Alençon in the direction of Rouen; you will therefore probably be able to bring up more troops from Rouen. With respect to railway transport, always apply to the railway authorities, who have received orders to hold four trains in readiness to convey troops from Rouen to Amiens.[13]

This exercise greatly impressed the correspondent of the *Daily News*:

It seems to me that the whole war hardly affords a more striking example of the military genius of von Moltke than the opportune railway trip he ordered for the 16th Brigade, forming part of the beleaguering army. Calculation had furnished him with evidence that von Goeben would make his mark at St Quentin all the deeper if he were strengthened with 4,000 or 5,000 men and a few guns; calculation and good information told him the hour at which this help would be good at need. The brigade quietly went away for the fight just as a lawyer goes down to Reading or Gloucester for the circuit; and, the work done, it comes back to its quarters before Paris just as the lawyer comes back to his cases in the Court of Queen's Bench. This device has simply for the time converted 5,000 men into 10,000 men.[14]

Reading Moltke's telegram as to the reinforcements being sent, Goeben's first reaction was that they would not be needed, but since the movement was already under way he thought it inappropriate to countermand it. Moltke had complete confidence in Goeben's leadership of the First Army, as he made clear in a long letter which he wrote in reply to Goeben's letter of January 15. In it he expressly approved all the latter's proposals, and left him a free hand to use the brigade from the Army of the Meuse as he saw fit. Giving an update of the situation elsewhere, Moltke wrote:

At Paris things are approaching a crisis. We await each day a desperate sortie en masse, perhaps the last. However, if it becomes necessary, it will still be possible to send you a second brigade by way of reinforcement.[15]

17

Tertry – Poeuilly

Once they had arrived at Nesle on January 17, Goeben and his staff had a busy evening. Apart from the correspondence with Moltke previously described, the key task was to issue the orders for the next day. These were drafted on the cautious assumption that Faidherbe had got further than was really the case. Kummer, with the 15th Division, was to march towards St Quentin, going by way of Tertry – Streillers. Von der Groeben, who was placed under Kummer's orders, was to march to Vermand. Barnekow with the 16th Division was to move on Jussy, and to take responsibility for Lippe's 12th Cavalry Division's reconnaissance. Prince Albrecht was to move up to Ham. The corps artillery was to move to Quivières – Ugny – l'Équipée; although this was close up to the marching divisions, it was not Goeben's intention, if Faidherbe was in position at St Quentin, to attack him on January 18. He intended first to establish his position by careful reconnaissance.[1]

Orders to von der Groeben were also sent direct by telegraph to Péronne. To Lippe, Sperling wrote that if he would place himself under the orders of the First Army, he would have the promised infantry brigade from the Army of the Meuse at his disposal. To Bentheim went confirmation of the news that the XIII Corps was marching from Alençon to Rouen. Another regiment, with one battery, was to be sent to Amiens; four trains were provided for this. Information came from the Army of the Meuse that the brigade to be detached would be the 16th Infantry Brigade (Colonel von Scheffler), and orders went to La Fère and Tergnier that it was to disembark at the latter place. With all these tasks completed, the staff were able to have only the briefest rest. At 9.00am next day they rode with Goeben from Nesle to Ham, to await news of Faidherbe's movements.

At Ham Roberts, who never missed an opportunity for a bit of tourism, paid a visit to the castle in which the young Napoleon III had been held as a prisoner. He noted the poor condition of the roads, but saw that in spite of the bad weather, it seemed to make little impression on the German troops: 'Infantry, cavalry, and artillery marched along as if struggling through mud was really a pleasure.' When he got to Ham, he found that reports were coming in fast and furious:

> So far it appeared that Faidherbe was playing a good and a sound game; the result was in the hands of his troops. This time it would not be the fault of the general; for even his enemies admired the manner in which he manoeuvred.[2]

The first report came in from Barnekow at 10.15am, to the effect that Roupy was unoccupied but that there were enemy outposts at L'Épine de Dallon, about 3 miles from the centre of St Quentin. Shortly after came a report written the night before: the French had not pursued Reinecke's detachment beyond Bouchy, and large columns of the enemy had been sent marching from Templeux, Herbecourt and Jeancourt towards St Quentin. Cavalry patrols confirmed this movement; Poeuilly, two miles west of Vermand, was strongly occupied. At 10.45 another report came in from Barnekow; Vermand was still occupied, as was Etreillers, and columns were seen moving southeast on Roupy, Happencourt and Seraucourt. Further west, Lippe had reached Vendreuil and Moy, on the Oise, without meeting the enemy. Although all this suggested that Faidherbe's main body had not yet reached St Quentin, the movement on Seraucourt suggested to the First Army staff that perhaps the French were already marching eastwards of St Quentin.[3]

In fact Faidherbe, whose march was headed by Lecointe's 22nd Corps, had made much slower progress than this. His leading division, that of Derroja, only reached Vermand on January 17, and although it pushed on next day the other division of the 22nd Corps (Bessol) was still in and around Vermand on January 18. These divisions, constituting the right flank of the Army of the North, were covering the march of the rest of the army. The troops that had been reported as moving on Seraucourt were from Isnard's brigade and had advanced south-westwards from St Quentin. Patry's battalion, well up with the leading units of Derroja's division, was soon on the road again:

> On the 18th at daybreak we were on the road to St Quentin. The weather was wretched, with cold rain, mud, a gloomy and penetrating mist and, to cap it all, in the distance to our rear from about ten o'clock onwards there was a muffled but well sustained cannonade which made us cock an anxious ear.[4]

The battalion reached St Quentin at noon; but just after it had begun to settle down, and start cooking, it was ordered back in the direction of Vermand to take part in the combat it had heard as it marched. By the time it reached the neighbourhood of Vermand, that battle was over, and the exhausted troops made their way back to St Quentin.

Goeben, cautiously, continued to make his dispositions on the basis that Faidherbe's main body might already be in or through St Quentin and on the march south-eastwards. Barnekow was at 12.30pm ordered to move northwards through Jussy and take up a position on the line Clastres – Montescourt – Remigny. Prince Albrecht's division, placed under Barnekow's orders, was to move east on St Simon and Flavy le Martel. Meanwhile Böcking, with the army reserve, arrived at Ham during the afternoon. With Kummer and Goeben marching eastwards, Goeben was well placed either to intercept Faidherbe if he continued his south-eastward march, or to launch his planned concentric attack if the French remained in St Quentin.

The sounds of battle that Patry had heard were from the engagement being fought between Tertry and Poeuilly. The line of march being taken by von der Groeben and Kummer meant, if they kept up their superior rate of progress, that they would catch up with the tail of the Army of the North as it made its way eastwards. At 8.00am on January 18 Bock's 29th Brigade, having crossed the Somme, set out from St Christ in the direction of Tertry, while Strubberg's 30th Brigade moved up from Brie to Estrées en Chaussée. From there Strubberg was to follow Bock in his advance. The 29th Brigade made contact with Bessol's rearmost units when it edged to its right towards Beauvois. Bock was anxious to do what he could to delay the French march. A large wagon train was at the tail of the French march and he ordered the 2nd and 4th squadrons of 7th

Hussars under Captain Rudolphi to charge and disperse it, a task which he carried out with great success. There were scenes of chaos, many wagons being overturned and others retreating north to Caulaincourt. This had precisely the effect which Bock had intended, bringing Foerster's brigade into action, as it turned back to engage the Germans. Bock took up a position with Dörnberg's 65th Regiment and three batteries at Trefcon. Artillery fire soon halted Foerster's advance, but French skirmishers all along the front inflicted serious losses on the gunners before the 1st Battalion of the 65th Regiment charged forward and drove the French from the scrub from which they were firing. At 2.30pm Foerster's unsuccessful attempts to dislodge Dörnberg came to an end, apparently when Bessol arrived on the scene to order the march south on Grand Seraucourt to be resumed.[5] According to Faidherbe, the cavalry first charged a battalion of Gardes Mobiles du Gard from the 1st Brigade of Bessol's division, and then a battalion of Gardes Mobiles from the 2nd Brigade. This brigade had already reached Roupy when the first contact was made. At all events Rudolphi rode on beyond Trefcon before being halted by heavy infantry fire.

Strubberg's 30th Brigade had duly reached Estrées en Chaussée but it was 11.45am before contact was made with von der Groeben's force advancing on the left of the German line. From Estrées, Strubberg could see long columns of wagons, escorted by infantry, marching east between Poeuilly and Vermand and, others south of Bernes. This was the tail of the left flank column of Paulze d'Ivoy's 23rd Corps; the right flank column, led by Payen's division, was already in Vermand. The proximity of the Germans meant that Paulze d'Ivoy must do something to check their advance, and Payen was ordered to swing around to attack Strubberg, advancing first on Poeuilly and then throwing out skirmishes towards Vraignes.[6]

The combat at Caulaincourt, by Pallandre. (Rousset/*Histoire*)

Paulze d'Ivoy at Vermand, by Bombled. (Grenest)

Payen's attack was led by Michelet's 1st Brigade, advancing through Caulaincourt against Strubberg's left flank. To cover this Kummer had sent the 8th Rifle Battalion to Cauvigny Farm, when it occupied the heights and the nearby buildings, while Strubberg moved the 1st Battalion of the 68th Regiment to Vraignes. Kummer now sent orders to von der Groeben to push his cavalry forwards at once in the direction of Vermand, as part of his efforts to detain Paulze d'Ivoy. Unfortunately von der Groeben's force, which consisted of Memerty's detachment and Dohna's Combined Cavalry Brigade, was not in the best position to assist. Dohna's cavalry had passed round Péronne to the north, but was still in the rear of Memerty's detachment. Nor had they moved as quickly as they might, and Memerty, anxious not to be separated too far from the cavalry, had delayed his march until Dohna had come into line.[7]

At noon Memerty heard the artillery fire at Tertry, and changed his line of march to that direction, while sending one squadron towards Roisel to cover his left. This brought him closer to Kummer's left wing. Soon after this, however, it appeared to von der Groeben that the sense of Kummer's orders to him meant that he should make Poeuilly his objective, and he instructed Memerty accordingly to attack the enemy there directly. Dohna was ordered up to Hancourt.

The advanced guard of Memerty's detachment was led by Pestel, and consisted of three squadrons of the 7th Uhlans, the 4th Regiment of Grenadiers and the 6th 4-pounder battery of the corps artillery. The gunners, advancing to the north of the Roman road, opened fire on the French troops in Poeuilly, which consisted of Lagrange's 2nd Brigade of Payen's division, at a range of about 2000 yards. Soon after this the rest of Memerty's

French infantry during the engagement at Caulaincourt, by Pallandre. (Rousset/*Les Combattants*)

artillery, consisting of three batteries, moved up and opened fire in support. The 4th Regiment now advanced to the attack and stormed into Poeuilly, taking about 100 prisoners, as Payen pulled his troops back towards Vermand.

To the east of Poeuilly there is a steep ravine, and Pestel's troops soon reached and crossed it, probing forward towards Vermand. When they reached the Soyecourt – Caulaincourt road they met such strong resistance that, although Pestel got most of his troops and guns across the ravine, no further progress was possible. Meanwhile two of Pestel's squadrons of Uhlans had been reconnoitring to the north, and identified some detachments of Robin's division between Soyecourt and Vendelles. Apart from Pauly's brigade, which had been making its way eastwards well in the rear of the rest of the Army of the North, Robin's division was the last of Faidherbe's units, and there must have been some danger of it being cut off or at least involved in a combat which, unless supported, it might not be able to cope with. It was an anxious time for Faidherbe and his senior commanders; all the German commanders were alive to the need to slow up the French movement, and were pressing forward wherever they could. On the other hand, as Palat pointed out, the movements of the German units had effectively divided the First Army into two parts, separated by about six miles which could theoretically give the French an opportunity.[8] Faidherbe, however, was concerned solely to concentrate his army in and around St Quentin, and he was certainly not about to embark on any rash adventures at this stage.

In fact Pestel's situation was indeed somewhat exposed. Both of Payen's brigades were in action, and Lagrange, who had fallen back only to Vermand, and Michelet, still in possession of Caulaincourt, outnumbered the forces immediately opposing them. Of Memerty's main body, only the 1st Battalion of the 44th Regiment had come up to support the advanced guard, and he assigned it to the task of covering his left flank towards Soyecourt. The rest of the regiment only arrived at about 4.00pm; until then Pestel's hard pressed infantry had been able to hold their position to the east of Poeuilly by virtue of the accurate fire of the artillery.

Pestel's advance had, however, had the effect of disengaging Bock's left flank at Trefcon. Bock's advance had led to Bessol recalling one battalion and four guns of Gislain's 2nd Brigade from Roupy to strengthen the position at Beauvois. Kummer, for his part, brought up the 1st 6-pounder battery of the corps artillery; dashing forward, it opened fire with considerable success, but it had gone too far, and was soon obliged to retreat to the position of the other battery. One of Strubberg's batteries joined them there, and to cover their right flank Bock brought up the 2nd Battalion of the 65th Regiment. The 1st Battalion was also soon committed to the fight, as Bessol extended his front in the direction of Lanchy, which he was able to do because of the gap between the two parts of the First Army. After a brisk action the two battalions drove the French out of the woods to the west of Beauvois.

Paulze d'Ivoy had been obliged to halt his march towards St Quentin, and found himself heavily engaged, from Vermand to Caulaincourt. Crucial to his position was his decision to post the battery of Captain Dupuich, which had lost its commander so embarrassingly on January 16, in front of the wood between Vermand and Caulaincourt, where it held its position all day under the leadership of the twenty year old Lieutenant Belvallette. Paulze d'Ivoy had personally chosen the site for the battery; that night he called the young lieutenant to him, and praised him as being the principal cause of the corps' success in withstanding the German attacks.[9]

Paulze d'Ivoy subsequently commented on Faidherbe's suggestion that he had thrown back the enemy:

> As to the affair at Vermand, when he (Faidherbe) says that I repulsed the enemy, this is not precisely correct. I did not repulse him; I merely took up good positions and I was able to hold them all day. I had to struggle with 5,000 men against 30,000 men. And certainly I would not wish to undertake again what I did that day.

Sergent also records that, when speaking of Vermand, Paulze d'Ivoy never failed to express his utter astonishment at being left unsupported by his commander in chief.[10] He may have decidedly exaggerated the enemy's numerical superiority, but it is evident that he was not at all happy with Faidherbe's leadership. The fact was that however successful Paulze d'Ivoy might have been in holding up the German advance, as far as the Army of the North's mission was concerned its goose was cooked the moment he and Lecointe had to stand and fight on January 18.

Kummer was anxious that Bock should not advance further towards Beauvois for the moment, since the French possession of Caulaincourt would expose his left flank. Since Memerty's right flank was bogged down in front of the village, and he was not making much further progress beyond Poeuilly, it was clear that Caulaincourt must be taken. The 1st Battalion of the 68th Regiment, which had been marching on Vraignes, was recalled; the 8th Rifle Battalion attacked north of Tertry and then moved on to the assault of Caulaincourt, supported by a 4-pounder battery that had been held in reserve and which at 3.00pm opened fire on the village from the crest of a hill to the west of Trefcon. There followed an intensive artillery exchange in which the German batteries soon gained the upper hand. The riflemen attacked Caulaincourt from the west, followed by the 1st Battalion of the 68th Regiment, while to the north of the village two battalions of the 44th Regiment charged forward. Within minutes the village was taken, with 120 prisoners and 14 provision wagons.[11]

Mindful of Goeben's determination not to get involved in a major battle that day, Kummer contented himself with holding Caulaincourt and not following up his success. This did, however, enable Bock at 4.00pm to resume his advance on Beauvois, which he entered with two battalions of the 65th Regiment, finding the place unoccupied. At Vermand, however, the French remained in strength in their positions, and Kummer detached two battalions from Strubberg's brigade to reinforce von der Groeben. Strubberg also pushed forward one and a half battalions of the 28th Regiment into Caulaincourt to strengthen the movement on Vermand.

Von der Groeben had ordered Dohna to bring his cavalry brigade into action on the extreme left of the German advance. When they arrived, the cavalry encountered large numbers of French infantry from Robin's division between Soyecourt and Vendelles. This force was so strong that Dohna had to give up his attempt to ride around the right wing of the Army of the North and fall on its rear. Its presence also moved von der Groeben to abandon his attempt to take Vermand that day; moreover, with a large part of his force on the eastern side of the ravine, he feared that they were seriously exposed, and he issued orders for a retreat to Poeuilly, leaving only pickets to watch the position. While this was going on, Robin's division attempted an advance on Memerty's left, which was driven back by the concentrated fire of the artillery.

At 5.00 the retreat across the ravine began, the artillery leading the way, followed by the infantry. Memerty rode over to the 2nd Battalion of the 44th Regiment on his right; as he did so he was severely wounded during an attempted assault by the French. Colonel von Massow took over the command. In spite of the darkness the French launched a further assault, but this too was repulsed.[12]

It had been a muddling battle. The French objective had of course been to press on with their march as rapidly as they could; Goeben's commanders had to do what they could to slow it down. In this, they were successful. At what time Faidherbe finally realised that he was not going to get beyond St Quentin without a fight is not clear. In his account of the campaign it appears that an eastward march was no longer in his mind as a possible option:

> The events of the 18th proved that the concentration of Prussian forces was already far too advanced to allow a march towards the north in order to have the support of the fortresses. Battle about St Quentin had to be accepted.[13]

Faidherbe, naturally, sought to put the best face he could on a day that had ended so badly. General Palat commented:

French troops repel German cavalry at Vermand, by Bombled. (Grenest)

The day was disastrous for the Army of the North. Its columns, surprised in open order by forces far less numerous, had fought without obtaining any result from their isolated efforts. Its movement on St Quentin had ended in the most regrettable conditions ... almost all reached their cantonments late into the evening.[14]

It had been, thought Palat, one further opportunity thrown away by Faidherbe. He had had the chance to attack an enemy in the best possible circumstances, caught 'en flagrant délit de concentration'. If the eastern march had evidently become impossible, he could and should have turned on his pursuers with the great superiority of force which he possessed.

In the course of the day Faidherbe suffered, according to his suspiciously vague account, about 500 casualties. This was plainly an underestimate; the French lost over 400 unwounded prisoners during the course of the day. German losses amounted to 19 killed and 199 wounded, with one missing.[15]

18

The Eve of Battle

Back in Versailles, Moltke was very conscious that the endgame of the war against the Government of National Defence had been reached. In the west, Chanzy's army had been wrecked; in the south-east Bourbaki was stumbling towards destruction; and the Army of Paris could plainly do no more to break out of the investment of the city. It was essential, however, that Faidherbe not be allowed to disrupt or delay the progress of the German armies towards total victory. The Army of the North had shown more than once that it was a force to be reckoned with. It substantially outnumbered the First Army, and there were indications that it was being reinforced. Its movement east towards St Quentin suggested that Faidherbe meant business. All, therefore, depended on Goeben. Moltke had already shown that he was prepared to reinforce the First Army with whatever it took to defeat Faidherbe; but his anxious wait for news was relieved by the total confidence that he had in Goeben as a commander.

Moltke's confidence was generally shared by those around him, although Blumenthal, the outspoken Chief of Staff of the Third Army, writing in his diary about Faidherbe's advance, observed: 'As I feared, this has made both the King and the Crown Prince anxious, though there is not the least ground for fear.'[1]

On January 18 there took place the proclamation of King William as German Emperor in the Salle des Glaces. For Moltke, who with all his senior colleagues of course attended the ceremony, the day was still a busy one, his principal concerns being the events in the north and in the south-east. First news of Goeben's intentions came in a telegram sent from his headquarters at 3.00pm:

> The army is concentrated westwards of St Quentin on the line Ham – Vendeuil, in readiness to attack the enemy tomorrow. The enemy had occupied St Quentin in force at midday, and was moving southwards; whether eastwards also has not yet been reported. Headquarters Ham.[2]

As this message indicated, it was still not entirely clear to Goeben where the Army of the North had got to, or what its intentions were. During the day an oral report from an orderly, Lieutenant Count Rothkirch, had brought the news that Kummer was in action, but it was not until 7.30pm that Kummer's report, that he had taken Poeuilly and Caulaincourt and was in cantonments on the line Devize – Tertry – Poeuilly, reached headquarters. Meanwhile a despatch had arrived at 4.00pm from Barnekow, written at 2.00pm, reporting that a strong French column had advanced from St Quentin and occupied Essigny le Grand. These troops appeared to be moving along the railway towards Montescourt, and Barnekow intended to advance to Lizerolles. Mindful of Goeben's intention not to start a battle that day, he was then going to go on to the defensive if the enemy advanced. At 6.45pm a report from Lippe, timed at 4.00pm, confirmed the enemy occupation of Essigny le Grand. The bridges over the Oise were practicable except for that at Chatillon. There appeared to be three regiments in the south-eastern suburbs of St Quentin, and also units in Neuville St Amand and Mesnil St Laurent.[3]

Meanwhile there was no news of the 16th Brigade, due to arrive from the Army of the Meuse. Captain Schell, who got to headquarters from La Fère at 3.30pm, reported that when he passed Tergnier at 11.00am there was no sign of the brigade, and an enquiry went to the Army of the Meuse. This brought the news that the 16th Brigade had marched to Gonesse on January 17, but it was 10.00 am on the following day before the first of its battalions left there and it was not expected that the whole of the brigade would be in place before the afternoon of January 19. Not much help, therefore, was to be expected from it in the early stages of the battle; Goeben confirmed that it should be under Lippe's orders.

Goeben had all along based his plans on the worst case scenario – that Faidherbe had concentrated his main body at St Quentin on January 17 and was hence able to move eastwards next day. The information available now indicated that the Army of the North was concentrated at St Quentin; Goeben assumed that the French troops in action at Vermand must have been a detachment covering Faidherbe's right flank. His concern now was that Faidherbe might, if an immediate attack was not launched, perceive his danger and get away to the north and the safety of his fortresses. There could, therefore, be no question of postponing the planned attack until the reinforcements arrived. At 8.00pm Goeben reported to Moltke that he would, on the following day, launch a concentric attack on the enemy.

When he had set out on his march eastwards, Faidherbe had reckoned that if he ran into superior forces he could fall back northwards and await Goeben under the guns of his fortresses. By January 18, however, he had reached the conclusion that his enemy had been too quick for him; the concentration of the First Army around St Quentin meant that it was too late to attempt a march northwards, and battle must be accepted in his present position.[4] The Army of the North now stood in two main groups, separated by the Somme, in a wide semicircle around St Quentin, facing to the south and the west. Schell observed the difficulties which limited the extent to which the French could strengthen the position which they had taken up:

> The heights, which surround the town at a distance of four kilometres, afforded very good defensive positions, but neither flank of the army had a suitable point d'appui, and all communications between the two divided halves of the army had to pass through St Quentin. The French army did not reach its positions until late on January 18, part of it not before nightfall, and had, therefore, no time to strengthen its positions materially by throwing up entrenchments. All that could be done was to barricade the main streets, and put some houses of the suburbs of St Quentin into a partial state of defence.[5]

General Palat reflected, with the benefit of hindsight, on the options open to Faidherbe as his troops trudged into position around St Quentin:

On the evening of January 18, Faidherbe was obliged to take a critical decision; the day's fighting had shown that he could no longer hope to outrun the enemy: to continue his movement to the east, with troops that were already exhausted, in the face of an enemy as mobile as this would be to court disaster.

To retire, without fighting, on the northern fortresses presented certain difficulties. The enemy was too close and our long columns would be vulnerable to his attack. Moreover this retreat would deprive Faidherbe of the fruits of his laborious march, and it would deeply trouble the morale of his young army and that of the populace. In addition, supposing that a retreat was possible, it would not have conformed with the instructions of M. de Freycinet. Having rejected these options, he had a choice between two others: to face the enemy in the defensive position around St Quentin, and thus derive the advantage of the proximity of a large town, or establish himself several kilometres to the north on the heights which overlook the canal, between Bellenglise and Croix. The first meant offering battle, separated into two parts by an impassable barrier, with the risk of being hurled into the Somme. The second required the abandonment of St Quentin, but this counted for little when the advantages were considered. The army would have its front covered by the canal and its retreat assured in case of a defeat. However, the first option was selected; Faidherbe chose to remain around St Quentin.[6]

Palat observed that the possibility of a retreat on the Bellenglise – Croix line did not seem to have been considered by Faidherbe. Whether it was a practicable option really

The Canal de St Quentin at Lehaucourt. (Duncan Rogers)

depends on when he finally realised that he was not going to be able to persevere in his lunge to the east. After the day's fighting on January 18, as his exhausted troops made their way into and around St Quentin, it was probably too late to redirect them northwards to the Bellenglise – Croix position. Even if he had been able to do so, Faidherbe's flanks there were somewhat exposed to Goeben's cavalry. As to a retreat from that position being 'assured', the most that can be said is that the Army of the North would not have so far to go to reach the safety of its fortresses. All the same, Palat is no doubt correct in suggesting that the position would have been better than that in which Faidherbe actually fought – if, that is, he had marched east for the sole purpose of offering battle to the First Army. As it was, that was the one thing he had hoped to avoid.

In 1871 the town which Faidherbe had thus opted to defend had a population of some 35,000. It took the form of an almost regular hexagon; its ancient fortifications had been replaced by wide boulevards, within which the town spread out on the slopes of a ridge which stretched north to the neighbouring heights. One of the highest of these was crowned by the Church of the Collegiate, visible from a long way off. The streets were generally wide, the houses brick built; factories were scattered in the residential areas. Beyond the exterior boulevards lay the substantial suburbs. Of these, the most important was that of Isle, beyond the Somme canal and the railway. It was linked by a continuous built up area to Neuville St Amand, where there was a major sugar refinery. This urban area lay astride the roads to Guise and La Fère. The hedges of the St Lazare Farm, and the high walls of the sugar refinery made it easily defensible, especially to the south and south-east; but a long ridge snaked around the position, assisting the approach of an attacker.

Beyond the Somme and its canal, to the west, which, with the pools and marshy meadows which bordered them, formed an impassable barrier, the suburb of St Martin stretched along the roads to Ham and Savy and the Roman road to Vermand. It was

The sugar refinery at Neuville St Amand, from a contemporary sketch. (Scheibert)

closely overlooked by the ridge on which stood the Rocourt windmills. The area between the Ham road and the Somme was covered with gardens bordered by hedges. Further north, the suburb of St Jean stretched along the Cambrai road on a ridge which provided defensible slopes to the north and north-west. Between this ridge and that of the Collegiate, the walls of Bagatelle and Monplaisir were easily adapted to defence.

Beyond this, the northern suburbs of the Cemetery and Remicourt overlooked the valley of the Somme. The long walls of the cemetery, and the hedges and walls of the large gardens and the nursery at the end of Remicourt commanded excellent views of the valley, and the roads from Omissy, Morcourt and Rouvroy. Beyond this again, between the Bohain road and that to Morcourt, the walled garden of the Sisters of the Cross provided an important defensive position. Ordinarily, the terrain neither obstructed the movement of infantry, but nor did it offer them shelter. However, the condition of the ground was decidedly unfavourable; the soggy mixture of chalk and clay had steadily deteriorated during the continual process of alternate frost and thaw, while the country roads were in any case completely broken up in winter by the passage of heavy farm traffic.

On the right bank of the Somme the ridge which ran around the Isle suburb reached the river near the village of Gauchy and the sugar refinery of La Biette. A second parallel ridge, separated from it by the little valley of Grugies, ran from Hancourt to Giffécourt. Finally a third hill, rising near Urvillers, ran to Contescourt; on it stood the village of Essigny le Grand. Beyond Mesnil St Laurent these three heights joined those above the Oise valley, through which passed the high road to Guise. These three heights considerably assisted the defence, although as it ended in the air, the position required a longer front than would otherwise have been the case.[7]

The plateau to the west of St Quentin ended in an acute angle, the sides of which were the valley of the Somme and that through which wound the road from Vermand. There were several copses. The large village of Savy was particularly defensible, its houses built close together; not so those in the Somme valley where the houses, like those on the left bank, were more scattered. South-east of Holnon a cluster of small villages, joined by a network of sunken roads, lay amid the farms and orchards. From the Holnon – Savy plateau ran two spurs; one, between the Roman road and the road from Vermand, was crowned by the Bois des Roses, a huddle of small houses surrounded by hedges; the other, on which stood the windmills of Coutte and de la Tour, joined the ridge of Fayet. In the centre of this latter village stood the Chateau de Fayet, which again could be easily defended.

The principal weakness of Faidherbe's position was of course the valley of the Somme; the river was up to 12 metres wide at St Quentin, running through marshy banks, while the St Quentin Canal was up to 20 metres wide. The available bridges were few; these were at Grand Seraucourt, Fontaine les Clercs, St Quentin itself, and those bearing the roads from Rouvroy, Morcourt and Omissy. The first of these was of critical importance, linking La Fère and Ham.

South of St Quentin, the left bank was divided by the railway line running to Tergnier; this crossed the ridges in a series of cuttings and embankments which were to prove crucial, and which formed an additional break in the communications of the various units engaged. There were three important roads into the town on the left bank, from La Fère, from Grand Seraucourt and, between them, the old Roman road known as the

Chaussée Brunehaut. The high road to Guise could serve as a line of retreat, but it ran north-east, and following it would expose the army to a flank attack. The best line of retreat for troops fighting on the left bank was through Isle and St Quentin, but this meant using two narrow bridges.

On the right bank, the position was crossed by four roads into the town; the high road from Ham, through Roupy and Rocourt to St Martin; the road through Savy; the old Roman road (in a particularly bad state) which ran through Holnon; and the Vermand road. On this bank, two lines of retreat were available. That to Cambrai ran from St Jean, crossing the St Quentin Canal near Bellenglise, and was particularly important. The other was the Bohain road, from the Cemetery suburb; it was in a poor state of repair.

All in all, the Army of the North must fight in a position that was strategically unsound, divided into two separate parts, with only the Cambrai and Bohain roads practically available for a retreat; and it risked being cut off from those if the First Army got round its flanks.[8] Nor could the condition of the French troops be described as battleworthy. Commandant Sergent, in giving an extract from the historical record of one battalion of the Mobiles du Pas de Calais, wrote that it was

> eminently appropriate to bring home the extreme misery of our brave soldiers, the shortages to which they were subjected, the vague and incoherent orders which they received, when they received any at all, in brief the deplorable conditions in which they found themselves, facing greatly superior forces, rested and fully provisioned, in the battle of Saint Quentin.[9]

Leaving on one side the inaccuracies in this comment the indignation of a French historian is perhaps understandable; but he might have gone on to reflect that the Army of the North had short and safe lines of communication and all the resources of north-eastern France on which to draw; its adversary, on the other hand, was operating at the end of lengthy and tenuous lines of communication which ran through potentially hostile territory.

The orders issued by Faidherbe during the evening of January 18 for the following day reflected the division of the battlefield into its separate sectors. Paulze d'Ivoy, whose 23rd Corps was reinforced by the Brigade Isnard, stood on the right bank of the river; Lecointe's 22nd Corps was responsible for the left bank. The 23rd Corps was established in an arc of which its left, consisting of Payen's 1st Division was on the Somme around Dallon, and its right, consisting of the 2nd Division under Robin, as far as the road to Cambrai. Isnard's brigade provided the connection between them. Lecointe's corps faced south, on a line which curved around from Grugies to the La Fère road. His 1st Division, under Derroja, was on the left and Bessol's on the right, resting on the Somme. In the orders he issued, however, Faidherbe appears to have contemplated that Lecointe would extend at least part of his line to a position on the right bank of the river:

> The troops will take up around Saint Quentin the positions set out below:
>
> The 22nd Corps will establish itself astride the canal, one division on the heights of Gauchy and Neuville facing south, with the other division on the right bank, between the canal and the Savy road, which it will overlap a little.

The 23rd Corps, reinforced by the Brigade Isnard, will establish itself facing west, between the Savy road and Fayet and will seek to occupy the best positions it can find.

The troops will occupy the woods and when there pitch tents and will cook soup. Headquarters will be in the Saint Martin suburb. The reserve artillery will be established in front of the same suburb.[10]

Unfortunately, this written order did not reach its destination; it was carried by Lieutenant Lagnier who was taken prisoner by an enemy patrol. In the classic tradition, the quick thinking Lagnier put the order in his mouth, chewed it, and succeeded in swallowing it. As a result the whole of the 22nd Corps prepared to face the coming battle on the left bank of the river.[11]

Faidherbe warned his corps commanders to expect the enemy to approach from the directions of Vermand, Ham, Chauny and La Fère. He indicated the roads to Cambrai and Bohain as the lines of retreat if necessary. The Brigade Pauly took post at Bellicourt to cover the first of these. As Palat pointed out, the effect of these orders was that the Cambrai road, the more important line of retreat, was protected by Robin's division and Pauly's brigade, the weakest units in the army. It was a disposition that might have disastrous consequences.[12]

Goeben issued his orders at 9.00pm. The army was, he said, to complete its victory on the following day, advancing all along the line at 8.00am. Kummer was to advance with his whole force, including all the corps artillery, by the Vermand and Etreillers roads, with a view to a concentric attack on St Quentin. On his left, von der Groeben was to extend his line as far as the Cambrai road. On the left bank, Barnekow was to advance with the 16th Division and Prince Albrecht's division on St Quentin along the railway

Preparing St Quentin for defence, by Pallandre. (Rousset/*Les Combattants*)

and by way of Essigny le Grand; Lippe, with his division and whatever troops of the 16th Brigade that might arrive from Tergnier, was to advance along the road from La Fère, aiming to turn the French left. The reserve under Böcking, which in the first instance Goeben intended personally to accompany, was to move out of Ham at 9.00am. Goeben was confident of victory:

> With the forces now assembled here and our superior artillery, all we have to do is to press forward vigorously; this will suffice to overthrow any force that the enemy can oppose to us ... If the enemy should not await our attack, we must strain every nerve to pursue him energetically, for experience has shown that it is not so much in the battle itself as in the vigorous pursuit afterwards that the greatest results are obtained against such loosely organised forces.[13]

The correspondent of the *Daily News* encountered a friend, the commander of a regiment, who was contemplating Goeben's orders for the day:

> 'This is von Goeben,' said he; 'I knew him well from 1866, when he was operating against the so-called South Army. The peculiarity of his disposition is the great exactness with which care is taken of all parts; none being neglected; each working for itself for a certain time, and scarcely knowing it is connected with a neighbour until the time comes when all act together as a whole. He cares comparatively little how many men perish on the march so long as the march is completed in the given time. And you will see today,' my friend added, 'the results he obtains. You will particularly notice that everybody will be not only in his right place, but also in due time.'[14]

The number of troops that would be engaged on each side has been the subject of considerable dispute. Faidherbe, not usually inclined to exaggerate his strength, put his total force at about 40,000.[15] It consisted of 67 battalions, with seven squadrons of cavalry and 99 guns, with three engineer companies. Of these, however, only 25 battalions were formed from regular units; 20 were composed of gardes mobiles and the remainder gardes nationales, or mobilisés. The artillery was organised in 15 batteries, apart from 10 guns attached to Isnard's brigade. General Palat reckoned that although it was impossible to determine it accurately, the strength of the Army of the North must have been between 30,000 and 40,000. Other writers have estimated 31,000 (Axel de Roppe) and 39,000 (Kunz).[16]

Goeben disposed of a total of 39 battalions, 48 squadrons, 161 guns organised in 27 batteries, and one engineer company. This includes one battalion of the 16th Brigade which arrived from Tergnier during the course of the day. Basing his estimate on an average battalion strength of 700 men, Palat arrived at a total of 27,700 infantry, with 5,580 cavalry and 2720 others, an overall total of 36,000. On the other hand, the Prussian Official History gives a total figure of 32,580.[17] Palat disputes this figure as not taking account of the gunners. Schell noted that many of the German infantry battalions had become very attenuated in the course of the constant fighting, some being no more than 500 strong; he put the total strength of the infantry at no more than 24,000. He also thought that Faidherbe's figure of 40,000 for the Army of the North did not include the brigades of Isnard and Pauly.[18]

19

St Quentin: The Southern Sector

January 19 dawned dark and misty, and the gloom persisted all day. The thaw continued, and an icy rain fell throughout the morning. Men and horses moved through the sodden ground with the greatest difficulty. Facing Barnekow, Lecointe's 22nd Corps had of course not received the orders issued by Faidherbe during the night of January 18/19, to defend the Somme valley on a line between the Ham and La Fère roads, while Paulze d'Ivoy's 23rd Corps and the reserve lay behind Lecointe's right flank. As it was, Lecointe's troops took up excellent positions in front of the villages into which they had wearily trudged during the night; and they were particularly well placed on the hills around Grugies, as well as holding Castres and Gauchy.[1]

Captain Seton had bought a handsome chestnut horse a few days earlier from an artillery officer. Now, on the morning of January 19, he felt he should, in case of accidents, pay for it: 'This was done by writing a cheque on the back of a leaf taken out of one of the railway account books at Montescourt station.'[2] This duly done, he rode forward to the head of the column, intending to remain with the 40th Regiment which he had accompanied throughout most of the campaign.

Barnekow set his troops in motion at 8.00am, but they had some way to go through the muddy fields before they could be in position to launch an attack on Lecointe's positions. Goeben did not leave Ham until 9.00, setting off towards Roupy with his headquarters staff and the army reserve under Böcking. Before he left Ham, Goeben sent off Captain von Schell to Barnekow to tell him that if Kummer, when he advanced with the 15th Division, found little opposition, he would be required to despatch one regiment and part of the corps artillery to Roupy, where they would be held in reserve as a support for Barnekow if necessary. Schell was ordered to remain with the right wing during the battle, and to send frequent reports to Goeben at Roupy.[3]

Goeben's orders had originally been drafted on the assumption that the bulk of the 16th Brigade, arriving at Tergnier, would be available to support Barnekow; it was the news that only one battalion of the brigade had reached Tergnier by midnight that prompted him to anticipate the possible need to shift troops from his left to his right. In fact, at 8.30am Barnekow, at that time between Lizerolles and Essigny le Grand, learned that the leading battalion of the 16th Brigade would reach Cérizy by 9.00am, and he reported this to Goeben, together with the news that his advanced guard had already got through Essigny le Grand. Goeben got this report at about 10.30am at Fluquières while still on his way to Roupy; and just at this time the sound of gunfire was heard, apparently from the direction of Essigny le Grand. Goeben was extremely sensitive to the dangers of the potential gap between the two wings of his army, and at 10.40 he decided to send Böcking and the reserve to Grand Seraucourt to support Barnekow's advance. This decision, of course, meant that the detachment from Kummer would certainly

Looking at Castres from the road to St Quentin. (Duncan Rogers)

now be required at Roupy.[4] First reports from the cavalry patrols operating in front of the advancing units of Kummer and von der Groeben suggested that the French were pulling back on this part of their line. Goeben continued on his way to Roupy, which he reached at about 11.00am. Listening for the sound of gunfire from Barnekow's sector, it seemed to him that the intensity of the conflict there had somewhat slackened; in fact, however, the reverse was true, as the 16th Division was by then heavily engaged.

Barnekow had been first concerned to secure Grand Seraucourt and Essigny le Grand, from each of which places the French had retreated. The leading units of his advance on Essigny le Grand were the 9th Hussar Regiment and Rosenzweig's 31st Brigade. The hussars had trotted on ahead, and were soon reporting that Grugies and the sugar factory south of the village were strongly held, and that other French columns were moving up. At 9.45am Barnekow ordered Rosenzweig to advance at once on Grugies, and at the same time ordered Hertzberg to concentrate his 31st Brigade beyond Essigny le Grand, while Prince Albrecht's 3rd Reserve Division was to halt south of that place. Prince Albrecht had already detached the Guard Hussar Regiment under von Hymmen with the 1st Battalion of the 19th Regiment, the Fusilier Battalion of the 81st Regiment and a 4-pounder battery to move through Artemps on Grand Seraucourt, thereby materially assisting communication between the two wings of the army.

It was clear to Barnekow that Grugies was the key point of Lecointe's position, and he trotted forward with the 31st Brigade as it prepared to attack. To prepare the assault he deployed the 5th Heavy and 5th Light Batteries, which at 9.30am crossed the shallow valley from Urvillers to Castres, keeping to the east of the main road into St Quentin and opened fire. Their immediate targets were a number of columns of French infantry moving southwards to the east of Gauchy. The French artillery, concentrated on the Tout

The sugar refinery today. (Duncan Rogers)

Vent windmill heights, replied. Rosenzweig's leading unit was the 2nd Battalion of the 69th Regiment, which now moved forward in company columns, preparing to attack the line of the railway. To its left the 2nd Battalion of the 29th Regiment moved forward to occupy the ground to the west of the railway line which, alternatively running through cuttings and along embankments, split the battlefield. There was a bridge carrying the embankment near the sugar factory, and further south, a bridge over a cutting close to Essigny le Grand.[5]

Meanwhile the French had brought up further artillery, deploying two batteries on another windmill hill between Grugies and Castres, which at about 10.00am opened fire, taking the German gun line in flank. Bessol's division was in and around Grugies, and had pushed forward three battalions to occupy Contescourt. Derroja's division stood somewhat behind Bessol, with Pittié's brigade at Gauchy, and Aynès' brigade still emerging from St Quentin. It was about this time that Bessol was mortally wounded by a shell which burst under his horse; he refused to leave his position, however, until he was sure that Foerster had taken over command of the division. It was some time before Lecointe was aware of this. Patry's regiment meanwhile had been in the suburb of Isle when he heard the sound of gunfire break out. His battalion set off at about 8.30 towards the heights of Tout Vent from which the French artillery were exchanging fire with the German batteries. It was soon apparent to him that battle had been joined in earnest:

> My company was at the head of the battalion which was then marching with its left flank to the front, as one says in military language. At first we followed the main road from La Fère before turning right into a farm road which, sometimes deeply embanked and sometimes in the open, wound across the fields to reach the hill. The

German shells which were missing our batteries came on to strike around us in the sodden clay and for the most part buried themselves in it without bursting, making a frightful whistling and sending up volcanoes of mud.[6]

When the battalion reached Tout Vent, it was concentrated behind the crest, while the officers went forward to see what was happening in their front.

The railway line was already beginning to have an important influence on the battle. Lecointe had evidently expected the principal German attack to develop to the west of the line, and initially took a position the left of which rested on the line itself. Schell described it thus:

> This line of railway divides the field of battle southward of St Quentin into two completely separate halves, for it crosses the heights which sweep from east to west in 30-50 feet deep cuttings, the steep banks and quickset hedges of which are almost everywhere impassable, even for skirmishers, so that all communication from one side of the line to the other is confined to a few narrow road crossings.[7]

Captain Seton came upon Barnekow and his staff as the former was directing the deployment of further batteries north of the La Manufacture farm, intended to support the attack of Rosenzweig's brigade. Seton noted that the southern face of the ridge behind which the infantry was massing to attack was not abrupt enough to give much cover against enemy artillery fire; when going forward the troops would be facing enemy troops in position on a plateau which commanded their line of advance. Seton had been riding with the commander and the adjutant of the 1st Battalion of the 40th Regiment:

> All three of us had been discussing in the morning the chances of the French waiting to receive the attack, now that a stop had been put to their march south, and great doubts had been expressed of a fight taking place. If these had not been dispelled by the flank fire, they presently were by a lot of shells coming at last from the windmill; one of them fell between Steinöcker and myself, covering us with mud, but not exploding. Another burst among the 3rd Battalion, and I am not sure but that it was this early stage of the action that Major von Holleben fell mortally wounded.[8]

Rosenzweig had pushed forward the 2nd Battalion of the 29th Regiment to the west of the railway line. Pressing on towards Grugies, at about 11.00am, the first of his units to pass to the assault was the 2nd Battalion of the 69th Regiment; the resistance at the sugar factory and the railway cutting was, however, so strong that the battalion could make no progress, even though it made four attempts to do so. Attacking across open fields, in the face of fierce Chassepôt fire, it was a daunting task even for the battle hardened and experienced infantry of the First Army. The repulse of these assaults emboldened Foerster to launch a counter attack with his brigade, advancing on both sides of the railway with six battalions against the almost isolated battalion which was running low in ammunition. Hastily Rosenzweig led forward six companies of the 1st Battalion of the 29th Regiment, which drove the French back on the sugar factory. Two companies of the regiment's Fusilier Battalion succeeded in occupying the high ground to the east

ST QUENTIN: THE SOUTHERN SECTOR 195

The Prussian 29th Infantry Regiment launches a bayonet attack during the Battle of St Quentin, by Roetzler. (Scheibert)

French Chasseurs take German infantry prisoner near the sugar refinery, by Bombled. (Grenest)

of the sugar factory at the point of the bayonet, forcing a battery which had come up on the west of the railway to fall back. The sugar factory, however, was strongly garrisoned, and the advance could not penetrate to it. By 12.30pm the two sides had, in this sector, settled into a fierce exchange of rifle fire, neither side for the moment attempting any further assaults.[9]

The bulk of the garrison of the sugar factory consisted of the 20th Chasseurs Battalion, led by Commandant Hecquet. He and his men had been roused at 3.00am and at 4.30am had set out to march southwards to Grugies, arriving there at dawn. Moving on, they reached the sugar factory which was at once seen as a defensive strongpoint of the highest importance, and as soon as it appeared that battle was about to commence, Hecquet deployed four companies in advance of the position between the railway line and the road to Contescourt. The records of the battalion show that casualties soon began to mount, especially among the officers; by 11.00am the garrison of the sugar factory was beginning to run short of ammunition.[10]

While Foerster's brigade was thus defending the sugar factory and Grugies, Gislain's brigade of Bessol's division was occupied to the west. Three battalions of this brigade had advanced, somewhat tentatively, from Castres in the direction of Essigny le Grand. Encountering three companies of the 2nd Battalion of the 29th Regiment, west of the railway line, they soon fell back in the direction of Contescourt. One of the three companies followed up the retreating French infantry, attacking the left of the position at Contescourt, which was by now also under attack by Hymmen's detachment advancing from Grand Seraucourt. This was led by the 1st Battalion of the 19th Regiment, which took up a position in the open fields south of Contescourt, supported by a battery which unlimbered behind it. Gislain's strength here, however, was such that for the moment no further progress was possible.[11]

Lecointe, having expected the attack on the west of the railway line, was soon obliged to extend his front eastwards as the advance of Lippe's 12th Cavalry Division began to make itself felt on the right of the 16th Division. Coming up the road from La Fère, it was a serious threat to Lecointe's position, and he ordered up Aynès' brigade at the double to occupy Neuville St Amand and the heights above Le Pontchu, just north of Urvillers. This brought Léonce Patry's battalion into action; Aynès galloped up to the battalion commander and ordered him to cross the La Fère road, where it halted. Aynès then required two companies, one of which was Patry's, to take up a position at a nearby farm:

> The Colonel, thereupon addressing himself to me as the most senior, said: 'Captain, you will go with these two companies to that farm which you see over there; you will occupy it strongly and you will defend it to the last extremity. The position is very important. It anchors our extreme left and it covers our only line of retreat.'

Patry, uncertain as to what was required of him, asked what was meant by the last extremity; Aynès' response left him in no doubt: 'You will not leave that farm except on a verbal or written order from me.'[12] The farm was well chosen as a defensive point, built in the classic French style with a square courtyard surrounded by high walls. Patry, and Fernandez, the other company commander, soon had their men in position. On their right stood the Raulieu farm, also by now garrisoned by men from Aynès' brigade, while on their left lay the village of Neuville St Amand, which now represented the extreme left of Lecointe's line. Patry was, for the moment, comforted to think that his flanks were secure.

Lippe, with only a limited number of infantry at his disposal, had halted the main body of his division at Cornet d'Or, on the La Fère road north of Urvillers. Lieutenant Colonel von Holtzendorff now led his 12th Rifle Battalion across the open ground towards the French position; and at this point the first of the reinforcements that had disembarked at Tergnier reached the battlefield. Lippe sent this unit, the 2nd Battalion of the 86th Regiment, supported by three guns of the 2nd Horse Artillery Battery, to move forward towards Neuville St Amand. At 1.30pm Holtzendorff's riflemen stormed the park, which had been holding up this advance, and shortly after took the Raulieu farm. In the fighting there Aynès was killed; the retreat of the garrison left Patry's right flank open and, soon after, the men of the 86th Regiment took Neuville St Amand. This meant Patry's position was totally exposed; he graphically described the scene inside the farmyard:

> The spectacle inside the courtyard was heartrending. The men wounded in the course of the action had sought refuge in the house and had taken off some of their clothing in order to tend themselves. Now as the flames reached them they tried to escape by dragging themselves along painfully, all bloody and dishevelled; but the flames overtook them and they were burned alive.[13]

The bulk of Patry's troops had already made their escape, falling back in disorder towards St Quentin, and Patry, with a small handful of the remaining men, was soon able to follow them into the suburb of Isle, where he learned that Aynès had been killed during the fighting at the adjoining farm. Lippe, still handicapped by his lack of infantry, did not for the moment attempt to pursue the retreating enemy into St Quentin, and concentrated his division on the main road and in Neuville St Amand.

Colonel Böcking, with the reserve, had received explicit orders from Goeben:

> To proceed forthwith to Grand Seraucourt and to join energetically in the action of the 16th Infantry Division wherever circumstances might demand it, at the same time reporting these orders to General Barnekow and placing himself at this general's disposal.[14]

Having sent off the reserve, Goeben found himself in a similar situation to that of Manteuffel at Amiens. As he sat his horse at Roupy, he was in the centre of his army's position, but between him and the enemy there stood only the 1st Squadron of the 9th Hussars, a situation that continued until Major Bronikowsky arrived with units detached from Kummer's division. These were two battalions of the 28th Regiment, the 8th Rifle Battalion and one battery. These marched into Roupy at about 11.30am, exhausted after a forced march through knee deep mud; it was clear to Goeben that they could not be committed without at least a half hour's rest. Since Bronikowsky had brought with him only one battery, Goeben sent to Kummer to request two more as soon as possible. By 12.00 noon the whole horse artillery division had arrived at Roupy.

Goeben had by now begun to feel rather out of touch as to what was happening on the ground, and sent off two staff officers to find out. Captain Rogalla von Bieberstein

The defence of St Quentin, by Armand-Dumaresq. (Rousset/Histoire)

rode off to meet Barnekow, going by way of Grand Seraucourt. His immediate mission was to tell Barnekow of the despatch of Böcking to that place, but also to emphasise that these troops represented the army's last reserve. Captain Baumann was sent to Kummer, to ascertain the situation in the western sector. Soon after his departure a written despatch arrived from Colonel von Witzendorff, the Chief of Staff of the VIII Corps, who was accompanying the left wing of the army. Timed at 10.30am, it reported on the commencement of the action on the western section, and that Dohna's cavalry had been pushed forward as far as Bellenglise without encountering anything of the enemy. He also sent some information which turned out to be thoroughly misleading; the capture of prisoners belonging to the 33rd, 65th and 75th Regiments of the line, and to the 2nd and 6th Battalions of Chasseurs, which belonged to the 22nd Corps, gave rise to an assumption that it was Lecointe's corps that was fighting in this sector. In fact, these were probably stragglers from the corps that had got separated from their units during the march to St Quentin.[15]

The despatch of Böcking to reinforce Barnekow was probably a prudent move in all the circumstances, since the 16th Division was for the moment being given a hard time. Michael Howard, however, found surprising Goeben's decision to reinforce his right wing, which had made little progress, rather than his left which was doing well, especially since a breakthrough in the western sector could have threatened Faidherbe's line of retreat.[16] As it was, Böcking's arrival was in due course to prove decisive in the struggle in the southern sector.

For the moment, Lecointe was doing rather well. Between 12.00 noon and 1.00pm Bessol's heavy numerical superiority forced Rosenzweig to retreat, losing the ground which he had hitherto gained; and although a temporary respite occurred when two

*The charge of the Prussian 70th Infantry Regiment at St Quentin, by Röchling. (Rousset/*Histoire*)*

companies of the 70th Regiment attacked Bessol's left wing, these were in their turn driven back and Rosenzweig, who had attempted to regain the lost ground, was also obliged again to retreat. However, the 10th and 11th Companies of the 40th Regiment from Hertzberg's brigade also came forward in support of the 31st Brigade, and succeeding in retaking a vital railway crossing to the south of the sugar factory, where they consolidated their position. This success enabled Rosenzweig, whose troops were exhausted after the long struggle, and were short of ammunition, to withdraw his three battalions in good order under the cover of heavy artillery.

The position was, however, still critical, and at 1.00pm Barnekow ordered Prince Albrecht to concentrate his division and advance over the open ground to the west of Essigny le Grand. Until now, he had been concerned to keep the 3rd Reserve Division in hand, in case Lippe ran into difficulties on the extreme right, but by now he had learned of the failure of the French advance towards Le Pontchu. What Barnekow did not know, however, was that Böcking had been told by Goeben that he was to get into action as soon as he could; all he knew was that the reserve was on its way to him. Barnekow ordered Hymmen to push forward towards Grugies as soon as Böcking arrived, while ordering the latter at 1.30pm to halt at Grand Seraucourt. In fact, however, Böcking had reached a position south-east of Contescourt by 12 noon; once his batteries had opened fire, the French fell back, and by 12.30pm he was possession of the village. The leading troops of the 41st Regiment, pressing on, soon took La Ferme Patte which stood on the road south-east of Castres, capturing 130 prisoners. 100 more prisoners were captured in the hollow way north of the farm, and a further 200 prisoners were taken when four companies of the 41st Regiment took the village of Castres. Gislain pulled back his brigade to the windmill hill south-east of Giffécourt, where he was able to take up a strong defensive position.[17]

20

St Quentin: The Western Sector

Kummer was uncertain as to the position actually taken up by the forces opposing him, but surmised that an advance by his left wing would, if directed through Vermand, enable him to turn Paulze d'Ivoy's right flank. Accordingly, his orders to von der Groeben were, in respect of the Combined Division, to advance from Poeuilly at 8.00am, marching through Vermand on St Quentin. As a result of the injuries to Memerty on the previous day, this was now led by Colonel von Massow. On his left Dohna's cavalry were stationed to cover his flank. The 15th Division was to move out from Beauvois through Etreillers, setting off at 8.45am, led by Bock's 29th Brigade, with Strubberg's 30th Brigade following. Strubberg, shortly to lose three battalions to form the army reserve, was also required to detach the Fusilier Battalion of the 68th Regiment to cover the corps artillery at Guizancourt, nearly four miles to the west of Beauvois.[1]

Bock, in order to maintain contact with Barnekow, sent the 9th Company of the 33rd Regiment, with a subdivision of hussars, to Roupy; when these troops got there, however, Böcking's reserve had already arrived, and Goeben sent back the detachment to rejoin Bock. At the same time Bock had effectively lost another battalion; due to a misunderstanding, the 1st Battalion of Dörnberg's 65th Regiment had fallen in behind Strubberg's brigade, so that as he advanced Bock's brigade was now reduced to four weak battalions. Ahead of his infantry, the 7th Hussars entered Savy. To the east of the village Captain Rudolphi, with five subdivisions, encountered a part of French cavalry. The correspondent of the *Daily News* described what ensued:

> I turned my horse round, and witnessed one of the finest and most gallant cavalry attacks I have ever seen. Immediately behind Savy several squadrons of French dragoons were drawn up against about an equal number of the King's Hussars. The former were extremely nice and clean; their horses well tended; saddles and bridles apparently a few days only in use; their white cloaks as if put on for the occasion. The hussars, on the other hand, as well as their horses, were covered with mud; their uniforms, usually so neat and shiny, were all soiled from the long and toilsome marches of the last few days. I was just instituting the comparison, when the hussars, like lightning, darted forward against the enemy, and overrode him in a pitiable manner. The first shock dismounted half of the French dragoons; their white cloaks covered the ground or were trodden into the earth; whilst those who remained on their horses fell under the heavy strokes of the hussars' sharp sabres, or were made prisoners. When brought in I conversed with some of them, and learned that they had entered the army only three weeks before, and that previously to that time they had never been on a horse's back.[2]

Faidherbe, whose accounts are not, unfortunately, very reliable when reporting the numbers of troops involved in an engagement, described the encounter as between a squadron of French dragoons and a regiment of Prussian cavalry.[3] Palat, giving a more balanced account, explains that the French dragoons had at first taken the hussars to be the rest of the French cavalry from which they had become detached; they got off one salvo from their carbines before the Prussians fell on them. The rest of the dragoons suffered further heavy casualties when retreating in front of the Prussian infantry. Palat was sharply critical of the way in which the modest cavalry resources available were used: 'This example shows how, all too often, our cavalry was employed with a complete lack of relevance or timing.'[4]

Apart from this colourful encounter, the hussars had also succeeded in locating the position of the French infantry. These were from Isnard's brigade, which occupied the two woods to the north of the road leading from Savy into St Quentin, and Bock immediately deployed his brigade to attack. Dörnberg, with the 2nd and Fusilier Battalions of his 65th Regiment and a 4-pounder battery, moved out of Savy at about 10.00am. It was not immediately clear what the French were about; although some French troops were seen to be moving into the woods, other columns appeared to be marching towards St Quentin. In fact, what was happening was that Isnard was taking up a position between the two divisions of Paulze d'Ivoy's 23rd Corps; Lagrange's brigade of Payen's division was on the Ham road to the south of Isnard, while to his north Robin's division had taken up a position between Fayet and Francilly.[5]

The French assault on Fayet, by Bombled. (Grenest)

Looking towards the rear of the French positions at Francilly. (Duncan Rogers)

What exactly was going on in Paulze d'Ivoy's front is unclear, as the French Official History pointed out. By 9.00am the combat on the left bank of the Somme was well advanced, and Bessol was heavily engaged there, contrary to Faidherbe's intentions:

> General Faidherbe was located in the Saint Martin suburb; he probably had heard by then that General Lecointe had not received his orders; he had to accept that the division of du Bessol must remain on the left bank, because of the impossibility of crossing the Somme below Saint Quentin, and because of the German advance on Contescourt. But did he then modify his previous dispositions in instructing General Paulze d'Ivoy to extend his left as far as the Crozat Canal? Or was the deployment of part of Payen's division between the Savy road and the Somme a personal initiative of Paulze d'Ivoy? It is impossible to say.[6]

North of Paulze d'Ivoy's corps came Pauly's brigade; it served to prolong Faidherbe's right well beyond the position which Kummer thought marked its northern extremity, as Dohna was soon to find out.

Dörnberg brought his battery up to the northeast of a windmill standing outside Savy to the east, and it at once opened fire on a French battery that appeared between the two woods.[7] He next sent the 2nd Battalion of the 65th Regiment forward towards the smaller wood, and the Fusilier Battalion on its left against the larger wood. For the moment the action of the infantry was confined to skirmish fire, while awaiting reinforcements to enable an assault to be mounted on the larger wood. It was clear that each of the woods was strongly occupied, the French infantry blazing away against their assailants.

Soon Bock was able to bring forward a 6-pounder battery, coming up on the right of the 4-pounder battery already in action; these were joined by a 6-pounder battery from Strubberg's brigade, which opened fire at 11.00am. With the support of these guns, Dörnberg's infantry advanced to the attack. By 12 noon they were well into both woods, where a violent struggle took place, particularly in the smaller wood to the south, where Isnard was bringing up strong reinforcements, evidently with the intention of trying to turn Dörnberg's right. To prevent this, Bock brought up the 1st Battalion of the 33rd Regiment on the right of the 65th. The vigorous artillery exchanges continued; the French fire was wild, and was mainly directed at the three German batteries which did not respond, concentrating their fire on the French infantry in the two woods. Strubberg, meanwhile, had moved up into a hollow to the south of Savy, where Kummer held it for the moment as a reserve for Bock's attack.

On his left, Massow had been delayed by the need to resupply his units with ammunition, a task which was not completed until 7a.m. His advanced guard, under Pestel, consisted of three squadrons of the 7th Uhlan Regiment, the Fusilier Battalion of the 44th Regiment and two battalions of the 1st Regiment, together with a 6-pounder battery. Moving from Poeuilly, Pestel entered Vermand at about 8.00am which he found unoccupied except by a few stragglers. Beyond Vermand, Pestel's cavalry met with a body of French infantry which it quickly dispersed. Altogether Pestel had, in these operations, picked up about 100 prisoners. On Pestel's left von der Groeben had sent forward four squadrons with four horse artillery guns. Pestel's cavalry, probing forward, now reported that Holnon was occupied by the enemy, and that some parties of French infantry were advancing towards the extensive woods west of that place. These consisted of the 2nd Battalion of Garde Mobiles of the Ardennes. At the time the Fusilier Battalion of the 44th Regiment was closing up to the western edge of the woods. Charging forward, the fusiliers beat the French to it, occupying the woods before driving the French back into Holnon. The 10th and 11th companies of the 44th Regiments, with the 7th Company of the 1st Regiment continued the advance moving into the northern part of Selency, supported by the horse artillery and the battery of the advanced guard. Their position there was, however, very precarious; the French still held the southern part of the village as well as Francilly, and at 10.00 am Massow reinforced them with two more companies of the 44th Regiment and part of the 2nd Battalion of the 1st Regiment.

While this had been going on, the cavalry posted by von der Groeben near Vermand had been reconnoitring towards Gricourt, which it reported as occupied by French infantry. The heights between Gricourt and Selency fall gradually down towards St Quentin, and it was obviously desirable to drive the French off them as soon as possible. On the ridge north of Selency stood two windmills; these, with their adjacent buildings, were held by Robin's division. The principal unit here was the 1st Battalion of the Voluntaires due Nord, under Commandant Foutrein.[8] Recognising that this was the key to this part of the French position, Kummer put together a substantial force to be ready to attack the position. This consisted of two battalions of the 44th Regiment, the 4th Regiment, and three batteries. On the heights between Holnon and Fayet, Major Munk, the artillery commander on the spot, had assembled 28 guns, which poured a heavy fire on the French columns retreating down the Roman road. They were able to keep up this

Looking west from the French lines in front of Fayet towards Holnon, and the direction of the German advance. (Duncan Rogers)

bombardment, however, for only half an hour before running out of ammunition. Their ammunition wagons had gone back to the column of the VIII Corps in order to fetch fresh supplies, and had not yet returned.[9]

The Moulin Conti farmstead, on the summit of the hill north of Selency, was stormed at about 10.30am by the 6th and 8th Companies of the 1st regiment, routing Foutrein's troops stationed there, capturing one gun, an ammunition wagon and a large number of prisoners. Foutrein wrote a report of this engagement which Palat laconically described as a fantasy:

> I arrived at the summit of a wooded hill between Holnon and Vermand, when I observed three squadrons of cavalry. I deployed my battalion and manoeuvred it to fire on them, but they made no further movement. Ten minutes later I saw the reason for this immobility; 50 metres away, hidden behind the trees in a fold of the ground, in a sunken road, an enemy division welcomed us with a murderous fire. It was then 8.00am. We held this division in check for an hour, sheltering ourselves as best we could; but in our isolated situation, separated by six kilometres from the army, with no hope of support, it was necessary to retreat, leaving on the battlefield 292 killed and wounded, among whom were 7 officers of whom 2 captains were killed.[10]

Foutrein's report continued at some length in the same vein, claiming that by holding up an enemy infantry division, with cavalry and artillery, for an hour, his battalion had rendered 'an incalculable service' to the right wing of the army; without this desperate resistance, the troops in the rear would not have had time to come up to take their place in the line. In carrying out this extremely thankless and perilous task, he wrote, he had had officers of 'an incontestable valour and an admirable composure.' Grenest's work contains a large number of other individual unit reports; regrettably not all of them can be relied on for an accurate account of the events they describe.

While Foutrein's troops were being chased off the height above Selency, the rest of the village had now fallen into the hands of the 44th Regiment. The Fusilier Battalion of the 1st Regiment had also now arrived there, and began to push skirmishers towards Francilly, which was for the moment still occupied by Isnard's men.

It was at about 12.00 noon that Major General von Gayl arrived at the battlefield. Goeben had designated him to succeed Memerty in command of the combined division when the latter was wounded; but Gayl, although reaching Ham from Rouen during the evening of January 18, had not been able to set off from Ham until the morning of the next day. After a ride of some 18 miles he reached the combined division, to find that it was heavily engaged. It clearly made no sense to change the command arrangements at this stage of the action, and Gayl sensibly left Massow to conduct the operations around Selency and Holnon.[11]

Meanwhile, Dohna's cavalry had been riding north and northeast from Vermand in order to ascertain the extent to which there were French troops beyond the First Army's left flank. Daussy described their movements:

The defence of the Bellenglise Canal, by Pallandre. (Rousset/*Histoire*)

Dohna's horsemen were launched as to part to the west, towards Vendelles – Jeancourt and Le Vergnier, where they encountered only some scattered stragglers; another part rode northeast towards Bellenglise to cut the road to Cambrai. But at this point the energetic response of one brave officer, Captain Tailhade, provost marshal of Robin's divisions, intimidated the enemy and saved us from great danger. Assembling close to the canal several companies of gardes nationales (the 2nd Battalion of the 44th Regiment de Marche), he skilfully placed them in carefully chosen locations, and by a vigorous rifle fire discouraged the advance of the cavalry who certainly lacked boldness.[12]

The French Official History also describes this incident, noting that Dohna withdrew to Maissemy to take up a position on von der Groeben's left flank.[13] However, no reference to this incident appears in either the German Official History or in Schell's account. It would seem that no serious attempt to sever Faidherbe's line of communications was contemplated. At any rate, all the sources agree that Dohna's movement was now towards Fresnoy le Petit.

Although by now the whole of the village of Selency was in German hands, it was certainly the case that the left wing of the First Army had not so far succeeded in driving back the 23rd Corps very far from its initial positions; Schell points out, however, that the forces available to Kummer and von der Groeben represented much the smaller portion of the available troops that had been engaged.

21

St Quentin: Victory on the Left Bank

For both commanders the fighting on the left bank had involved more resources than they had originally intended. In the case of the Army of the North it was because Faidherbe's orders to Lecointe, assigning Bessol's division to a position on the right bank of the Somme, never reached the corps commander. And it was this, indirectly, which led to Goeben committing his reserve under Böcking to the left bank, having originally located it in the western sector; the very effective resistance being put up by Bessol to Barnekow's advance was partly the reason for Goeben's decision to strengthen his forces facing Lecointe. This had also been prompted, as we have seen, by the tardy arrival on the battlefield of the 16th Brigade. As a result of this emphasis on the southern sector, the area adjoining the left bank witnessed some of the fiercest fighting of the battle.

The defensive position south-east of Giffécourt, behind the windmill hill known as Hill 103, had held up Böcking for a while, particularly as there were parties of enemy troops in the ravines to the south of the dell running from Castres towards the railway. In order to soften up the defenders of Hill 103, first the 4-pounder reserve battery with Hymmen's detachment, and then Böcking's two batteries opened fire on the French position. Gislain's artillery had pulled back from there to a point east of Gauchy. As the bombardment continued, the two 6-pounder batteries of the 3rd Reserve Division came up on the right of those already engaged at 2.00pm, and joined the cannonade. Watching closely, it seemed to Böcking the enemy artillery fire had considerably slackened, and that some of the enemy infantry were falling back. At 2.15pm he launched an attack by Hüllessem's 41st Regiment, working around Gislain's right, which ultimately succeeded in taking the hill. It was an important success, since it took Böcking's advance to a point at which it outflanked the sugar factory and the French troops still occupying a position to the south of it.[1]

Lecointe, who had been accompanying Gislain during this phase of the battle, had called on Foerster to reinforce the troops on Hill 103, while at the same time taking the belated decision to pull back his right towards the heights of Giffécourt. The units retreating from Contescourt and Castres had poured back through Giffécourt under the fire of the 30 German guns that were bombarding the position, and which had crushed the Battery Chastang, forcing it to retreat to Grugies before the 17th Chasseurs, which had been holding a position around the mill, were in their turn swept off the heights. Gislain succeeded in collecting together the wreckage of three battalions behind the Tout Vent windmill.[2]

Lecointe now ordered Pittié's brigade to begin a series of counter attacks, which were pressed home so vigorously that Barnekow had to cast about for units to strengthen his front line. Böcking, now in secure possession of Giffécourt, turned the fire of the five German batteries on the sugar factory. Both here and in the positions to the south, the defenders continued to hold their ground in spite of the energetic attacks of the Prussian infantry.[3] Barnekow had in the meantime ordered the two battalions of the Reserve Division still at Essigny, under Colonel von Goeben, to move up to the front line, together with Rosenzweig's three battalions which had now been resupplied with ammunition.

It was at this moment that at about 3.00pm Pittié launched the most serious of his counter attacks, strong columns pushing forward between the railway and the high road from Essigny le Grand to Saint Quentin from the heights to the south of the sugar factory, and the French guns east of Gauchy opened up again. Swarms of tirailleurs lined the crest of Hill 108, firing from behind piles of beetroots which covered the fields. Barnekow, realising that the attack was extremely serious, called up von Strantz and the Reserve Cavalry Brigade from Urvillers. Strantz, with five squadrons, trotted forward towards the advancing enemy, which at the same time were being raked in their right flank from Böcking's five batteries.

Barnekow had got so far forward that he found himself between the opposing lines of skirmishers. He led forward all the infantry he could collect towards Hill 108 and then returned to Strantz, ordering him to charge over the crest of the hill. Strantz brought forward his two leading squadrons, the 1st and 2nd Squadrons of the 1st Reserve Dragoon Regiment, holding the three squadrons of the 3rd Reserve Hussar Regiment in reserve for the moment. Covered by a dip in the ground, the dragoons rode forward and were joined as they prepared to charge by Barnekow himself. Captain Seton, who had been riding with Barnekow, witnessed what followed:

> The dragoons came up first and trotted past in very pretty order, the officers saluting. The hussars followed, but were ordered to remain in reserve under the ridge, while the divisional commander told the dragoons to cross the same, and charge towards the enemies' batteries. I drew a long breath, for I feared a repetition of part of the afternoon scenes on the Spicheren, and at Gravelotte, and the squadrons were very weak. They ascended the ridge in column but close to the top, by some blunder, a wrong signal was sounded, and the rear squadron went about, coming down the ridge in some disorder – for all this was going on under some amount of fire. I was horrified at first, but presently reassured by seeing them get together again, and the three (sic) squadrons dash over the brow. I could not resist the inclination to gallop after them, and on clearing the ridge was well rewarded by the splendid sight before me. The slope down into the valley was here easy and unbroken by ravines, but the opposite ascent somewhat steeper. A few hundred yards in front were the dragoons in full career, just on the point of wheeling round short of the trees and hedge, from which came rifle fire kept up by the few French who made any stand; otherwise the lower part of the slope on this side, and the whole face of the opposite, were covered with fugitives in utter disorder, making for Tous-Vents, the batteries near which had now ceased working … I don't remember ever witnessing a sight so distinctly representing victory. I hardly think the dragoons sabred many men in their charge; and it was the moral effect of their sudden appearance and dash forward that was so beautiful.[4]

An episode of the Battle of St Quentin, by Navlet. (Rousset/*Histoire*)

An episode of the Battle of St Quentin, by Navlet - a watercolour study. (Rousset/*Histoire*)

Barnekow's horse had been wounded under him during the charge, but on his return he at once ordered Hertzberg to advance with his whole brigade in pursuit of the retreating enemy along the high road towards St Quentin.

While this was going on, Foerster's long defence of the sugar factory was coming to an end. The last five available companies of the 19th and 81st Regiments, from Colonel von Goeben's combined Infantry Brigade, had advanced from Essigny le Grand on Grugies to the east of the railway. Behind them came two squadrons of the 2nd Guard Uhlan

Regiment, followed by Rosenzweig's three battalions. Meanwhile, to the west of the railway the Prussian troops that directly faced the sugar factory began to advance. These were the 2nd Battalion of the 29th Regiment, half a battalion of the 40th Regiment and the 8th Company of the 69th Regiment. Storming forward under the heavy covering fire of the artillery, they forced their way into the building at about 3.15pm, taking a large number of prisoners and driving the remainder of the defenders northwards in disorder.[5]

At the same time Böcking launched the 41st Regiment against Grugies, sweeping into the village with its first rush. Here, too, numerous prisoners were taken. The morale of Lecointe's corps was beginning to disintegrate, as the French Official History noted:

> Already there was great confusion due to the demoralisation caused by the sight of the relentless progress of the enemy on the right bank of the Somme ... The Germans took large numbers of prisoners. At Grugies they captured 20 officers and 330 men, among whom was part of L Company of marines.[6]

Böcking was by now in direct command of all the units in this sector, which had become extremely intermingled, and he prepared for an immediate further advance on

French engineers deployed as infantry during the Battle of St Quentin, by Bombled. (Grenest)

the Tout Vent heights. His two batteries and two from Prince Albrecht's division took up a fresh position on the hill south of Grugies, from where they opened fire on the French artillery on the Windmill Hill 121 and on the rear-guard at Gauchy that Gislain had posted to cover his retreat to Tout Vent. To deal with the French position there Böcking also had available the five battalions of Goeben and Rosenzweig which had come up from Essigny le Grand.

He did not, however, have the whole of the 41st Regiment; it had been his intention that it should advance on Gauchy, but in the confusion following the occupation of Grugies several companies of the regiment had of their own accord advanced along the railway cutting. They were now followed by the rest of the regiment in two columns, the larger of these under Hüllessem on the railway itself, and the smaller one west of the line. The advance was supported by the troops that had taken the sugar factory.[7]

The French gunners posted on Hill 121 briefly did their best to check this advance but, under the concentrated fire of the German artillery, were forced to pull back from their position. Switching targets, Böcking now ordered his batteries to concentrate their fire on the columns of infantry that could be seen falling back towards Saint Quentin. The French were by now in considerable confusion; here and there small parties of infantry endeavoured to make a stand, but were soon hustled out of the way by Böcking's advancing troops. In one clash by Hill 121 half a squadron of the 2nd Guard Lancer Regiment rode down a line of French skirmishers.[8]

Behind these units Rosenzweig's brigade had now come up; the rest of the 16th Division, on the far side of the railway, was advancing up the Essigny le Grand – Saint Quentin road. The 9th Hussar Regiment moved up to the front line to the right of the road where it encountered a swampy ravine which it got through only with great difficulty. Riding forward, the hussars attempted to overtake a large body of French troops on the other side, but these just had time to reach a group of buildings at the junction of the roads to Grand Seraucourt and Essigny le Grand, and succeeded in beating off the attack of the hussars.

On the extreme right of the German line Lippe had been waiting to see what the outcome would be of the attack launched by Pittié's brigade before he attempted to get round Lecointe's left flank. When it was clear that the attack had failed, and that the two cavalry regiments which he had available for a turning movement would not be required to support the 16th Division, Lippe prepared to advance. He first opened a heavy fire on the French infantry who could be seen retreating into Saint Quentin; and then directed Major General Senfft von Pilsach to advance with the 17th and 18th Uhlan Regiments, the 1st Horse Artillery Battery and three guns of the 2nd Horse Artillery Battery to Neuville St Amand. Colonel von Carlowitz, with the Guard Cavalry Regiment and the rest of the 2nd Horse Artillery Battery, came up the La Fère road and past Cornet d'Or.

Lippe's attempt, however, to cut off the line of Lecointe's retreats was frustrated by the latter's occupation of the villages of Harly and Homblières. In addition Lecointe had prudently located a considerable force of artillery on the heights at Bellevue, between the two villages. These French guns opened fire with such effect that Senfft was obliged to pull back his own artillery from the position by Neuville St Amand. That village was held by two companies of the 86th Regiment until the end of the battle. Senfft now moved his troops to the west as far as the La Fère road, up which another company of the 86th Regiment had begun a successful attack on the outermost houses of the Isle suburb.[9]

A rather fanciful impression of German cavalry attacking French Gardes Mobiles at St Quentin, by Amling. (Fehleisen)

As the short winter day came towards its end, the German advance continued all along Barnekow's front. The first troops to reach the Isle suburb, at a point close to the railway, were those of Hüllessem. Parties of French troops were encountered in the copses and ditches of the meadows of La Biette, immediately south of St Quentin, and Hüllessem pushed forward the 6th and 7th Companies of the 41st Regiment to clear them away. As darkness fell he pressed on along the line of the railway, and reached the railway station at about 5.15pm. After a short struggle, the station buildings were taken by three companies of the 41st Regiment and one of the 81st Regiment, and Hüllessem moved into the Isle suburb. By 5.30pm he had reached the bridge over the canal and crossed into St Quentin itself without opposition.[10]

As the French rearguard retreated through the town, Gislain recalled a conversation which he had had during the day with Commandant Zédé, to the effect that Faidherbe had demanded a relentless struggle prolonged to the absolute limit, and that there was to be no retreat, but that ultimately the direction that might be taken was towards Cambrai. Crossing through the town, he found the Commander in Chief in the main square, and having collected up the debris of five battalions pressed on up the road to Cambrai, reaching Le Catelet at about 11.00pm.[11] Foerster, meanwhile, with most of the rest of the division, avoided the centre of the town, passing more to the east, and crossing the canal near Romancourt. There were chaotic scenes on the roads northwards, as Foerster reported:

> We found the roads encumbered with vehicles, among which were scattered utterly exhausted parties of soldiers. I succeeded however in keeping together an escort for my batteries which, on the following day, arrived with 2,000 men in the vicinity of Cambrai.[12]

Patry, meanwhile, retreating into St Quentin, had found Derroja endeavouring to construct barricades to hold up the German advance. As night fell they began to retreat, under fire from the Germans in the railway station, and Patry found himself alone in a deserted square, uncertain of the direction to take to get away to the north:

> All the houses were shut up tight. In vain I rained blows on several doors, thumped on venetian shutters or ground floor windows. Nothing. The German batteries were already beginning to bombard the town, and the bursting shells had so terrified the inhabitants that not one dared show himself. I gave way to melancholy reflections, believing that before long I would be taken prisoner, for I was so tired that I literally could no longer drag myself along.[13]

Luckily at this moment he encountered his friend Doctor Michel, the regimental medical officer, and his orderly, and they made their way to safety via the Valenciennes road.

Derroja, once he had concluded that resistance within St Quentin would be useless, collected his division together and, in accordance with the orders he received from Lecointe, set off in the direction of Le Cateau. He reported subsequently that the march was conducted in good order although much hampered by the obstacles of all sorts which he encountered on the road northwards. The troops, he wrote, without food and some barefoot, were completely exhausted, which accounted for the disorder of the following day. However, he was proudly able to report that 'not one cannon, not one vehicle nor any baggage fell into the hands of the enemy, and one can say that the day of January 19 was glorious for our troops.'[14]

Barnekow rode across the canal bridge and entered the town at 6.00pm at the head of Hertzberg's brigade. His troops were no less exhausted than the French, and to give them a break he halted their march in an open space west of the canal. Hüllessem, meanwhile, had been mopping up, pushing forward columns through the dark streets of the town, taking a large number of prisoners. There were not only stragglers from Lecointe's retreating columns, but also complete bodies of troops falling back from their final positions south and southwest of the town.[15]

It was not until 8.00pm that Goeben heard that Barnekow's troops had entered St Quentin; Captain Schell had stayed with Barnekow until quarters had been sorted out for the night, and then rode to the southwest entrance to the town to look for the First Army headquarters. At about 7pm he encountered troops of the 15th Division preparing to enter the town, completely unaware of it being already occupied. They were followed by detachments from Bronikowsky's force, he having been ordered to provide for the security of the First Army headquarters. When Schell told him of the situation in St Quentin, they both rode off to report to Goeben at L'Epine de Dallon.

22

St Quentin: The End of the Battle

Goeben was making a very effective use of his staff officers, relying on them to send reports which enabled him to have a comprehensive view of the developing situation across the battlefield. Close by his headquarters at Roupy, the reserve force under Bronikowsky was recovering its strength after its exhausting march, and would shortly be fit to move forward. Uncertain of the situation around Fontaine les Clercs, Goeben sent two officers to ascertain the position. While he was awaiting their report, Baumann returned from Savy at 12.15pm with news of the fighting in the woods north-east of the village, and the advance of von der Groeben. Next he heard from Schell at about 12.30pm; his message, timed at 11.15pm, had reported the momentary stalemate in Barnekow's front, and prompted a reply to tell Barnekow that Böcking was moving with the reserve to his support.[1]

It was not long before Bronikowsky was required to move. From its position west of Roupy his force was ordered at 12.30pm to advance to clear away large numbers of French skirmishers that were pestering the right wing of the 15th Division. The 1st Battalion of the 28th Regiment advanced along the Roupy – St Quentin road and captured the farmhouse which stood about a mile north-east of Roupy on the Savy – Fontaine les Clercs ridge; Bronikowsky brought up to this point the rest of his force, being the 2nd Battalion of the 28th Regiment, the 8th Rifle Battalion, the 2nd 4-pounder Battery of the VIII Corps, and the Horse Artillery Division. Kummer, meanwhile, had at 12.45 pm posted two other batteries of the Corps Artillery on the north side of the farmhouse. Bronikowsky's artillery took as its targets the enemy infantry retreating towards L'Epine de Dallon, and the batteries seen on the heights to the east of Savy between Dallon and Francilly. Goeben was concerned that Kummer's two batteries might need reinforcement, or at least some cover, and sent at 2.00 an officer to enquire whether this was needed. In the event, however, it was found that the French skirmish line had now retreated a long way off. Just prior to this, Major Lentze, the general staff officer of the 15th Division, had arrived to tell Goeben of the taking of Selency, and the advance of von der Groeben.[2]

Since the 15th Division was still experiencing difficulty in advancing through the woods, the energetic Bronikowsky now pushed forward the two battalions of the 28th Regiment from the farmhouse on up the St Quentin road. After an intensive artillery preparation they had by 2.00pm stormed into L'Epine de Dallon; the French troops that had held the village retreated under fire to the heights north of Oestre, losing many prisoners.[3] This does not appear to have been a very substantial force; according to the French Official History it was composed of troops from the 24th Chasseurs, the 33rd Regiment and the 65th Regiment, and amounted to no more than 350 men in all.[4]

Goeben now moved his headquarters to the farmhouse, and it was here at 2.30pm that Bieberstein returned with news of the progress which Barnekow had been making up till about 2.00pm, when he left him. At the same time Witzendorff sent a report from Selency with the welcome news that Francilly was now in German hands, and that von der Groeben's advancing units were now in touch with the 15th Division. It also brought information about the extreme right of the French line; four hostile battalions were apparently advancing on Gricourt. These, as would be seen, were the troops of Pauly's brigade.[5]

The attack on Francilly had been carried out under Gayl's direction; while leaving Massow to conduct the operations on the left, he had assumed command of the right wing of von der Groeben's forces. Six companies of the Crown Prince's Grenadier Regiment under Major von Elpons advanced from Selency and Holnon, and six companies from the 4th and 44th Regiments on the right moved forward against the French infantry emerging from the larger wood. Elpons was soon able, in spite of heavy fire from the defenders, to storm into Francilly, capturing many prisoners and an ammunition wagon.[6]

With Bronikowsky's success immediately before him, and aware of the progress being made on the left bank, Goeben ordered Kummer to renew his attack with the 15th Division. This, however, Kummer had already resolved to do, ordering Bock to take the heights in front of him with the 29th Brigade. The movement was at once supported by von der Groeben, who pushed forward from Francilly to the south of the Roman road. Before, however, Gayl's troops could follow up their success at Francilly, they were obliged to cope with a new development, as the French Official History recorded:

> It was then that events took an unexpected turn, thanks to the initiative of General Pauly; his brigade of mobilisés, energetically led, debouched on the flanks of the Combined Division. The result of this intervention was that parts of the brigades of Isnard and Michelet, assembled to the south of Bois des Roses, were able to take possession of this key point and obliged General von Gayl, who was advancing victoriously on the plateau, to suspend his march in order to lean more towards his left.[7]

This surprising move by Pauly's brigade thus had a significant effect on the progress of the battle in this sector. He had been able to launch his attack because the reports from the German cavalry of his presence and forward movement had not been effectively followed up:

> The commander of the German squadron posted at Bellenglise having reported the position of the Brigade Pauly at about 2.00pm, the whole of the regiment of Uhlans was concentrated to the south of Pontruet, where the men armed with carbines dismounted; but their long range fire was not supported by Dohna's two guns. This support had been called for, but in vain, and the mobilisés continued their march undisturbed. En route they cut across four battalions and the artillery of Division Robin, which they judged it useless to follow, and then met, further on, behind Fayet, the 1st and 3rd Battalions of the 4th Regiment de Marche, which prolonged their right.[8]

Pauly's attack fell in the first instance upon the 2nd Battalion of the 44th Regiment and two companies of the 1st Battalion. These held their position, although on their right the farmhouse of Bois des Roses had to be abandoned. Other French troops now advanced from Fayet, greeted by the fire of the two 6-pounder batteries, while the two 4-pounder batteries were brought forward to concentrate their fire on Pauly's troops. The two guns of Dohna's cavalry brigade also came into action, while the cavalry was assembled in readiness to charge if necessary.[9]

Meanwhile Michelet's brigade had also advanced in the direction of Selency, forcing back the German troops in their front; it was only when Gayl, supported by ten guns at and to the south of Francilly, launched an attack that the threat from this quarter was removed. Michelet fell back rapidly towards to the line Fayet – Saint Quentin, pursued only by the fire of the German artillery, having got out of range of the fire of the infantry. To Michelet's right the concentrated fire of the 26 guns that had been pounding Pauly's troops had begun to take effect, and in the gathering twilight the mobilisés retreated rapidly in the direction of Gricourt and Fayet.

The latter village was now ablaze; and although night had begun to fall von der Groeben resolved to launch an attack on it at once, pushing forward the 1st and 2nd Battalions of the 4th Regiment and the 2nd Battalion of the 4th Regiment. When they

French dragoons form a dismounted skirmish line during the closing stages of the Battle of St Quentin, by Bombled. (Grenest)

entered Fayet, however, they found it to have been abandoned by the enemy, and they took up their quarters there for the night (having presumably extinguished the flames). The rest of von der Groeben's Combined Division found quarters in the surrounding villages.[10]

Goeben had remained for the moment in ignorance of these events, his latest information at 3.45pm being news from Captain Ahlborn of the situation as it was at 3.00pm – in other words, before Pauly's attack had developed. At the same time, however, Kummer had been pushing forward the attack of Bock's 29th Brigade with success, advancing towards the heights between Francilly and L'Epine de Dallon. His attack was launched on either side of the Savy – St Quentin road, with the 65th Regiment to the left of it and two battalions of the 33rd Regiment to the right; between them came the 2nd Battalion of the 68th Regiment. The rest of Strubberg's brigade followed in reserve. The attack was supported by six batteries of artillery, three on each side of the road.

Kummer's troops were by now enjoying themselves, driving the enemy back from position to position as the latter fell back towards St Quentin under the heavy fire of artillery. Darkness was, however, falling, and the fighting soon came to an end, although Kummer pushed forward the 2nd Battalion of the 68th Regiment with half of a battalion of the 33rd Regiment and the 1st Squadron of the 7th Hussars over the heights to the west of the suburb of Saint Martin.[11]

Goeben had by now moved his headquarters forward to L'Epine de Dallon where at 4.00pm he received a further report from Schell. This was, however, timed as early as 1.30, and told only that Barnekow's front was for the moment stationary, but that Böcking and Hymmen were advancing towards Grugies, while there seemed to be indications of a retreat of the French troops in front of Lippe's division. Soon after this Goeben rode forward again towards Rocourt; on his way he met an officer sent by Prince Albrecht to maintain contact with the left wing of the army, and he sent him back with news of the success that had been achieved.

Bronikowsky, meanwhile, had resumed his advance up the St Quentin road with the whole of his infantry on the height immediately north of Oestre. Both this hill and the village itself were carried at about 4.00pm, and Bronikowsky pressed on to attack the strongly defended village of Rocourt. This was, at 5.00pm, stormed at bayonet point with the support of troops from the 33rd Regiment, on the right wing of the 15th Division, who burst out of the ravine to the west of the village. Several attempts to retake the village were made, but repulsed, and as night fell Bronikowsky pushed forward a company of riflemen to the Saint Martin suburb. To his left, the 29th Brigade also closed up to the outermost buildings and gardens.[12]

The intervention of Pauly's brigade had slowed up the advance of the extreme left of the First Army to the extent that, once the brigade was obliged to retreat, it was able to regain the Cambrai road. There, it joined the general movement that was developing, including the former defenders of Fayet; the 7th and 9th Garde Mobile battalions, two battalions of the Mobilisés du Nord and the marines were beating a retreat northwards. While these were getting away, however, the brigades of Isnard, Lagrange and Michelet, pinned down in front of St Quentin, were beginning to disintegrate under the attacks of the 15th Division and Bronikowsky's detachment.[13]

Paulze d'Ivoy had pulled back his artillery, according to him because night was coming on fast; but having been ordered to hold the road from Roupy to St Quentin 'a outrance', he had positioned the 6th Battalion du Nord and part of the 73rd Regiment opposite Rocourt, to the south of the mill and covering the entrance into Saint Martin.[14]

Faidherbe had spent the morning with Lecointe's troops on the left bank. At about noon he departed to assess the position of the 23rd Corps, being reasonably confident that the 22nd Corps would be able to hold its positions. At that point in time this was a reasonable assumption. After spending the early afternoon with Paulze d'Ivoy's corps, however, he began to realise that it probably could not hold on. He was profoundly fearful about the difficulties of a night time retreat, yet he was still more concerned at the risk that his army might be shut up in St Quentin. He had witnessed part of Pauly's offensive, which might for the moment have given him some encouragement, but overall he knew in his heart that the battle was lost. It was in this state of mind that, accompanied by Colonel Charon, his artillery commander, he had a meeting with Paulze d'Ivoy's Chief of Staff, Lieutenant Colonel Marchand. A note of their conversation was made by Captain Courson in terms which Faidherbe later told the Commission of Enquiry were more or less correct:

> 'Mon Général, until now we have held up the enemy but that cannot continue; we are going to be surrounded, what should we do?'
> 'Reprovision the cartridge belts and the ammunition wagons and hold on.'
> 'But we are going to be forced back into Saint Quentin, mon Général.'
> 'I realise that, Colonel.'
> 'And what do we do then?'
> 'We will begin the struggle again tomorrow.'
> 'But, mon Général, that is Sedan.'
> 'Not at all: we will fire off our cartridges, we will make use of all our weapons, and when we run out of ammunition we will defend ourselves with our bayonets. We will not surrender.'
> 'Is that your final word, mon Général?'
> 'Yes; the newspapers make fun of us and say that we are always retreating; well, this time we won't retreat.'[15]

With these not very helpful sentiments he left the hapless Marchand, and made his way back into the centre of St Quentin. He was perfectly convinced that his troops, exhausted by two days of forced marches and two days of combat, were incapable of effecting an orderly retreat. On the other hand, he absolutely rejected the idea that he might have to capitulate. He was amazed to find, when he reached the town centre, that Lecointe's corps was already conducting its retreat; he was especially, and most agreeably, surprised to find that 'they were in a good state; battalions and batteries were marching down the roads in perfect order. The retreat was thus possible!'[16]

Paulze d'Ivoy, to whom Marchand had presumably reported his meeting with Faidherbe, was doing his best to extricate what he could of the 23rd Corps. He had by no means been kept fully informed of the situation in St Quentin. He wrote in his report of the difficulties which he encountered:

> I then rallied all that I could find of my corps, which consisted only of the wreckage of the Division Payen; I formed a single column, putting myself in the middle of it, and set it on the road to Cambrai. But the Prussians had got

ST QUENTIN: THE END OF THE BATTLE

Faidherbe at St Quentin, by Knötel. (Pflug-Harttung)

French troops in action in the market place at St Quentin, by Knötel. (Pflug-Harttung)

round Saint Quentin from the east, and occupied the exit from the town on the Cambrai road; also the column had halted, and all those in front of me had grounded their arms, while the rear of the column was attacked, surrounded and captured by enemy detachments that had entered the town by the Roupy road, from where the troops had abandoned the positions which I had assigned them for the night. I only escaped myself, as did General Payen and our chiefs of staff thanks to an inhabitant of the town who led us, by a little side road, to rejoin the Cambrai road outside Saint Quentin.[17]

Barnekow's troops soon made themselves at home in St Quentin, once the fighting had stopped. Captain Seton joined the 1st Battalion of the 40th Regiment as it was engaged in mopping up the parties of French troops left in the town, who were happy enough to surrender; the battalion then crossed the canal and established itself in the nearest square:

A general illumination commenced, and several of the inhabitants appeared at the doors with bottles of wine and glasses. The Chablis at one house was so good, that Rosen decided on taking up his quarters there, and although the owner objected at first to the horses standing in his granary, we were entertained at table by himself, wife, and the friend of the family, as if we had been matter of course guests. The number of prisoners being found was rather embarrassing; a staff officer, who came in while we were at dinner, said that on going into a room by himself, he found five French officers, who quietly surrendered to his order. Some drinking went on in the town that night, but I heard of no excess taking place.[18]

While Faidherbe was entitled to feel profound relief that his troops were able to avoid being penned up in St Quentin, the situation was not one which left all the French commanders very happy. Paulze d'Ivoy, for instance, continued to be resentful at the way in which the 23rd Corps had been treated, as he later made plain to the Commission of Enquiry in terms which prompted a lengthy response from Faidherbe:

General Paulze d'Ivoy complained bitterly to the Commission of Enquiry that he had been sacrificed, intentionally, by the commander in chief; the account I have given proves that this was not the case, and that circumstances outside the control of the commander in chief laid upon General Paulze d'Ivoy all the weight of the retreat of the army. If General Lecointe had held his position for another three quarters of an hour, and he could have, because although taken in flank by several enemy guns on his right, he had the canal to cover him on this side … the 23rd Corps would have been warned in time, and General Paulze d'Ivoy would not have found himself in such a critical situation.

Even in beating the spontaneous retreat that he did, if General Lecointe had taken steps for his rearguard to hold up the Prussians for half an hour more in the suburb of Isle, General Paulze d'Ivoy would have been able to get out of his dangerous situation, and the enemy would not have had the satisfaction of taking prisoner a thousand soldiers of the 23rd Corps, who were obliged to lay down their arms because they had been surrounded.[19]

It is regrettable that Faidherbe chose to try to cast blame on Lecointe in this way; quite apart from the fact that he faced a lot more than 'several enemy guns', and that the canal was, in his situation, in no sense a cover for his battered corps, Lecointe's skilful defence for many hours during January 19 deserved far better of Faidherbe.

While Faidherbe was dealing with the consequences of his army's defeat, Goeben was catching up with what had been happening. At 5.00pm a further report from Schell set out the situation as it was at 3.30pm. From this it was evident that Barnekow had won a significant victory, and that his leading troops were on the point of entering Saint Quentin. To this Major Hassel, the general staff officer of the 16th Division, added the news of the fall of Grugies, and the advance of Prince Albrecht and Böcking. The

The French withdrawal at St Quentin, by Knötel. (Lindner)

The left flank of the German positions on the evening of January 19. The left middle distance shows troops from the German 3rd Cavalry Division with a battery of horse artillery. To the far right is the road to Péronne, threading its way through Savy. The prominent Tout Vent windmill heights can be seen just to the left of centre in the distance. (Hiltl)

situation in the centre, at Rocourt and on the roads adjoining was already apparent to Goeben, and he returned to L'Epine de Dallon to establish his headquarters there. At 6.30pm he sent a telegram to Moltke to report on the day's events:

> Have attacked the French Army of the North in its position in front of Saint Quentin, driven it from all its positions in a seven hours' fight and forced it back upon Saint Quentin after an obstinate resistance. As yet ascertained, two guns taken fighting, above 4,000 unwounded prisoners. The operations which night has interrupted will be continued tomorrow.[20]

At this point Goeben did not appreciate that Barnekow's victorious troops had already occupied St Quentin, and that the Army of the North was making its way northwards with all speed. It was about 7.00pm that Schell, having left Barnekow in the town, met the leading troops of the 15th Division as they prepared to march in; shortly after he also encountered some parties of Bronikowsky's detachment. None of these knew that St Quentin was already in German hands, and Schell rode on to tell Goeben of this, followed shortly after by Bronikowsky. When he heard the news, Goeben sent a further report of this to Moltke at Versailles.

23

Aftermath

Looking at the completeness of the First Army's victory, Schell commented that 'our losses were not considerable when compared with such a result.' Writing in 1873, he put the German casualties as 395 killed, 1,977 wounded and 134 missing, a total of 2,506. The German Official History, published ten years later, arrived at a slightly different figure: 447 killed, 1,858 wounded and 71 missing, a total of 2,376. The French Official History put the total German losses at 2,158. Faidherbe, writing with his usual breezy disregard for accuracy, suggested that the Germans had lost 5,000 men on January 18 and 19. When it came to the French losses, neither Schell nor the German Official History could do better than guess at a total of about 15,000. Faidherbe characteristically suggested a figure of 3,000 killed and wounded and 6,000 stragglers, 'most of them Mobiles and Mobilisés, but the majority escaped and rejoined their corps after several days.' The French Official History, published in 1904, concluded that the total of French killed and wounded was 3,402, with 14,338 missing.[1] Not surprisingly Goeben had quite a lot to say about Faidherbe's inaccuracy on the subject of casualties. Writing in 1873, he calculated the total German casualties as 2,503, no doubt relying on Schell's figures. As to the French losses, he pointed out that 3,000 wounded were found in Saint Quentin alone. As to prisoners, the figure rose steadily during the night of January 19/20; the figure of 9,000 was, he thought, doubtless still very low:

> The number has never been accurately ascertained, because on the one hand, the convoys of them were despatched at once, even as early as during the battle, to the rear; and indeed, part by Péronne to Amiens, part to Ham, part in fine to La Fère – on January 20 to this point alone 5,400 prisoners – while on the other hand they were rapidly sent farther by the authorities in those places without, as later enquiries showed, the numbers being always noted.[2]

Commenting on his adversary's remarks about stragglers, Goeben was generous in his praise of the French troops:

> General Faidherbe, however, does his own troops great injustice, when he asserts that we picked up swarms of stragglers during the pursuit. I declare on the contrary with pleasure my full recognition of the way in which the French army after such a defeat was able to effect its retreat. Thus the corps directed on Cambrai, the nearest fortress, distant five German miles from Saint Quentin, according to assertions of the French newspapers indeed arriving in complete disorder, did nevertheless reach the place in spite of all, and our troops, which arrived as early as noon on January 20 in front of the fortress, picked up only a few hundred completely exhausted men.

And it was just the same in the direction of Valenciennes, whither the remainder of the French troops had betaken themselves.[3]

On any view, it had been a remarkable victory, and certainly not one that could be taken to have been inevitable, as the leading historian of the Franco-Prussian War has pointed out:

> The result of the battle of St Quentin was not a foregone conclusion. In infantry Goeben had only about half his opponent's strength, and the open hills round the town made any attack doubly difficult. The circumstances of the battle were no less favourable to the French than they had been in the battle of the Hallue. But Faidherbe's army, though numerically stronger, was far weaker in morale than it had been a month before. Wearied and dispirited by its marches in the rain, disordered by the fighting of the previous day, it looked forward with reluctance to battle.[4]

Goeben had wasted no time in preparing orders for his army's operations on the day after the battle, issuing at midnight on January 19/20 a general order of which the key sentence read: 'The next thing now to be done is to make the most of this victory; today we have fought, tomorrow we must march to complete the defeat of the enemy.'[5] His intention was himself to ride to Le Catelet, where he expected reports from his divisional commanders.

However, next morning he changed his mind about this, deciding not to ride north until a clearer picture had emerged of Faidherbe's movements. He was keeping Bronikowky's detachment in hand as a reserve, and accordingly ordered that it move only from its overnight bivouacs at Rocourt and L'Epine de Dallon into St Quentin. At 10.00am Goeben and his staff rode into the town, there to await news of the enemy. It was not long in coming, and the first reports reaching Goeben made it clear that Faidherbe had got more or less clean away, and that the advancing Germans units had failed to catch them. Since many of them were starting from a position south of St Quentin, this is perhaps not altogether surprising, although Roberts thought Faidherbe's escape was a 'marvel':

> It has been said that one of the most difficult manoeuvres is that of withdrawing beaten and disorganised troops from before a victorious enemy. This General Faidherbe certainly achieved most marvellously. He removed his long trains of munitions, his artillery, and his infantry in a most masterly and, considering the circumstances, orderly manner.[6]

Perhaps, thought Roberts, the German cavalry did not move as quickly as they should have. The infantry, on the other hand, exhausted as they were by the previous day's exertions, had to struggle through the sodden ground with mud up to their knees. As a result the Army of the North gained the safety of Cambrai during the night and early morning.

Roberts, as he rode into St Quentin, was shocked by the numbers of French wounded, and by the conduct of their medical teams:

Exhausted and ill, Faidherbe is carried to his quarters at Cambrai following the Battle of St Quentin, by Tiret-Bognet. (Deschaumes)

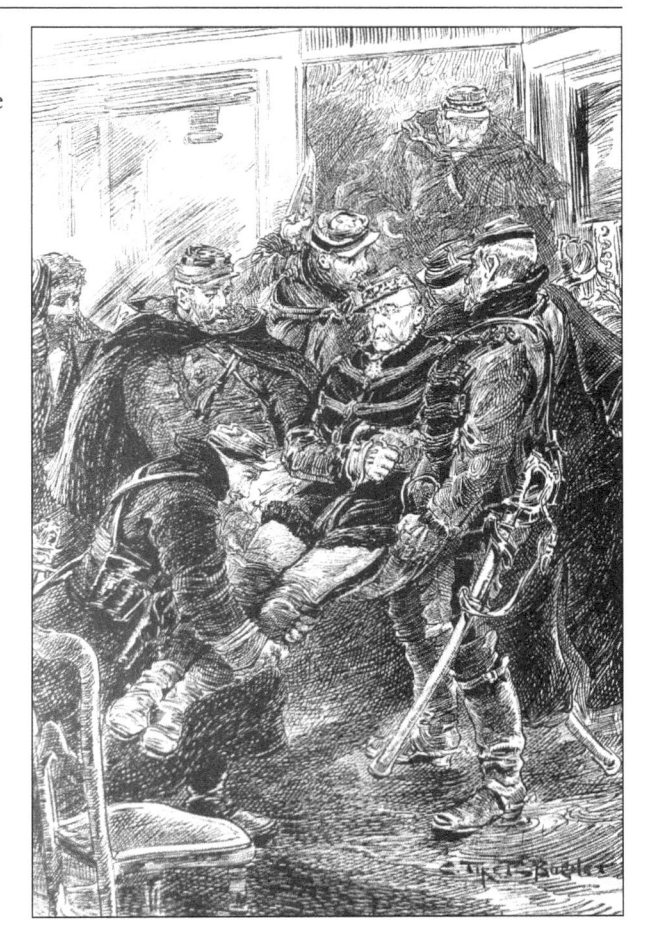

I do not exaggerate when I say that the conduct of the French military medical men here was, with a few exceptions, beyond contempt. In Saint Quentin alone there lay 2000 wounded – the theatre was full, and they were still pouring in from the villages around; yet you might go into the cafés and find French military surgeons lounging about, smoking, drinking, and playing billiards, whilst their countrymen, who had done their duty like men, lay groaning upon beds of pain.[7]

Goeben was, by 2.00pm, in no doubt that Faidherbe had got away. Barnekow reported from Sequehaut, nine miles north of St Quentin at 1.45pm; he had not met the enemy anywhere and in those circumstances wondered, in view of the state of the roads, if it was still mandatory to reach Clary and Coudry by nightfall. Goeben, ever a realist, left it up to him. Kummer, prior to this, had reported from Pontruet on the west side of the Schelde canal that his advance guards were picking up a lot of stragglers. Prince Albrecht from Lesdins, four and a half miles from St Quentin, reported that part of the French army had retreated to Bohain, and that Faidherbe, with about 10,000 men, was said to have gone to Landrecies. It was far from clear in which direction the main body of the

French had gone, and Goeben pushed forward his cavalry in all directions to find out. He himself set off with his headquarters to Bellicourt, arriving at about 6pm.

In his history of the campaign Schell was somewhat defensive about the failure of the First Army to fall upon the wreckage of the Army of the North; he pointed to the state of the roads, which had prevented the completion of the full extent of the march which Goeben had ordered for January 20, but noted that in spite of this the army had marched 18 miles during the day. A pursuit on the night of the battle was impracticable, as he explained:

> General Goeben had already commenced a vigorous pursuit of the enemy on the morning after the victory. The want of intact reserves and the extreme fatigue of all the troops made it impossible to pursue the beaten enemy to any distance on the night of the battle. The fatiguing marches which the troops had made the preceding days on the miry roads, and the hard fight and the soft soil of the battlefield had exhausted the strength of the army. Added to this, a great part of the troops were but insufficiently provisioned on the evening after the battle, as it had not been in all cases possible to bring up supplies from the trains in the rear of the army.[8]

Moltke might have been disappointed that Faidherbe had got away; in his laconic telegram of congratulations to Goeben at 12.30pm on January 20 he made, as usual, a reference to following up the beaten enemy: 'His Majesty the Emperor congratulates Your Excellency on your success, and recommends rigorous pursuit. The 16th Infantry Brigade is to be sent back here as soon as it can be spared.'[9] Moltke was having to get used to referring to William as the Emperor; it had been only two days earlier that the German Empire had been proclaimed in the Salle des Glaces at Versailles.

Moltke addressed the question of the pursuit after a victory in his own history of the war, drawing attention to the reality of the situation usually faced by a successful commander:

> According to theory, the pursuit should invariably clinch the victory – a postulate assented to by all, and particularly by civilians; and yet in practice it is seldom observed. Military history furnishes but few instances, such as the famous one of Belle Alliance. It requires a very strong and pitiless will to impose fresh exertions and dangers upon troops who have marched, fought and fasted for ten or twelve hours, in place of the longed-for rest and food. But even given the possession of this will, the question of pursuit will yet depend on the circumstances under which the victory has been won. It will be difficult of execution when all the bodies on the field, as at Königgrätz, have become so intermixed that hours are required to re-form them into tactical cohesion; or when, as at Saint Quentin, all, even the troops last thrown into the action, have become so entangled that not one single tactically complete body of infantry remains at disposition. Without the support of such a body, cavalry at night will be seriously detained before every obstacle and each petty post of the enemy, and thus alone its exertions will rarely be repaid.[10]

Meanwhile Faidherbe, in Douai, was contemplating the position in which the scattered units of his army had found themselves. Not surprisingly, he found that the morale of his soldiers was extremely low, and he found it necessary to issue an extremely bombastic order of the day 'in order to lessen the depression which ran through an army forced to retreat after having suffered much.' In it, he told his troops that they could be proud of themselves, and that they had well merited their country. They had, he said, proved that the Prussians were not invincible. He ended with words that he probably did not believe: 'Several days of rest, and those who have sworn the ruin of France will find us right back at them.'[11] Goeben forebore to comment on these observations.

Meanwhile Gambetta had arrived in Lille, and Faidherbe, accompanied by Farre, made his way there to meet him. In the course of their conversations Faidherbe conceded that it might be possible to re-enter the campaign in ten days, but he made it clear that in his opinion the struggle could not be kept up for more than a month. Coming from the lips of one of the few generals in whom he had complete confidence, Gambetta must

'The rearguard of the Army of the North', by Sergent. (Rousset/*Histoire*)

have been dismayed; it did not, however, prevent him from delivering an impassioned address to the citizens of Lille on January 22. In the course of this, he expressed his profound conviction that in the weeks and months to come they would see the annihilation of the invading armies, and that the ruin of Prussia would be immediate, in the face of 38 million French who had sworn to conquer or die.[12] Sir Charles Dilke thought that the speech was the 'finest oratorical display' which he had ever heard.

Faidherbe, of course, for all his brave words to his troops, and his subsequent historical inaccuracies, was a realist. Roberts recorded an aspect of this, when commenting that no one could suppose that men like Faidherbe and Bourbaki could have imagined that it would be possible to drive the Prussians out, but something might be done to improve the subsequent peace terms:

> Upon one occasion two Prussian officers saw General Faidherbe upon some business. When the interview was concluded, General Faidherbe's last words to them were, 'Au revoir, messieurs,' and an aide who was standing by added, 'Oui, a Berlin;' but the general turned away with a mournful shake of the head.[13]

With Faidherbe's army safely ensconced in and behind the northern fortresses, there was clearly no point in Goeben advancing further. It cannot have been far from his mind that the war was certainly almost at an end, and he had no intention of hazarding his men's lives to no purpose. There was nothing to be gained by attacking the fortresses; there was no siege artillery available, and it had been demonstrated on more than one occasion that field artillery on its own could not quickly bring about a capitulation. Nor was it practicable to invest any of them for a long time. Their military significance lay only in the protection which they afforded the Army of the North, from which there was little more to be feared, and in any case Goeben had no plans to occupy the area north of the Somme on a permanent basis. The orders that he issued for January 22 reflected the beginning of a reshuffle of the badly mixed units of the First Army, to restore them to their original commands, while at the same time ensuring that the most forward positions were those most convenient to check any forward move by the Army of the North.[14]

In fact on January 22 von der Groeben's patrols reported that the suburbs of Cambrai appeared no longer to be occupied, and that barricades at their entrances had been removed; at the gates of the fortress the patrols had not been fired on. In the hope that this indicated that the inhabitants might be prepared to capitulate, von der Groeben sent Lieutenant Voigt to the commandant of the fortress with a summons to surrender; this was, however refused, and no attack took place.[15] A similar situation arose at Landrecies, which Lippe found to contain few French troops; the news that two battalions were on the way there led him to make an attempt to seize the little fortress by a *coup de main* before they arrived. On January 23, therefore, two columns led by Hüllessem and Krug von Nidda respectively advanced on the place from the south; although they got as far as the railway station, it was seen that the two enemy battalions were already entering the town from the north, and Lippe called off the attempt.[16]

Over the next few days the First Army gradually retired to the line of the Somme. By January 29 it had more or less occupied this position. It was with his troops thus deployed that Goeben heard first the news that the guns had fallen silent at Paris since midnight on January 26/27. This was followed by another dispatch sent by Moltke at

11.45pm on January 28 to the effect that a truce had been signed which was to come into force at noon on January 31, or earlier if the French should ask for this. In order to ensure that an armistice on the basis of the status quo should leave the First Army in the most advantageous position, Goeben at 10.00am on January 29 ordered the 29th Brigade to advance to a position ten miles north of Amiens and the 30th Brigade to Albert. Later that day the detailed text of the armistice agreement arrived, and at 2.00pm next day Goeben sent Faidherbe to ask if the terms were accepted.

Faidherbe had already, before seeing the detailed terms, sent Villenoisy to Amiens to conduct the negotiations. Villenoisy later described his reception by Goeben as having been extremely courteous, the latter complimenting Faidherbe on the part he had played.[17] When he was shown the text of the armistice terms, Villenoisy realised that they did not accord with his own instructions; in particular, they provided for the evacuation of Abbeville, which he could not accept. On January 31 it was agreed that this could be left in abeyance for the moment, and a convention was signed on this basis. Moltke approved this; three days later a general agreement as to the lines of demarcation was agreed with the Government of National Defence. As a mark of respect for Faidherbe, Goeben agreed that the French garrison could remain in Abbeville until February 6, and that no war contributions would be levied on the town.[18] Elsewhere there had been, predictably enough, some issues arising between local commanders; but they were resolved without further bloodshed.

It was, at last, all over in the North. Gambetta would have fought on everywhere, but it would have been entirely futile, as Testelin had bluntly pointed out to him on January 20:

> Understand for sure that the mass of the nation is going to hold the Republic, and you, responsible for our grievous disasters, and will fall at the feet of the first person who will bring peace; that is sad, but it is true.[19]

Appendix I

Order of battle of the First Army, November 15 1870

COMMANDER-IN-CHIEF: GENERAL BARON v. MANTEUFFEL
Chief of the Staff: Major-General v. Sperling
Quartermaster-in-Chief: Colonel Count v. Wartensleben
Commanding Artillery: Lieut-General Schwartz
Commanding Engineers and Pioneers: Major-General Biehler
Inspection General of Etappen
Inspector-General: Lieut-General Malotki v. Trzebiatowski
Chief of the Staff: Major v. Ditfurth

I ARMY CORPS

General Commanding: General Baron v. Manteuffel
(after November Lieut.-General v. Bentheim)
Chief of the Staff: Lieut.-Colonel v. d.Burg
Commanding Artillery: Major-General v.Bergmann
Commanding Engineers and Pioneers: Major Fahland

1st Infantry Division

Commander: Lieut.-General v. Bentheim
General Staff: Major v. Schrötter

1st Infantry Brigade, Major-General v. Gayl
    1st Grenadiers, Colonel v. Massow
    41st Regiment, Lieut.-Colonel Baron v. Meerscheidt-Hüllessem

2nd Infantry Brigade, Major-General Baron v. Falkenstein
    3rd Grenadiers, Colonel v. Legat
    43rd Regiment, Colonel v. Busse

Divisional troops:
    1st Rifle Battalion, Lieut.-Colonel v. Ploetz
    1st Dragoons, Lieut.-Colonel v. Massow
    1st Field Division, 1st Field Artillery Regiment (1st and 2nd Heavy, 1st and 2nd Light Batteries, Major Munk

2nd Field Pioneer Company with Entrenching Tool Column, Captain Neumann
3rd Field Pioneer Company, Captain Riemann

2nd Infantry Division

Commander: Major-General v. Pritzelwitz
General Staff: Captain v. Jarotzki

3rd Infantry Brigade, Major-General v. Memerty
    4th Grenadiers, Colonel v. Tietzen u. Hennig
    44th Regiment, Colonel v. Böcking

4th Infantry Brigade, Major-General v. Zglinitzky
    5th Grenadiers, Colonel v. Einem
    45th Regiment, Colonel v. Mützschefahl

Divisional troops:
    10th Dragoons, Colonel Baron v. d.Goltz
    3rd Field Division, 1st Field Artillery Regiment (5th and 6th Heavy, 5th and 6th Light Batteries), Major Müller
    Int Field Pioneer Company with Light Field Bridge Train, Captain Ritter

Corps Artillery, Colonel Jungé

H. A. Division, 1st Field Artillery Regiment (2nd and 3rd H. A. Batteries), Major Gerhards
2nd Field Division, 1st Artillery Regiment (3rd and 4th Heavy, 3rd and 4th Light Batteries), Lieut.-Colonel Gregorovius

Columns Division, 1st Field Artillery Regiment, Major Kaunhoven
Artillery Ammunition Columns, Nos. 1 to 5, Infantry Ammunition Columns, Nos. 1 to 4, Pontoon Column

1st Train Battalion, Major Kalau v. Hofe

VII ARMY CORPS

General commanding: General v. Zastrow
Chief of the General Staff: Colonel v. Anger
Commanding Artillery: Major-General v. Zimmermann
Commanding Engineers and Pioneers: Major Treumann
Commander of the Headquarter Guard: 2nd Lieut. Count v. Villers, 15th Hussars
Present at headquarters: Captain the Hereditary Prince George of Schaumburg-Lippe

13th Infantry Division

Commander: Lieut.-General v. Bothmer
General Staff: Major v. Werder

25th Infantry Brigade, Major-General Baron v. d. Osten Sacken
   13th Regiment, Colonel v. Frankenberg-Ludwigsdorff
   73rd Fusiliers, Lieut.-Colonel v. Loebell

26th Infantry Brigade, Major-General Baron v. d. Goltz
   15th Regiment, Colonel v. Delitz
   55th Regiment, Colonel v. Barby

Divisional troops:
   7th Rifle Battalion, Major v. Kamecke
   8th Hussars, Lieut,-Colonel Arent
   3rd Field Division, 7th Field Artillery Regiment (5th and 6th Heavy, 5th and 6th Light Batteries), Major Wilhelmi
   2nd Field Pioneer Company, with Entrenching Tool Column, Captain Goetze
   3rd Field Pioneer Company, Captain Cleinow

14th Infantry Division

Commander: Lieut-General v. Kameke
General Staff: Major Baron v. Hilgers

27th Infantry Brigade, Colonel v. Pannwitz
   39th Fusiliers, Colonel Eskens
   74th Regiment, Lieut.-Colonel v. Kamecke

28th Infantry Brigade, Major-General v. Woyna, IInd
   53rd Regiment, Colonel v. Gerstein-Hohenstein
   77th Regiment, Colonel v. Conrady

Divisional troops:
   15th Hussars, Colonel v. Cosel
   1st Field Division, 7th Field Artillery Regiment (1st and 2nd Heavy, 1st and 2nd Light Batteries), Major Baron v. Eynatten
   1st Field Pioneer Company with Light Field Bridge Train, Captain Junker

Corps Artillery, Lieut.-Colonel Minameyer

Horse Artillery Division, 7th Field Artillery Regiment (2nd and 3rd Horse Artillery Batteries), Major Coester
2nd Field Division, 7th Field Artillery Regiment (3rd and 4th Heavy, 3rd and 4th Light Batteries), Major Matthias

Columns Division, 7th Field Artillery Regiment, Major v. Fragstein-Niemsdorff
Artillery Ammunition Columns Nos. 1 to 5, Infantry Ammunition Columns Nos. 1 to 4, Pontoon Column

7th Train Battalion, Major Baron v. Bothmer

VIII ARMY CORPS

General commanding: General v. Goeben
Chief of the Staff: Colonel v. Witzendorff
Commanding Artillery: Colonel v. Kameke
Commanding Engineers and Pioneers: Lieut.-Colonel Schulz
Commanding Headquarter Guard: 1st Lieut. Suermondt, 8th Cuirassiers

15th Infantry Division

Commander: Lieut.-General v. Kummer
Staff Officer: Major Lentze

29th Infantry Brigade, Colonel v. Bock
    33rd Fusiliers, Lieut.-Colonel v. Henning
    65th Regiment, Lieut.-Colonel Barol v. Dörnberg

30th Infantry Brigade, Major-General v. Strubberg
    28th Regiment, Colonel v. Rosenzweig
    68th Regiment, Colonel v. Sommerfeld

Divisional troops:
    8th Rifle Battalion, Major v. Oppeln-Bronikowsky
    7th Hussars, Colonel Baron v. Löe
    1st Field Division, 8th Field Artillery Regiment (1st and 2nd Heavy, 1st and 2nd Light Batteries). Major Mertens
    2nd Field Pioneer Company with Entrenching Tool Column, Captain Eichapfel

16th Infantry Division

Commander: Lieut.-General Baron v. Barnekow
Staff Officer: Captain Hassel

31st Infantry Brigade, Major-General Count Neidhardt v. Gneisenau
    29th Regiment, Lieut.-Colonel v. Blumroeder
    69th Regiment, Colonel Beyer v. Karger

32nd Infantry Brigade, Colonel v. Rex
    40th Fusiliers, Lieut.-Colonel Reinicke
    70th Regiment, Colonel Mettler

Divisional troops:
    9th Hussars, Colonel v. Wittich or v. Hinsmann-Hallmann
    3rd Field Division, 8th Field Artillery Regiment (5th and 6th Heavy, 5th and 6th Light Batteries) Lieut.-Colonel Hildebrandt
    1st Field Pioneer Company with Light Field Bridge Train, Captain Pagenstecher
    3rd Field Pioneer Company, Captain Richter IInd

Corps Artillery, Colonel v. Broecker

Horse Artillery Division, 8th Field Artillery Regiment (1st, 2nd, 3rd Horse Artillery Batteries). Lieut.-Colonel Borkenhagen

2nd Field Division, 8th Field Artillery Regiment (3rd and 4th Heavy, 3rd and 4th Light Batteries), Major Zwirnemann

Columns Division, 8th Field Artillery Regiment, Captain Eggers
Artillery Ammunition Columns Nos. 1 to 5, Infantry Ammunition Columns Nos. 1 to 4, Pontoon Column

8th Train Battalion, Colonel v. d. Marwitz

3rd Reserve Division

Commander: Major-General Baron Schuler v. Senden
General Staff: Major v. Lettow-Vorbeck, 70th Regiment

Combined Line Infantry Brigade, Major-General v. Blanckensee
    19th Regiment, Colonel v. Goeben
    21st Regiment, Colonel v. Sell

3rd Reserve Cavalry Brigade, Major-General v. Strantz
    1st Reserve Dragoons, Major v. Keltsch
    3rd Reserve Hussars, Colonel v. Glasenapp

Combined Artillery Division (1st and 2nd Heavy, Light Reserve Battery), Major v. Schweinichen

3rd Cavalry Division

Commander: Lieut.-General Count v.d. Groeben
General Staff: Captain Count v. Wedel

6th Cavalry Brigade, Major-General v. Mirus
    8th Cuirassiers, Colonel Count v. Roedern
    7th Lancers, Lieut.-Colonel v. Pestel
7th Cavalry Brigade, Major-General Count zu Dohna
    5th Lancers, Colonel Baron v. Reitzenstein
    14th Lancers, Colonel v. Lüderitz

1st Horse Artillery Battery, VIII Army Corps, Captain Schrader

Appendix II

Distribution of the German Forces for the Battle of St Quentin, January 19 1871

RIGHT WING, Lieut.-General Baron v. Barnekow

16th Infantry Division
Lieut.-General Baron v. Barnekow

Advanced Guard
31st Infantry Brigade, Colonel v. Rosenzweig, commanding 28th Regt.
    29th Regiment (exc. the 7th Co.)
    2nd Battn. 69th Regiment
    2nd, 3rd and 4th sqns., 9th Hussars
    5th Heavy and 5th Light Batteries, 8th F. A. Regt.

Main Body
32nd Infantry Brigade, Colonel v. Hertzberg, commanding 68th Regt
    40th Fusiliers
    3rd, 4th Cos. and Fus. Battn., 70th Regiment
    4th sqn., 1st Reserve Dragoons
    6th Heavy and 6th Light Batteries, 8th F. A. Regt.

3rd Reserve Cavalry Brigade, Major General v. Strantz
    1st, 2nd and 3rd sqns., 1st Reserve Dragoons
    1st, 2nd and 3rd sqns., 3rd Reserve Hussars

Reserve: 3rd Reserve Division, Lieut.-General Prince Albrecht of Prussia (son)
Combined Line Infantry Brigade, Colonel v. Goeben, commanding 19th Regt.
    2nd and Fus. Battns., 19th Regiment (exc. the 6th Co.)
    1st Battn., 81st Regiment

4th and 5th sqns., 2nd Guard Lancers
1st and 2nd Heavy Reserve Batteries, Vth Army Corps

Left Flank Detachment, Lieut.-Colonel v. Hymmen, commanding Guard Hussars:
    1st Battn., 19th Regiment
    Fus. Battn., 81st Regiment
    1st, 4th and 5th sqns., Guard Hussars
    Light Reserve Battery, Vth Army Corps

12th Cavalry Division, Lieut.-General Count zur Lippe

Advanced Guard
Colonel v. Carlowitz, commanding Saxon Guard Cavalry Regt.
    1st and 3rd Cos., 12th Rifle Battalion
    Saxon Guard Cavalry Regiment
    2 guns 2nd H. A. B., 12th F. A. Regt.

Main Body
Major-General Krug v. Nidda, commanding 23rd Cav. Brig.
    2nd Battn., 86th Fusiliers
    2nd and 4th Cos., 12th F. A. Regiment
    17th Lancers
    3 guns 2nd H. A. B., 12th F. A. Regiment

Reserve
Major-General Senfft v. Pilsach, commanding 24th Cav. Brig
    18th Lancers
    1st H. A. B., 12th F. A. Regt.
    1st Battn., 96th Regt. (arrived at noon)

LEFT WING, Lieut.-General v. Kummer

15th Infantry Division, Lieut.-General v. Kummer

29th Infantry Brigade, Colonel v. Bock.
    Advanced Guard: Lieut.-Colonel Baron v. Dörnberg, Commg, 65th Regt.
        2nd and Fus. Battns., 65th Regiment
        ¼ 2nd and 4th sqns., 7th Hussars
        1st Light Battery, 8th F. A. Regt
    Main Body, Lieut.-Colonel v. Henning, commanding 33rd Fus.
        1st and 3rd Battns., 33rd Fusiliers
        1st Battn., 65th Regt. (By mistake it marched in rear of 30th Brigade)
        ½ 2nd sqn., 7th Hussars
        1st Heavy Battery, 8th F. A. Regt.

30th Infantry Brigade, Major-General v. Strubberg
    28th Regiment
    1st and 2nd Battns., 68th Regt.
    8th Rifle Battns.
    1st and 3rd sqns, 7th Hussars. (attached to 29th Brigade during the march)

2nd Heavy and 2nd Light Batteries, 8th F. A. Regt.
2nd Field Pioneer Co., VIIIth Army Corps

Corps Artillery, with escort, Colonel v. Broecker
    Fus. Battn., 68th Regt.
    ¼ 2nd sqn., 7th Hussars
    H. A. Divn., 8th F. A. Regt. (1st, 2nd and 3rd H. A. B.)
    2nd F. Divn., 8th F. A. Regt. (3rd and 4th Heavy, 3rd and 4th Light Batteries)

Lieut.-General Count v. d. Groeben's Detachment

Combined Division Ist Army Corps, Colonel v. Massow, commanding 1st Grenadiers (afterwards Maj.-General v. Gayl, commanding 1st Infantry Division)

Advanced Guard, Lieut.,Colonel v. Pestel, commanding 7th Lancers.
    2nd and Fus. Battns. 1st Grenadiers
    Fus. Battn. 44th Regiment
    1st and 4th sqns., 5th Lancers
    1st, 2nd and 4th sqns, 7th Lancers
    5th Heavy Battery, 1st F. A. Regt.

Main Body, Major Bock, 44th Regiment
    4th Grenadiers
    1st and 2nd Battns., 44th Regt. (exc. the 3rd Co.)
    2nd and 4th sqns., 14th Lancers
    4th Heavy, 4th and 6th Light Batteries, 1st F. A. Regt.

Combined Cavalry Brigade, Maj.-General Count zu Dohna, commanding 7th Cav. Brigade
    8th Cuirassiers
    2nd sqn., 5th Lancers
    1st and 3rd sqns, 14th Lancers
    ⅓ 1st H. A. B., 7th F. A. Regt.

ARMY RESERVE, Colonel v. Böcking, commanding 44th Regt.
41st Regiment
1st and 3rd sqns., 2nd Guard Lancers
1st sqn., 9th Hussars
3rd Heavy and 3rd Light Batteries, 1st F. A. Regt.

Absent:
    7th Co., 29th Regt., at Ailly sur Noye
    1st and Fus. Battns., 69th Regt., at Péronne
    1st and 2nd Cos., 70th Regt., at Ham
    2nd Battn., 70th Regt., at Amiens
    2nd Battn., 33rd Fusiliers, on march from Amiens

6th Co., 19th Regt., with wagon-park at Chaulnes
2nd Battn., 81st Regt., at La Fère
2nd sqn., Guard Hussars, at Picquigny
4th sqn., 3rd Res. Hussars, at Nesle
1st Battn., 1st Grenadiers, on Rouen-Amiens Railway and at Picquigny
3rd Co., 44th Regt., with regimental train
3rd sqn., 5th Lancers, at Péronne
3rd sqn., 7th Lancers at Amiens
3rd Saxon Cav. Regt., at Clermont
1st F. Pion. Co., VIIIth A. C., at Jussy and St. Simon bridges
3rd F. Pion. Co., VIIIth A. C., at Péronne

Appendix III

Order of Battle of the Army of the North, mid-January 1871

Commander in Chief: Lieutenant General Faidherbe
Second in command (major-géneral): Lieutenant General Farre
Assistants (major-généraux adjoints): Colonel Cosseron de Villenoisy of the engineers, Major Lucase de Peslouan, Mélard
Commander of artillery: Lieutenant Colonel Charon
Commander of engineers: Colonel Milliroux
Chief of Staff: Lieutenant Colonel de la Sauzaie

Troops attached to headquarters:
Cavalry (Colonel Barbault de Lamotte): 11th Provisional Dragoons: Lieutenant Colonel Baussin: four and a half squadrons
Provost (Major de Courchamp des Sablons): two provisional squadrons of police
Artillery reserve (Naval Lieutenant Giron): 1st mixed battery (12-pounders) – Naval Lieutenant Rolland (La Chapelle); 2nd mixed battery (12-pounders) – Naval Lieutenant Gaigneau d'Étiolles (Meusnier); 1st battery of *Mobiles* of Seine-Inférieure (4-pounders): Captain de Belleville (Dieudonné)
Engineer reserve: 12th company *bis* of the 2nd Regiment (Captain Grimaud)
Engineer park: Captain Grimaud
Free corps: reconnaissance battalion – Captain Jourdan (Major Bayle); Volunteer Sharpshooters of the Nord – Captain Delaporte, *Zouaves éclaireurs du Nord* – Captain Trouvé; free company of the battalion of *Mobilisés* of Saint-Quentin – unknown commander

22ND ARMY CORPS

General commanding: Lieutenant General Lecointe
Chief of Staff: Lieutenant Colonel of Infantry Aynès (detached to 1st Brigade of 1st Division); Captain of Engineers Farjon
Artillery commander: Major Pigouche
Engineer commander: Major Thouzelier

1st Infantry Division
Commander: Lieutenant General Derroja
Chief of Staff: Major Jarriez
Artillery commander: Captain Cornet

Engineer commander: Captain Sambuc

1st Brigade, Lieutenant Colonel Aynès (killed 19 January 1871)
2nd Provisional Chasseur Battalion (Major Boschis). 67th Provisional Infantry Regiment (1st and 2nd battalions of the depot of the 75th Line Infantry Regiment, 1st Battalion of the depot of the 65th Line Infantry Regiment) (Lieutenant Colonel Fradin de Linières. 91st Provisional regiment (5th, 6th, 7th battalions of the *Gardes Mobiles* of Pas-du-Calais) (Lieutenant-Colonel Fovel {captain in the 33rd Line Infantry Regiment}).

2nd Brigade, Colonel Pittié
17th Provisional Chasseurs (Major Moynier). 68th Provisional Infantry Regiment (1st and 2nd battalions of the depot of the 24th Line Infantry Regiment, 1st Battalion of the depot of the 33rd Line Infantry Regiment) (Lieutenant-Colonel Cottin, then Tramond). 46th Provisional Regiment (1st, 2nd, 3rd battalions of the *Gardes Mobiles* of the Nord) (Lieutenant Colonel J. de la Lalène-Laprade)

Divisional troops:
Artillery: 1st battery *bis* of 15th Artillery Regiment (4-pounders) (Captain Collignon {Ravaut}), 2nd battery *bis* of 15th Artillery Regiment (4-pounders) (Captain Bocquillon), 3rd battery *bis* of 12th Artillery Regiment (8-pounders) (Captain Lannes de Montebello, then Captain Robert). Total 18 cannon.
Engineers: 2nd Company of 2nd Engineer Regiment (Captain Sambuc).

2nd Infantry Division
Commander Major General Dufaure du Bessol
Chief of Staff: Major Zédé
Artillery commander: Major Chaton
Engineer commander: Captain Cantagrel

1st Brigade, Colonel Foerster
20th Provisional Chasseurs (Major Hecquet). 69th Provisional Infantry Regiment (1st and 2nd battalions of the depot of the 43rd Line Infantry Regiment, 3rd Provisional Battalion of the *infanterie de marine*) (Lieutenant Colonel Pasquet de la Broue {*infanterie de marineI*}), 44th Provisional Infantry Regiment (2nd, 3rd and 3rd *bis* {or 5th} battalions of the *Gardes Mobiles* of the Gard) (Lieutenant Colonel Lemaire {Saignemorte}).

2nd Brigade, Lieutenant Colonel de Gislain
18th Provisional Chasseurs (Major Pichat). 72nd Provisional Infantry Regiment (1st and 2nd battalions of the depot of the 91st Line Infantry Regiment, 3rd Battalion of the depot of the 33rd Line Infantry Regiment) (Lieutenant Colonel Delpech). 101st Provisional Infantry Regiment (4th Battalion of the *Gardes Mobiles* of the Somme, 3rd of the Marne, mixed Somme-Marne battalion) (Lieutenant Colonel du Brouard [major of infantry].

Divisional troops:
Artillery: 2nd battery *ter* of 15th Artillery Regiment (4-pounders) (Captain Marx {Benzou}), 3rd battery *bis* of 15th Artillery Regiment (4-pounders) (Captain Chastang), 3rd battery of 12th Artillery Regiment (12-pounders) (Captain Beauregard). Total 18 cannon.
Engineers: 1st depot company of the 3rd Engineer Regiment (Captain Cantagrel).

23RD ARMY CORPS

General commanding: Lieutenant General Paulze d'Ivoy
Chief of Staff: Lieutenant Colonel of Infantry Marchand
Assistant chief of staff: Major Benoit de Laumont
Artillery commander: Major Grandmottet
Engineer commander: Major Allard

1st Infantry Division

Commander Post Captain Payen
Chief of Staff: Lieutenant Colonel of Infantry Jacob
Artillery commander: Captain Ravaud
Engineer commander: Captain Mangin

1st Brigade, Lieutenant Colonel (A) Michelet
19th Provisional Chasseurs (Major Wasmer, killed 18 January 1871). Regiment of *fusiliers marins* (1st and 2nd battalions provided by the port of Brest, 3rd Battalion by the port of Toulon) (Lieutenant Commander Granger), 48th Provisional Infantry Regiment (7th, 8th and 9th battalions of the *Gardes Mobiles* of the Nord) (Lieutenant Colonel Degoutin).

2nd Brigade, Lieutenant Commander de Lagrange
24th Provisional *Chasseurs* (Major de Négrier, wounded 19 January, then Captain Joxe). Provisional Infantry Regiment (1st Battalion of the depot of the 33rd Line Infantry regiment, 2nd Battalion of the depot of the 65th Line Infantry Regiment; 5th Battalion of the *Mobilisés* of Pas-de-Calais) (Major Rameaux {Lieutenant Colongel Jacob}. 47th Provisional Infantry Regiment (4th, 5th, 6th battalions of the *Gardes Mobiles* of the Nord) (Lieutenant Colonel Lebel).

Divisional troops:
Artillery: 3rd battery *ter* of 15th Artillery Regiment (4-pounders) (Captain Halphen), 1st battery of the *Gardes Mobiles* of the Pas-de-Calais (4-pounders) (Captain Belvalette {Dupuich}), 4th battery *bis* of 15th Artillery Regiment (12-pounders) (Captain Dieudonné). Total 18 cannon.
Engineers: 2nd depot company of the 3rd Engineer Regiment (Captain Mangin)

2nd Infantry Division

Lieutenant General (A) Robin (former captain of *infanterie de marine*)

Chief of Staff: Colonel (A) Astré
Artillery commander: Major de Saint-Wulfranc
Engineer commander: unknown

1st Brigade, Colonel of *mobilisés* Brusley
1st Battalion of Voltigeurs of the Mobilisés of the Nord (Major Foutrein). 1st Provisional Regiment (1st, 2nd and 3rd battalions of the 1st Legion of Nord) (Lieutenant Colonel Loy) (former sergeant major). 2nd Provisional Regiment (1st, 2nd and 3rd battalions of the 2nd Legion) (Lieutenant Colonel Dubois de Courval)

2nd Brigade, Colonel of *mobilisés* Amos
2nd Battalion of Voltigeurs (4th of the 5th Legion) (Major Lacourte-Dumont), 1st Battalion of Voltigeurs (4th of the 1st Legion) (Major Monnier), 3rd Provisional Regiment (1st, 3rd and 5th battalions of the 3rd Legion, (Lieutenant Colonel Chas). 4th Provisional Regiment (5th, 6th and 7th battalions of the 9th Legion) (Lieutenant Colonel Brabant).

Divisional troops:
Artillery: 2nd battery of the *Gardes Mobiles* of Seine-Inférieure (4-pounder mountain) (Captain Montaigut), 4th battery of the *Gardes Mobiles* of Seine-Inférieure (4-pounder mountain) (Captain de Launoy), 1st battery of the *Gardes Mobiles* of Finistère (4-pounder mountain) (Captain Benoit). Total 18 cannon
Cavalry: a half squadron of *eclaireurs mobilisés du Nord* (Captain Leclaire).

Isnard Brigade (also termed Cambrai Mobile Column)
(attached on 15 January to 22nd Corps)
3rd Battalion of the depot of the 24th Line Infantry Regiment (Major Morlet). 73rd Provisional Infantry regiment (depot battalions of the 3rd and 40th Line Infantry Regiments) (Lieutenant Colonel Castaigne). Provisional Regiment (1st and 2nd *bis* battalions of the *Gardes Mobiles* of Ardennes (Lieutenant Colonel Giovanninelli). 4th Battalion of the 7th Legion of the *Mobilisés* of Nord (Major Plaideau)
Artillery: two smoothbore howitzers from the 15th Artillery Regiment, eight 4-pounder mountain guns (Lieutenant Wisshoff).

Brigade Pauly
Aide-de-camp: unknown
1st Battalion of *chasseurs mobilisés* (1st of the Legion of Arras) (Major Garreau) 1st Provisional Regiment (1st, 2nd and 3rd battalions of the Legion of Béthune (Lieutenant Colonel Poupard). 2nd Provisional regiment (4th and 5th Battalions of the Legion of Béthune, 5th Battalion of the Legion of Arras) (Lieutenant Choquet)
Artillery: one battery of *mobilisés* of Pas-de-Calais (four 6-pounder Armstrong cannon)

Appendix IV

Moltke's Instructions to Manteuffel and Frederick Charles

Headquarters, Versailles, December 17 1870

The general situation renders it desirable that the pursuit of the enemy, after the victory which has been gained, should only be continued to the extent necessary mainly for the dispersion of his masses, and for the prevention of their reassembly for a considerable period. We cannot follow him to his last points of support, like Lille, Havre, and Bourges, nor permanently occupy distant provinces like Normandy, Brittany, or La Vendée, but must make up our minds to evacuate also Tours, so as to concentrate the bulk of our forces at a few main points.

These latter should be occupied as far as possible by entire brigades, divisions or corps. From them the neighbourhood, but only the immediate neighbourhood, should be cleared of franc-tireurs by moveable columns; at them we must wait until the hostile levies have become again embodied into formed armies, so as to proceed to their encounter by short offensive movements.

By these means our troops will presumably be guaranteed the long rest of which they stand in need, so that they may recover strength, bring up their reinforcements of men and ammunition, and replenish their equipments.

His Majesty the King has, therefore, been please to command as follows:-

> For the future investment of Paris, the main forces of the First Army will towards the north be assembled at Beauvais (subsequently at Creil, if the railways can be placed in working order for large transports of troops). Rouen, Amiens, and St. Quentin will be occupied, and v. Senden's Division will shortly move off to the latter place. The left bank of the Seine is to be abandoned by the First Army; on the other hand this stream is to be watched as far as Vernon.
>
> Towards the west, after the termination of the pursuit now in progress, the Grand Duke's Detachment is to assemble at Chartres, a strong detachment at Dreux.
>
> Towards the south, the main forces of the Second Army will concentrate at Orléans. It will abandon the occupation of the country on the left bank of the Loire, and will limit itself to watching towards the Cher. On the other hand, we must hold, if not Tours, at any rate Blois and Gien. (The passages up stream should, as far as possible, be destroyed.)
>
> The main points here mentioned should, in the event of a hostile attack, be supported as far as can be foreseen, in good time from their respective central

positions; in any case they should form points of retreat for repulsed detachments, whence to renew the offensive.

But, as an offensive movement of Bourbaki's Army on the right bank of the Loire may render necessary still larger forces than may be available at Orléans (leaving there the necessary garrison, I Bavarian Corps), and at Gien, the Corps of General v. Zastrow is to be directed with its main body on Auxerre, where it is *a portée*, if necessary, for joining the Second Army at Montargis in the event of battle.

To the Army Headquarters all further arrangements (also as regards the Detachment of His Royal Highness the Grand Duke of Mecklenburg) are hereby committed with the very respectful remark, that the preceding observations are only intended for the information of the Headquarters of Armies, and, consequently, should only be communicated to the Corps' Headquarters, to the extent that my appear desirable for the execution by the latter of the tasks allotted to them.

[Further it is respectfully remarked that it would be in accordance with the intentions of the Royal Headquarters, if the present distribution of the I Bavarian Corps were preserved for the next few days.]

(Signed) COUNT V. MOLTKE
To the Headquarters of the First and Second Army.

NOTE – The words written between parentheses [ ] only occur in the copy addressed to the Second Army.

From: Official History IV, Appendix CVIII.

Appendix V

The Chassepôt and the Needle Gun

In considering the relative performance of the Army of the North and the First Army, it must be borne in mind that there was a substantial discrepancy between the standard infantry weapons used by each side. Although in 1864 and 1866 the Prussian army had gone to war with a rifle that was vastly superior to that employed by each of its opponents, in 1870-71 the position was completely reversed. Technological advantage was now decidedly on the side of the French, the Chassepôt substantially outperforming the Dreyse needle gun.

This had been demonstrated throughout the early campaigns and nowhere more dramatically than during the battle of Gravelotte-St Privat. Attacking an enemy securely ensconced in a good defensive position the Guard Corps suffered no less than 8,000 casualties in the space of 20 minutes, a third of its effective strength. Admittedly the assault was badly mismanaged, but the experience had a chilling effect on German commanders for the rest of the war.

The needle gun was first introduced into service with the Prussian army in 1848. Its inventor, Johann Nikolaus von Dreyse, had first perfected a muzzle-loading rifle in which a needle like firing pin fired the percussion cap at the base of the bullet. He then adopted the bolt-action breechloading principle, which gave it a much higher rate of fire. It fired a 15.5mm calibre bullet and weighed 4.7kg. It possessed, however, a number of serious defects, the most important of which was its effective range, which was no more than about 650 yards. Its rate of fire was 10-12 rounds per minute. A significant amount of gas escaped at the breech when it was fired with a paper cartridge, seriously reducing its muzzle velocity. After firing several times, the rifle's breech would not fully close, exposing the infantryman to the risk of burning from the escaping gas; as a result he would frequently choose to fire from the hip. The pin itself was also relatively fragile, often requiring replacement after some 200 shots, while the residue of the black powder charge that built up meant that the barrel needed cleaning after 60 – 80 shots.

The Chassepôt, named after its inventor Antoine Alphonse Chassepôt, was designed in 1866 and introduced into service with the French army during the following year. It was a bolt-action breechloading rifle, firing a bullet of 11mm calibre. It weighed slightly less than the needle gun, at 4.6kg. Its rate of fire was 8 – 15 rounds per minute. Where it excelled was in its range, which at 1,300 yards was double that of the needle gun. It had a substantially higher muzzle velocity. It did, however, suffer from the fouling of the chamber and bolt mechanism by burnt paper residues and black powder.

Overall, the Chassepôt gave the undertrained troops of the Government of National Defence a huge advantage in combat which to a considerable extent compensated for their lack of experience when compared with their tough and battle hardened opponents. The latter, however, to some extent counterbalanced this by the effectiveness of the German artillery, which in the campaign against the Army of the North, as elsewhere, played a substantial part in their success.

Appendix VI

Major Garnier explains himself to General Faidherbe

Péronne, 11th of January

General / Dear Sir

I regret to inform you that yesterday I sadly had no choice but to surrender the town of Péronne to the enemy after a 13-day bombardment.

The walls surrounding the place were barely attacked and thus haven't been too damaged but the town itself is no more than a heap of ruins. Any building not burnt down has been demolished, riddled with projectiles or weakened. (I cannot confirm) that not a single building remains untouched. The destruction is huge and for a large part of the population their ruin is complete.

At noon on December 28, I received a summons from the enemy, warning me that, if I was not going to agree to surrender, a bombardment would begin at 2pm. Before even having received my reply, delayed by half an hour, the enemy general ordered six field batteries positioned within a 1000 – 2000 metre radius to open fire on the town. The delay was due to my decision to send back the envoy in order to hide him from the population and thus avoid having insults at him,.

The hospital with two Geneva Convention flags flying on its roof and the church were the first to be attacked. The patients were carefully moved from the hospital to the barracks. Then in the evening the church was set ablaze and the destruction of the town spread to all areas.

A very intense blaze went on for 24 hours, slowly dying down afterwards to finally go out totally at the end of the third day. The response of our artillery was vigorous: it put out of action a large number of the enemy cannons and killed many of its men. The artillery itself suffered only a few broken gun carriages.

The enemy then positioned a battery of mortars and howitzers near the village of Briaches and opened fire again on January 2 at 10am which carried on without intermission until January 9 at 10am. By that time an envoy had arrived bringing with him a new summons to surrender the place, warning us of the setting up of siege batteries and of the continuation of the bombardment.

According to intelligence, reinforcement had well and truly arrived around the place with new cannons ready to fire.

I then sent envoys to the Prussian General. Their mission was to persuade the General to allow the civilians to leave the place. The General was inflexible. However, owing to the long and strong defence of the place he agreed on a certain number of propositions which I deemed honourable regarding the capitulation.

Despite my willingness to prolong the defence I had to give up:

1. to avoid the total destruction of the few houses still standing
2. because I feared that the remaining civilians, who were hiding in cellars, would rush on the bunkers and posterns already overcrowded with the garrison.
3. because I dreaded the thought of people being made homeless and facing harsh months to come.
4. because I feared the deterioration of the already poor health conditions, caused by an extended overcrowding of dank and unventilated premises by the civilians and the garrison. Cases of smallpox were increasing every day and several cases of insanity had been reported.
5. and finally, I must say, because I was not sure of the continued commitment of most of the garrison which by this time had been influenced by a population fully hostile to the defence.

However, if the fervour had become dulled amongst some corps of the garrison, I feel it my duty to state it had remained undiminished:

1. in the marine company
2. the detachment of the 43rd Line Regiment
3. the 2nd Artillery Battery of the Somme

Losses recorded for the garrison:
16 killed or died from fatal injuries
52 wounded

Major of the fortress of Péronne
Garnier

From: Guerre IV, docs annexes.

Appendix VII

Report of Colonel Degoutin of the 48th Regiment of the Mobiles Du Nord, for January 18 1871

The experiences of the 48th Regiment of the Mobiles du Nord on January 18, were typical of those encountered by Faidherbe's army as it struggled east and south-east. The regiment, led by Colonel Degoutin, headed the march of the 1st Brigade of Payen's division, leaving Roisel at 7.00am. The brigade linked up with the 2nd Brigade at Hervilly, and the entire division continued its progress towards St Quentin. Colonel Degoutin described in his report the events of the day:

> Towards midday the whole of the 2nd Brigade had passed Vermand. The 48th Regiment was still wholly within the village, when the sound of gunfire could be heard from the south-west. The column immediately halted its march, and the order was given to move back, concentrating on its left. The regiment left the village and established itself on the road to Caulaincourt, whence came the sound of the guns. The struggle intensified and the brigade advanced. The regiment's three battalions, formed in dense columns, advanced towards Caulaincourt, passing on the west the woods between that village and Vernand. The 7th Battalion faced west and took up a position in the clumps of trees on the heights between the Tertry and Vermand road. The 8th and 9th Battalions were directed by Colonel Degoutin to march on Trefcon, when they were recalled and formed up facing west on the Vermand road, the left resting on Caulaincourt.
>
> The 7th Battalion, commanded by Captain Steverlynck, engaged in a vigorous struggle with the enemy riflemen attempting to turn from the west. The exchange of rifle fire was intense. The enemy batteries directed their fire beyond this position, reaching the other two battalions on the Vermand road. The sailors continued to fight in front of and to the east of Caulaincourt.
>
> Towards 3.00pm, the enemy forces being considerably strengthened, the 7th Battalion was obliged to fall back on the other two; the sailors at the same time executed a retreat. The brigade found itself pressed back beyond Caulaincourt. Colonel Degoutin, at the head of the 8th and 9th Battalions attempted an advance to disengage the brigade and to keep the enemy beyond the Vermand road. This was successful, but it was very difficult to maintain the position.
>
> In the face of these strong enemy forces, General Paulze d'Ivoy gave the order to take up a position to the rear, retreating en echelon. The regiment gained the woods

between Caulaincourt and Vermand and passed through them without the enemy daring to follow, in spite of the disorder in which the movement took place.

In his report Degoutin commended Captains Steverlynck, Lestien and Bouxin, his battalion commanders, for their intelligence and sangfroid.

From: Grenest, pp.415-417.

Appendix VIII

Report of Commandant Hecquet, of the 20th Battalion of Chasseurs, for January 19 1871

I have the honour to report to you the part played by my battalion in the battle of January 19.

On January 19 the 1st Brigade arrived at Grugies; at the entrance to the village was found a sugar factory, in the spacious buildings of which I was ordered to establish my battalion; I was to maintain a close surveillance of the road from Hancourt – Urvillers to Saint Quentin from the plateau in front of which my battalion was placed. I immediately posted one company there as an outpost.

The railway line crossed the plateau in an embankment, level with the sugar factory in a deep cutting which separates the part which we occupied from the rest, which was more extensive and higher.

Scarcely had the outpost taken up its position when it signalled to me that columns of infantry and artillery were debouching from Itancourt, and taking post in front of us.

An attack was clearly imminent.

My battalion immediately stood to arms and I reinforced the outpost with two companies in order to ensure that part of the plateau the other side of the railway remained in our hands, which seemed to me the most important. Indeed, the enemy directed his first attack on this point, but met in front, and at the same time taken in flank, by the fire of the skirmishers hidden behind the hedge of the railway line, they suffered serious casualties, halted and took a position behind a fold in the ground, from where they maintained a vigorous fire.

I deployed the rest of my battalion in such a way as to make it appear stronger than it was, and remained in my position awaiting support. The 1st Division soon sent help, and I was able to make good my ammunition which had begun to run out. While this was going on, which had slowed our rate of fire, the enemy skirmishers had made ground and had reached the top of the plateau.

Before giving them time to establish themselves, I launched a counter attack, in the confidence given by the arrival of a regiment behind me. Indeed, the Prussian lines beat a retreat and, pursued by our fire from behind them and in their flank, they suffered heavy losses. In this movement we took 12 prisoners.

The enemy, giving up any attack on this side, crossed the railway and moved to his left; I followed this movement and posted my battalion to the right of the railway; it was in this position that, having driven back those in front of us, I received the order to retire.

I called in any skirmishers and retreated by the railway line, leaving two companies to move through the village in accordance with your orders; my five companies were reunited behind the village, and escorted a battery of four guns.

It was in this way that I effected my retreat as ordered.

At the end of the day of battle in exceptionally exhausting conditions, we headed for Cambrai, where we arrived next day at 8.00am.

Allow me, mon Colonel, to draw your attention to one fact to the honour of the 20th Battalion; it is that after such a fierce struggle it abandoned not one knapsack or rifle belonging to the men that you brought back under the walls of Cambrai.

From: Guerre IV, docs annexes, pp.106-107.

Appendix IX

Report of Lieutenant Belvalette, Commanding the Battery Dupuich, for January 18 1871

On January 18 at about 1.30pm, the mobile battery of Arras, halted behind the village of Vermand with a part of its division, received the order to move to the right of the village where the battle was raging. After being held for some time in reserve, the order was given for the battery to take up a position on a plateau dominating a deep valley, between the villages of Caulaincourt and Marteville.

The battery, protected by a line of skirmishers lying about 200 metres in front of it, directed its fire against the enemy columns marching on the heights opposite Beauvois when suddenly, an enemy battery which had allowed our guns to establish themselves undisturbed, and which had taken up a position on our left, on the heights above Marteville, opened a violent fire upon our guns which were taken in flank. To respond to this sudden attack, we had to effect a change in our front on our right and thus received the fire of the enemy infantry which our skirmishers had not been able to push back. This movement had not been completed when a new battery revealed itself on the hill and suddenly fired several shots taking us the flank. Exposed in this way to the enemy crossfire we were obliged to retreat.

Having taken the road from Caulaincourt to Vermand for 300 metres, the battery was ordered to cross the field and take up a position 1000 metres from that road. Scarcely was it in position when several enemy guns came to the road where we had left it and opened a heavy fire. It was now about 3.30pm.

Until nightfall our guns successfully replied to those of the enemy whose fire slackened gradually. The time-fused shells fired at 1000 metres were entirely successful.

The order to cease fire was given at 5.00pm, and the battery took the road to Saint Quentin, where it was billeted in the suburb of Saint Jean.

Next day, at 8.00am, the battery was ordered to take from a nearby battery two munition wagons and to take up a position in front of Fayet, in order to rejoin the rest of the brigade. When it got there the battery was to go to the heights opposite that village, on the left of the road. To get to this point it was necessary to climb a very steep slope, which the bad state of the ground made even more difficult. Only five guns were able to make it, with the help of the gunners; the sixth remained behind; the munition wagons could not follow.

The five guns formed a battery to the left of the farm on the hill, and opened fire at 1800 metres against a battery that was twice obliged to change its position.

The enemy skirmishers advancing in large numbers, a number of shells compelled them to withdraw; but our ammunition had run out, and the two ammunition wagons not being able to follow on, the order was given to go into reserve and resupply the guns.

We were then posted in front of Saint Quentin, on a plateau 800 metres from the town to support one of our batteries located on our left, against which the enemy was delivering a violent fire.

At 3.00pm Commandant Bodin came to ask for two guns; the 3rd Section left with Lieutenant Delalé, and rejoined us next day at Cambrai at about 1.00pm.

At about 4.30 the order came for us to go to the left of a marine battery of 12 guns, at the entrance to the town, on a hill overlooking the suburb. Scarcely had we got there when we became entangled with that battery which was returning to the town. As the skirmishers were retreating, it was impossible to hold the position indicated. Accordingly we followed the column into the town and then took the road to Cambrai which we reached next day at 4.30am.

From: Guerre IV, pp.121-123.

Appendix X

General Goeben's Orders for the Pursuit

At midnight General Goeben issued the following Army orders for January 20:

The French Army of the North is totally beaten, St. Quentin is occupied by the divisions of Generals von Barnekow and H.R.H. Prince Albrecht: two cannons have been captured, and more than 4,000 prisoners are in our hands; I congratulate the troops which I have the honour to command on the victory they have gained. The next thing now to be done is to make the most of this victory; today we have fought, tomorrow we must march to complete the defeat of the enemy. The latter seems to have retreated partly upon Cambrai and partly upon Guise; we must overtake him before he reaches the line of his fortresses. For this purpose I establish as a rule that all troops march 22½ miles tomorrow; wherever it is possible the packs of the infantry will be carried on carts.

General Kummer will march on Cambrai with the 15th Infantry Division, Count Groeben's detachment, the staff of the Corps Artillery, and the 2nd field Artillery Division. The numerous passages over the Schelde (Escaut) will give him the opportunity of combining several of his marching columns and cutting off the enemy's retreat to Cambrai.

General Barnekow will march by Sequehart upon Clary and Caudry with the 16th Infantry Division, Prince Albrecht's Reserve Division, and Colonel Böcking's detachment, which is placed under his orders.

Count Lippe's Division will march on Bohain and Le Cateau Cambresis, detaching at the same time troops in the direction of Guise to watch whatever forces of the enemy may have retreated in this direction.

I shall ride in the first instance to Le Catelet, and shall arrive there at midday; I expect to find reports there from the above-mentioned commanding officers. Major Bronikowsky's detachment, including the Horse Artillery Division of the Corps Artillery, will follow me to the same place and remain at my disposal.

All the divisions will start at 8 a.m.

All prisoners that have not been already sent to Péronne will be sent under escort to La Fère. The number of them is to be reported by midday tomorrow at Le Catelet.

The 16th Division and H.R.H. Prince Albrecht's Division will complete their ammunition at Grand Seraucourt, General von Kummer's troops at Etreillers.

From: Schell, pp.175-176.

Appendix XI

Order of the day from the Commanding General after the Battle of Saint-Quentin

Douai, 21 January
Soldiers!

It is a pressing necessity for your general to render you justice before your fellow citizens. You can be proud of yourselves, and you have well merited your country.

You have suffered what those who have not seen it can never imagine, and there is no one to blame for this suffering; circumstances alone caused it.

In less than a month you have fought three battles and several actions with an enemy which all Europe fears. You have held him; you have seen him fall back many times before you, you have proved that he is not invincible and that the defeat of France was no more than an incident caused by the ineptitude of an absolute government.

The Prussians have found in young, badly clothed solders and in the *Gardes Nationales* adversaries who can beat them. Who cares if they gather up stragglers and boast of it in their bulletins! These famous takers of guns have not touched one of your batteries.

Honour to you!

Several days of rest, and those who have sworn the ruin of France will find us right back against them.

From: Faidherbe, Appendix N, p.101.

Notes

Chapter 1: The Army of the North
1. J.P.T. Bury, *Gambetta and the National Defence* (London 1936) pp.94-95.
2. Ibid., p.109.
3. Ibid., p.111.
4. Harold Stannard, *Gambetta* (London 1921) pp.59-60.
5. Bury, p.127.
6. Quoted Bury, p.154.
7. Stannard, p.84.
8. Quoted Bury, p.154.
9. Pierre Lehautcourt, (pseudonym of General Barthelemy Edmond Palat) *Campagne du Nord en 1870-1871* (Paris 1897) p.30.
10. General L. Faidherbe, *Campagne de l'Armée du Nord* (Paris 1872) (translated S. Sutherland as *The Campaign of the Army of the North*, (Solihull 2010) (cited together as Faidherbe) p.9.
11. Léonce Patry, *The Reality of War*, translated D. Fermer (London 2001) p.286.
12. Stannard, p.80.
13. Faidherbe, p.9.
14. Ibid.
15. Quoted Lehautcourt, p.41.
16. Ibid., p.42.
17. Patry, p.179.
18. Lehautcourt, p.43.
19. Faidherbe, p.12.
20. German General Staff *Official Account of the Franco German War 1870-1871*, trans Maj. FCH Clarke (London 1883) IV p.2 (cited as Official History).
21. Lehautcourt, p.52.
22. Michael Howard, *The Franco Prussian War* (London 1962) p.292.
23. Quoted Lehautcourt, p.58.

Chapter 2: The Advance of the First Army
1. Colonel H. von Wartensleben, *Operations of the First Army under General von Manteuffel*, translated by Colonel C. von Wright (London 1893) p.4; Field Marshal H von Moltke, *Correspondence Militaire* Vol II (Paris n.d) p.432 (cited as MMC).
2. Quintin Barry, *The Franco Prussian War 1870-71: After Sedan* (Solihull 2007) p.52.
3. Fritz Hoenig, *Twenty Four Hours of Moltke's Strategy* (Woolwich 1895) p.101.
4. MMC II pp.423-425.
5. Wartensleben, p.8.
6. Ibid., p.10.
7. Ibid., pp.14-15.
8. Ibid., p.11n.
9. Ibid., p.18.
10. Sir Randal H. Roberts, *Modern War: Or the Campaigns of the First Prussian Army 1870-71* (London 1871) p.307.
11. Wartensleben, p.22.

12. Ibid., p.26.
13. Ibid., p.31.
14. Official History, IV p.1.
15. Roberts, p.327.
16. MMC II p.494; Wartensleben, p.42.
17. Wartensleben, p.46.
18. Ibid., p.45.
19. Ibid., p.48.
20. Alain Coursier, *Faidherbe* (Paris 1989) p.131.
21. Howard, p.391.
22. *Dictionnaire du biographie francaise*, Vol 10 (Paris 1965).
23. Ibid., vol 11.
24. Faidherbe, p.14.
25. Wartensleben, pp.51-52.

Chapter 3: The Battle of Amiens
1. Wartensleben, pp.52-53.
2. Captain J.L. Seton, *Notes on the Operations of the North German Troops in Lorraine and icardy* (London 1872) p.185.
3. Major General J.F. Maurice (ed.) *The Franco German War 1870-71* (London 1900) p.334.
4. Maurice, pp.334-336.
5. Wartensleben, pp.54-55.
6. Official History, IV p.3.
7. Wartensleben, pp.57-58.
8. Official History, IV p.4.
9. General A. von Goeben, *Contributions to the History of the Campaign in the North West of France*, translated by Capt. J.L. Seton (London 1873) pp.14-15.
10. Wartensleben, pp.59-60.
11. Lehautcourt,m p.59.
12. Roberts, p.382.
13. Official History, IV pp.7-8.
14. Wartensleben, pp.70-71.
15. Official History, IV pp.8-9.
16. Ibid., p.11n.
17. Wartensleben, p.71.
18. Ibid., p.66.
19. Patry, p.188.
20. Goeben, pp.15–16.
21. Wartensleben, p.70.
22. Official History, IV p.13.
23. Roberts, p.336.
24. Ibid., pp.356-351.
25. Wartensleben, p.72.
26. Roberts, p.337.

Chapter 4: La Fère
1. Faidherbe, p.23.
2. Roberts, p.339.
3. Ibid., p.340.
4. Official History, IV p.16; Faidherbe p.19.

5. Faidherbe, p.25.
6. Lehautcourt, p.77; Captain H.M. Hozier, *The Franco Prussian War* (London n.d) p.161.
7. Goeben, p.21.
8. Faidherbe, p.26.
9. Ibid., p.27.
10. Lehautcourt, pp.78-79.
11. Goeben, pp.22-23.
12. Ibid, p.23.
13. Colonel B. von Tiedemann, *The Siege Operations in the Campaign against France,* (London 1877) p.99.
14. Official History, IV p.17.
15. Lehautcourt, p.81.
16. Ibid.
17. Lehautcourt, p.82; Official History, IV p.17.
18. Official History, IV pp.17-18.
19. Tiedemann, p.100.
20. Lehautcourt, pp.83-84; Official History, IV p.18; Tiedemann p.100.
21. Adolph Goetze, *Operations of the German Engineers and Technical Troops during the Franco-German War 1870-71*, translated by Colonel G. Graham (London 1875) p.207; Lehautcourt, p.84.
22. Tiedemann, p.101.
23. Wartensleben, pp.74-75.
24. MMC, IV pp.536-537.
25. Wartensleben, p.79.

Chapter 5: Rouen
1. Wartensleben, p.89.
2. Official History, IV p.19.
3. Maurice, p.339.
4. Offical History, IV p.20.
5. Wartensleben, p.84.
6. Ibid..
7. Ibid., p.85.
8. Ibid., p.89.
9. Official History, IV p.21.
10. Ibid., p.22.
11. Wartensleben, p.93.
12. Roberts, p.356.
13. Official History, IV p.22.
14. Roberts, p.359.
15. Ibid., p.360.
16. MMC, II p.549.
17. Ibid., pp.550-551.
18. Wartensleben, pp.109-110.
19. Ibid., pp.110-111.
20. Ibid., p.111; Official History, IV p.23.
21. Official History, IV p.24.
22. Wartensleben, p.106.
23. Ibid., p.107.
24. Goetze, pp.216-218; Wartensleben, p.107.
25. Roberts, p.364.

26. Official History, IV p.25.
27. Hozier, II p.217.
28. Roberts, p.382.

Chapter 6: The Arrival of Faidherbe
1. Faidherbe, p.85.
2. Patry, p.221.
3. Faidherbe, pp.31-32.
4. Patry, p.193.
5. Wartensleben, pp.124-125.
6. Lehautcourt, p.99.
7. Patry, p.193.
8. Ibid., p.201.
9. MMC II, pp.579-580.
10. Official History IV p.26.
11. Wartensleben, p.133.
12. Goetze, p.220.
13. *'Daily News', Correspondence of the War Between Germany and France* (London 1871) p.406.
14. Dora Raymond, *British Policy and Opinion during the Franco-Prussian War* (New York 1871) p.283.
15. Moritz Busch, *Bismarck: Some Secret Pages of his History* (London 1898) p.174.
16. Faidherbe, p.33.
17. Wartensleben, p.136.
18. Ibid..
19. Official History, IV p.107.
20. Wartensleben, p.138.
21. Faidherbe, p.34.
22. Lehautcourt, p.109.
23. Ibid., p.110.
24. MMC II pp.586-587.
25. Wartensleben, p.143.
26. MMC II pp.594-595; Official History IV Appendix CVIII
27. Ibid.

Chapter 7: The Battle of the Hallue
1. Seton, p.196.
2. Faidherbe, p.34.
3. Patry, p.345.
4. Wartensleben, p.155.
5. Howard, p.394.
6. Wartensleben, pp.149-150.
7. Wartensleben, p.156; Howard, p.394.
8. Wartensleben, p.152.
9. Ibid.
10. Official History, IV p.110.
11. Patry, p.210.
12. Wartensleben, pp.154-155.
13. Roberts, p.13.
14. Wartensleben, pp.157-158.
15. Hozier, II p.219.

16. Wartensleben, p.159.
17. Ibid.
18. Roberts, p.404.
19. Official History, IV p.113.
20. Patry, pp.211-212.
21. Official History, IV p.114.
22. Patry, p.213.
23. Official History, IV p.115.
24. Ibid.
25. Lehautcourt, p.133.
26. Wartensleben, p.160.
27. Lehautcourt, p.135.
28. Ibid., p.134.
29. Wartensleben, p.162.
30. Faidherbe, p.40.
31. Lehautcourt, p.136.
32. Goeben, pp.27-32.

Chapter 8: Retreat
1. Wartensleben, p.162.
2. Patry, p.214.
3. Seton, p.203.
4. Official History, IV p.117.
5. Wartensleben, p.163.
6. Ibid., pp.164-165.
7. Ibid., p.166.
8. Faidherbe, p.41.
9. Official History, IV p.118 and Appendix CXIV.
10. Patry, p.219.
11. Roberts, pp.410-411.
12. Faidherbe, p.42.
13. Official History, IV p.119.
14. Ibid..
15. Wartensleben, pp.187-188.
16. Official History, IV pp.121-122.

Chapter 9: The Investment of Péronne
1. Wartensleben, p.174.
2. Tiedemann, p.191.
3. Goetze, p.234.
4. Official History, IV p.248.
5. Ibid., p.249n.
6. Faidherbe, p.50.
7. Wartensleben, pp.175-176.
8. Ibid., p.176.
9. Goeben, p.43.
10. Faidherbe, pp.51-52; Lehautcourt, p.169.
11. Wartensleben, p.179.
12. Official History, IV p.250.
13. Tiedemann, p.192.

14. Lehautcourt, p.170.
15. Ibid.
16. French General Staff *La Guerre de 1870-71, publiée par la Revue d'Histoire, rédigée a la section Historique de l'Etat – Major de l'Armée* (Paris 1901-13) (cited as Guerre) IV p.2.
17. Guerre II p.134.

Chapter 10: Bapaume
1. Patry, pp.219-220.
2. Wartensleben, p.186; Official History IV p.120.
3. Patry, pp.280-281.
4. Wartensleben, pp.189-190.
5. A. Schell, *The Operations of the First Army under General von Goeben* (London 1873) pp.14-15.
6. Roberts, pp.423-424.
7. Official History, IV p.234.
8. Patry, p.227.
9. Official History, IV p.234.
10. Faidherbe, p.44.
11. Goeben, p.38.
12. Schell, pp.35-36.
13. Lehautcourt, p.179.
14. Schell, p.23.
15. Faidherbe, p.41; Schell, p.23; Official History Appendix CXXVII
16. Patry, pp.229-230.
17. Schell, p.26; Official History, IV p.237.
18. Schell, p.27.
19. Ibid., p.28.
20. Official History, IV p.240.
21. Roberts, p.435.
22. Patry, p.232.
23. Schell, pp.30-31.
24. Schell, p.36; Faidherbe, p.48; Official History, IV Appendix CXXCII
25. Patry, p.233.
26. Wartensleben, p.198.
27. Faidherbe, p.47.
28. Lehautcourt, p.193.
29. Major W. Bigge, 'The Campaign of the First Army in the North of France' in *The Franco German War 1870-71* (London 1900) p.355.
30. Wartensleben, p.199.
31. Faidherbe, p.88.
32. Goeben, p.35.

Chapter 11: Goeben Takes Command
1. Wartensleben, pp.200-201.
2. Schell, pp.51-53; Wartensleben, p.202.
3. Schell, pp.54-55.
4. MMC, II p.656.
5. Ibid., pp.662-663.
6. Ibid., p.663.
7. Ibid., p.664.
8. Roberts, pp.451-452.

9. Howard, pp.403-404.
10. 'Daily News' pp.503-504.
11. Schell, p.63.
12. Lehautcourt, pp.210-211.

Chapter 12: The Fall of Péronne
1. Tiedemann, p.193.
2. Goetze, p.237.
3. Official History, IV p.252.
4. Schell, pp.38-39; Official History, IV p.252.
5. Goetze, p.236.
6. Official History, IV pp.252-253.
7. Schell, p.40.
8. Ibid., p.42.
9. Ibid., p.43.
10. Lehautcourt, pp.201-202.
11. Schell, p.46.
12. Ibid., p.48.
13. Ibid., p.49.
14. Goetze, p.237.
15. Lehautcourt, p.202.
16. Schell, p.49.
17. Ibid., p.64.
18. Lehautcourt, p.202.
19. Ibid., p.203.
20. Schell, p.65.
21. Ibid.
22. Ibid., p.66.
23. Roberts, p.448.
24. Tiedemann, p.193.
25. Goetze, p.238.
26. Lehautcourt, p.204.
27. Quoted Faidherbe, p.56.
28. Quoted Elihu Rich, *A History of the Franco German War* (London 1884) p.459.

Chapter 13: Robert-le-Diable
1. Official History, IV p.243.
2. Bigge, p.359.
3. Official History, IV p.244.
4. Wartensleben, p.193.
5. Wartensleben, p.194; Official History, IV p.244.
6. Official History, IV p.245.
7. Ibid., pp.245-246.
8. Schell, p.77.
9. Ibid.
10. MMC, IV p.677; Schell, p.85.
11. Schell, p.98.

Chapter 14: Faidherbe Advances Again
1. Schell, pp.69-70.
2. Lehautcourt, p.214.

3. Schell, p.76.
4. Ibid.
5. Official History, IV p.256.
6. Schell, p.77.
7. Ibid., p.83.

Chapter 15: The Plan to Move East
1. Faidherbe, p.59; Guerre, IV p.7.
2. Lehautcourt, p.221.
3. Ibid., pp.222-223.
4. MMC, IV pp.676-677.
5. Guerre, IV p.7.
6. Ibid, p.2.
7. Ibid, p.6.
8. Goeben, p.45.
9. General Louis Faidherbe, *Réponse á la Relation du General von Goeben* (Paris 1873) p.20.
10. Guerre, IV p.6.
11. Isnard to Faidherbe, Guerre IV Documents p.31.
12. Guerre, IV pp.12-13.
13. Faidherbe, p.59; Guerre IV p.13.
14. Guerre, IV p.15.

Chapter 16: The March Begins
1. Lehautcourt, p.225.
2. Hozier, II p.226.
3. Faidherbe, p.62.
4. Goeben, p.45.
5. Ibid., p.46.
6. Schell, p.89.
7. Official History IV p.259.
8. Schell, pp.99-100.
9. Roberts, p.457.
10. Patry, p.240.
11. Schell, p.101.
12. Eugene Desiré Eduard Sergent (Grenest) *Les Armées du Nord et de Normandie* (Paris 1897) p.413.
13. MMC, IV p.676.
14. '*Daily News*' pp.508-509.
15. MMC, IV pp.677-679.

Chapter 17: Tertry-Poeuilly
1. Schell, pp.101-102.
2. Roberts, p.458.
3. Schell, p.106.
4. Patry, p.241.
5. Official History IV, p.261.
6. Schell, p.112.
7. Ibid., p.113.
8. Lehautcourt, p.231.
9. Grenest, pp.428-430.
10. Ibid, p.430.
11. Schell, p.116-117.

12. Ibid., pp.117-118.
13. Faidherbe, p.61.
14. Lehautcourt, p.237.
15. Schell, p.119.

Chapter 18: The Eve of Battle
1. Field Marshal Count K. von Blumenthal, *Journal for 1866 and 1870-71* (London 1903) p.279.
2. Schell, p.108.
3. Ibid., p.122.
4. Faidherbe, p.62.
5. Schell, pp.127-128.
6. Lehautcourt, pp.238-239.
7. Ibid., p.243.
8. Ibid., p.246.
9. Grenest, p.440.
10. Guerre, IV p.79.
11. Lehautcourt, p.251.
12. Ibid, p.249.
13. Schell, pp.125-126.
14. '*Daily News*' Correspondence, p.503.
15. Faidherbe, p.62.
16. Lehautcourt, pp.246-247.
17. Official History, IV p.264.
18. Schell, p.172.

Chapter 19: St Quentin: The First Phase in the Southern Sector
1. Howard, p.405.
2. Seton, p.244.
3. Schell, p.129.
4. Ibid., p.130.
5. Official History, IV p.265.
6. Patry, pp.241-243.
7. Schell, p.133.
8. Seton, p.246.
9. Schell, p.135; Official History IV p.265.
10. Grenest, p.455.
11. Official History, IV p.266.
12. Patry, pp.244-245.
13. Ibid., p.248.
14. Schell, p.143.
15. Ibid., pp.144-145.
16. Howard, p.405.
17. Schell, p.147.

Chapter 20: The Western Sector: The First Phase
1. Schell, pp.137-138.
2. '*Daily News*', p.505.
3. Sutherland, p.85.
4. Lehautcourt, p.262.
5. Official History, IV p.267.
6. Guerre, IV p.116.

7. Schell, p.140.
8. Grenest, p.491.
9. Official History, IV p.269.
10. Grenest, pp.491-492.
11. Schell, p.142.
12. H. Daussy, *La Ligne de la Somme pendant la Campagne 1870 -1871* (Paris 1875) pp.313; Lehautcourt, p.261.
13. Guerre, IV p.136.

Chapter 21: Victory on the Left Bank
1. Schell, p.149; Official History IV p.271.
2. Guerre, IV pp.102-103.
3. Schell, p.149.
4. Seton, pp.252-253.
5. Schell, p.167; Off Hist, IV p.272.
6. Guerre IV pp. 103-104
7. Schell, p.168.
8. Official History, IV p.273.
9. Schell, p.170.
10. Official History, IV p.273.
11. Guerre IV, pp.108-109.
12. Ibid., Documents p.102.
13. Patry, p.250.
14. Guerre, IV Documents p.99.
15. Schell, p.170.

Chapter 22: The End of the Battle
1. Schell, pp.157-158.
2. Ibid., p.158.
3. Official History, IV p.173.
4. Guerre, IV p.135.
5. Schell, pp.158-159.
6. Official History, IV p.274.
7. Guerre, IV p.136.
8. Ibid., p.138.
9. Schell, p.160; Official History, IV p.274.
10. Schell, p.161.
11. Official History, IV p.275; Schell, p.162.
12. Official History, IV p.272; Schell, p.162.
13. Guerre, IV pp.142-143.
14. Ibid., pp.144-145.
15. Ibid., p.145.
16. General L. Faidherbe, *Note Supplementaire a la Commission d'Enquete* (Paris 1873) p.14.
17. Guerre, IV pp.147-148.
18. Seton, p.255.
19. Faidherbe, *Note Supplementaire*, pp.15-16.
20. Schell, pp.164-165.

NOTES

Chapter 23: Aftermath
1. Official History, IV Appendix CXXVII; Schell p.173; Guerre IV Documents pp.132-136; Faidherbe, p.68.
2. Goeben pp.58-59.
3. Ibid., p.60.
4. Howard, pp.404-405.
5. Schell, p.175.
6. Roberts, p.468.
7. Ibid., p.466.
8. Schell, pp.171-172.
9. MMC, II pp.682-683.
10. Field Marshal Count von Moltke, *The Franco German War*, 3rd Edition (London 1907) p.323.
11. Faidherbe, p.101.
12. Guerre, IV p.155.
13. Roberts, p.471.
14. Schell, pp.186-187.
15. Ibid., p.189.
16. Official History, IV p.279.
17. Guerre, IV p.158.
18. Schell, p.201.
19. Guerre, IV p.3.

Bibliography

Abbott, J.S.C., *Prussia and the Franco Prussian War* (London 1871)
Allnutt, H., *Historical Diary of the War Between France and Germany 1870-71* (London 1871)
Baldick, R., *The Siege of Paris* (London 1864)
Barry, Q., *The Franco Prussian War 1870-71* (Solihull 2007, 2 volumes)
Bigge, Major W., 'The Campaign of the First Army in the North of France' in *The Franco German War 1870-71* (London 1900)
Bleibtreu, C., *Amiens – St Quentin* (Stuttgart 1902)
Blume, W., *The Operations of the German Armies in France* (London 1872)
Blumenthal, Field Marshal Count K von, *Journal for 1866 and 1870-71* (London 1903)
Bonie, Lieut. Colonel, 'The French Cavalry in 1870' in *Cavalry Studies from Two Great Wars* (Kansas City 1896)
Brockett, L.P., *The Franco German War of 1870-71* (New York 1871)
Bucholz, A., *Moltke and the German Wars* (New York 2001)
Bucholz, A., *Moltke, Schlieffen and Prussian War Planning* (New York 1991)
Bury, J.P.T., *Gambetta and the National Defence* (London 1936)
Bury, J.P.T. & Tombs, R.P., *Thiers 1797-1877: A Political Life* (London 1971)
Busch, M., *Bismarck in the Franco German War 1870-71* (London 1898)
Chabot, Colonel J. de, *La Cavalerie Allemande pendant la Guerre de 1870-71* (Paris 1899)
Chanzy, General A., *La Deuxième Armée de la Loire* (Paris 1871)
Coursier, A., *Faidherbe* (Paris 1989)
Creveld, M. Van, *Supplying War* (Cambridge 1977)
'*Daily News*', *Correspondence of the War Between Germany and France* (London 1871, 2 volumes)
Daussy, H., *La Ligne de la Somme pendant la Campagne 1870-71* (Paris 1875)
Dictionnaire du Biographie Francaise, Vol 10 (Paris 1965)
Faidherbe, General L., *The Campaign of the Army of the North*, translated by S. Sutherland (Solihull 2010)
Faidherbe, General L., *Réponse a la Relation du General von Goeben* (Paris 1873)
Faidherbe, General L., *Note Supplementaire a la Commission d'Enquête* (Paris 1873)
Fermer, D., *France at Bay 1870-71* (Barnsley 2011)
Franklyn, H.B., *The Great Battles of 1870 and Blockade of Metz* (London 1887)
Frederick William, Crown Prince, *The War Diary of the Emperor Frederick III*, translated by A R Allinson (London 1927)
French General Staff, *La Guerre de 1870-71: Campagne de l'Armée du Nord* (Paris 1901-1913, 4 volumes)
Freycinet, C. de, *La Guerre en Province* (Paris 1901)
Gensoul, L., *Souvenirs de l'armée du Nord* (Paris 1914)
German General Staff, *Official Account of the Franco German War 1870-71*, translated by Major FCH Clarke (London 1883, 5 volumes)
Goeben, General A. von, *Contributions to the History of the Campaign in the North West of France*, translated by Capt. J.L. Seton (London 1873)

Goetze, Captain A., *Operations of the German Engineers and the Technical Troops during the Franco German War 1870-71*, translated by Colonel G Graham (London 1875)
Goltz, C. von der, *Leon Gambetta und Seine Armeen* (Berlin 1877)
Grenest (pseudonym of E. Sergent), *Les Armées du Nord et de Normandie* (Paris 1897)
Hoenig, F., *Twenty Four Hours of Moltke's Strategy* (Woolwich 1895)
Hoenig, F., *Enquiries Concerning the Tactics of the Future*, translated by Capt. H.M. Bowes (London 1899)
Horne, A., *The Fall of Paris* (London 1965)
Howard, M., *The Franco-Prussian War* (London 1962)
Hozier, Captain H.M., *The Franco-Prussian War* (London n.d., 2 volumes)
Kunz, Major H. von, *Der Feldzug der Ersten Deutschen Armee im Norden und Nordwesten Frankreichs 1870-71* (Berlin 1900)
Lecluselle, A., *La Guerre dans le Nord 1870-71* (Cambrai 1898)
Lehautcourt, P. (pseudonym of General B.E. Palat) *Campagne du Nord en 1870-71* (Paris 1872)
Levi, C., *La Défense Nationale dans le Nord* (Paris n.d., 4 volumes)
Lonlay, Dick de, *Francais et Allemands* (Paris 1890, 4 volumes)
Maurice, Major General F. (ed.), *The Franco German War 1870-71* (London 1900)
Moltke, Field Marshal H. von, *Correspondence Militaire* (Paris n.d)
Moltke, Field Marshal H. von, *The Franco German War of 1870-71* (London 1907)
Moltke, Field Marshal H. von, *Strategy: Its Theory and Application* (Westport CT 1971)
Ollier, E., *Cassell's Illustrated History of the War Between France and Germany* (London n.d., 2 volumes)
Ortholan, H., *L'Armée du Nord 1870-71* (Paris 2011)
Patry, L., *The Reality of War,* translated by D Fermer (London 2001)
Raymond, D., *British Policy and Opinion during the Franco-Prussian War* (New York 1921)
Rich, E., *A History of the Franco German War* (London 1884)
Roberts, Sir R., *Modern War: Or the Campaigns of the First Prussian Army 1870-71* (London 1871)
Schell, Major A. von, *The Operations of the First Army under General von Steinmetz* (London 1873)
Schell, Major A. von, *The Operations of the First Army under General von Goeben* (London 1873)
Seton, Capt J., *Notes on the Operations of the North German Troops in Lorraine and Picardy* (London 1872)
Showalter, D., *Railroads and Rifles* (Hamden, CT 1975)
Stannard, H., *Gambetta* (London 1921)
Stone, D., *First Reich* (London 2002)
Tiedemann, Colonel B. von, *The Siege Operations in the Campaign against France,* translated by Major Tyler (London 1877)
Verdy du Vernois, General H. von, *With the Royal Headquarters in 1870-71* (London 1924)
Wartensleben, Colonel H. von, *Operations of the First Army under General von Manteuffel* (London 1873)
Wawro, G., *The Franco-Prussian War* (Cambridge 2003)
Whitton, Lieut Colonel F.E., *Moltke* (London 1921)

Index

Abbeville, 22, 66, 78-79, 117, 123, 137, 146, 161, 229
Ablainzeville, 127
Acheux, 88, 137
Achiet le Grand, 54, 117, 119, 122, 124, 127, 132
Ahlborn, Captain, 217
Ailly, 41, 50, 82, 237
Albert, 48, 54, 66, 76, 79, 82-83, 86, 88-90, 107, 110, 122, 126, 132, 138-139, 159, 161-162, 166, 168-169, 229
Albrecht, Prince, Junior, 25, 83, 87, 105-106, 113, 123, 126-127, 131-132, 138-139, 143, 159, 175,176, 189, 192, 199, 211, 217, 221, 225, 235, 255
Allonville, b83, 89-90, 101
Amiens, 16, 22, 28, 33, 35, 37-49, 51-58, 60, 62-66, 70-74, 76-89, 91, 96, 104, 106, 108-112, 118-119, 133, 137-140, 142, 145, 147-148, 159, 161, 163-165, 170, 172-173, 175, 197, 223, 229, 237-238, 243
Argeuil, 65, 67, 69
Arras, 18, 37, 56, 66, 70, 76, 78-80, 105, 107-108, 113-114,117-119, 126-127, 132-133, 138, 146-147, 152, 159, 167, 242, 253
Artemps, 192
Athies, 117
Auffray, 71
Avesnes les Bapaume, 122, 124, 126, 128, 132, 165
Aynés, Colonel, 88, 126, 193, 196-197, 239-240

Bancourt, 126, 129
Bapaume, 78-79, 110, 113, 117, 119-135, 137-138, 140, 142-14, 147, 150, 152, 159-162, 165, 171
Barentin, 87
Barnekow, Lieutenant General Albert von, 30, 48-50, 53, 69, 72, 78, 89, 94-96, 98, 106, 123, 138, 143-145, 147-150, 159, 161-162, 169-171, 175-176, 183, 189, 191-192, 194, 197-200, 207-209, 212-215, 217, 220-222, 225, 233, 235, 255
Baumann, Captain, 198, 214
Bavelincourt, 85, 98-99, 104
Bayonvillers, 48

Bazaine, Marshal François, 16, 28, 36
Beaucourt, 40, 96, 98-99, 101, 105, 161
Beaulencourt, 128-129
Beauvais, 33, 65, 78, 81, 83-84, 87, 243
Beauvois, 176, 180-181, 200, 253
Béhagnies, 119-121, 131-132, 159
Béhencourt, 85, 88, 95, 97-98
Bellenglise, 185-186, 188, 198, 205-206, 215
Bellicourt, 169, 189, 226
Belvallette, Lieutenant, 180
Bentheim, Lieutenant General Georg von, 28, 32, 34, 41-42, 46-48, 67-68, 70-72, 74, 78, 87, 108-109, 138, 153-158, 161, 175, 230
Bergerie, 89
Bergmann, Major General, 153-154, 156, 230
Bernay, 70, 72-73, 108
Bernes, 171, 177
Bernières, 108
Bessol, Major General Joseph du, 36, 39, 42, 48, 53, 75, 85, 88, 99-100, 121-122, 124, 126, 129, 132, 161, 168, 171, 176-177, 180, 188, 193, 196, 198-199, 202, 207, 240
Beugnâtre, 121-123, 126, 129, 131-132
Biaches, 111, 114
Bieberstein, Captain Rogalla von, 197, 215
Biehler, Major General, 72, 230
Bienvillers aux Bois, 121
Bigge, Wilhelm, 134
Bihucourt, 122, 124, 132-133
Bismarck, Count Otto von, 15, 26, 79
Blanckensee, Colonel von, 28-29, 233
Blois, 243
Blondin, M., 112-114, 149
Blumenthal, Lieutenant General, 183
Blumroeder, Colonel von, 98, 233
Bock, Colonel von, 50, 71
Böcking, Colonel, 172, 176, 190-191, 198-200, 207-208, 210-211, 214, 217, 221, 231, 237, 255
Bodin, Commandant, 254
Bohain, 137, 187-189, 225, 255
Bois des Bacquets, 143
Bolbec, 71, 73, 108, 156-157
Bonavy, 150
Bouchoir, 39, 41-42
Boos, 69

Bosc Berenger, 68
Bosc le Hard, 68
Bouchy, 175
Boulogne, 123, 137
Bourbaki, General Charles, 16-17, 19-24, 35, 183, 228, 244
Bourgachard, 71, 108, 154-157
Bourges, 84, 243
Bourgtherolde, 157
Bouxin, Captain, 250
Bouzeaucourt, 150
Boves, 39-40, 50-51
Bray, 48, 86, 106, 112-113, 142, 162-163, 168
Breteuil, 40, 67, 80-83
Briand, General, 65, 67, 69-71, 73, 83, 87
Brie, 144, 170, 176
Brionne, 72, 78, 155-157
Bronikowsky, Major von, 89, 93, 129, 197, 213-215, 217, 222, 233, 255
Bruntel, 113
Buchy, 67-69
Bucquoy, 108, 113, 117, 119, 132, 160
Bury, J P T, 16
Busse, Captain, 127
Busse, Colonel von, 65, 153-156, 230
Bussy, 85
Bussy les Daours, 91

Cachy, 39-40, 42, 46, 54
Caix, 41
Cambrai, 36, 60, 66, 108, 113, 118, 127, 132, 137-138, 147, 150, 162, 166-167, 187-189, 206, 212-213, 217-218, 220, 223-225, 228, 242, 252, 254-255
Camon, 89
Cardonette, 101
Carlowitz, Colonel von, 211, 236
Cartigny, 113, 144-145
Castres, 191-193, 196, 199, 207
Caudebec, 72, 156
Caulaincourt, 170, 177-181, 183, 249-250, 253
Chanzy, General, 158
Charles, Prince Frederick, 84, 243
Charon, Lieutenant Colonel, 53, 218, 239
Chartres, 71, 243
Chassepôt, Antoine, 194, 245
Châtillon-sur-Seine, 109
Chaulnes, 159, 238
Chauny, 76, 167, 189
Cherbourg, 71, 73, 140
Clary, 225, 255
Clères, 87, 157
Cléry, 113-114, 170
Combles, 113, 119, 123, 138, 168, 171
Compiègne, 25, 31-35, 60, 166-167

Conflans, 71
Contay, 85-86, 88, 95-99, 105, 107
Contescourt, 187, 193, 196, 199, 202, 207
Corbie, 37-38, 47-48, 53, 82, 85-86, 88-89, 100, 104-106, 142
Cornet d'Or, 197, 211
Cottenchy, 50
Coucy, 41
Coudry, 225
Coulmiers, 37
Courson, Captain, 218
Crécy, 119
Crèmieux, Adolphe, 15-16
Crèvecoeur, 83
Croisilles, 139
Croix, 185-186

Dallmer, Major, 42, 44
Danizy, 60, 62
Daours, 85, 88-89, 91-92, 94, 99-101, 105-106, 142
Davenescourt, 82
Degoutin, Colonel, 241, 249-250
Dehaussy, Captain, 149
Démuin, 42
Derroja, Major General Jean, 36, 39, 48, 50, 53, 75, 85, 88, 98, 106-107, 119, 121-122, 124, 126, 128-129, 132, 159, 161, 168, 170-172, 176, 188, 193, 213, 239
Dieppe, 70-71, 73-74, 78-79, 81, 84, 157
Dilke, Sir Charles, 228
Dohna, Major General zu, 70-71, 78, 81, 89, 97, 105, 122, 127, 131, 161, 164, 168, 178, 181, 198, 200, 202, 205-206, 215-216, 234, 237
Doingt, 113-114, 144
Domart, 41-42, 47, 117
Dommartin, 50
Dompierre-Becquincourt, 138
Dörnberg, Colonel von, 91, 177, 200-203, 233, 236
Douai, 20-21, 107, 113, 118, 167, 226, 256
Douchy, 139
Dreux, 70, 243
Dreyse, Johann von, 245
Duclair, 78, 87, 157
Dupuich, Captain, 169, 180, 241, 253
Dury, 38, 49-50, 52

Ecouis, 65
Elbeuf, 71, 87, 108, 153-154, 156
Epehy, 171
Eppeville, 77
Ervillers, 139, 159
Essertaux, 41, 49
Essigny, 147, 208

Essigny le Grand, 183-184, 187, 190-193, 196, 199, 208-209, 211
Essigny le Petit, 76
Estrées en Chaussée, 176-177
Eterpigny, 150-151
Etreillers, 176, 189, 200, 255
Eugénie, Empress, 16
Evreux, 70-72, 157

Faidherbe, General Louis, 17, 19, 35-36, 38, 54, 58, 75-83, 85-89, 91-92, 96, 98-104, 106-107, 111-117, 122-124, 127, 132-143, 145, 148-152, 156, 159-172, 175-177, 179-191, 198, 201-202, 206-207, 212, 218-221, 223-229, 239, 247, 249, 256
Falckenstein, General Vogel von, 26, 29
Farre, Lieutenant General Jean Joseph, 18-19, 22-23, 35-37, 39, 41-42, 53-54, 60, 75, 85, 115-116, 165-166, 227, 239
Fauville, 156
Favre, Jules, 15-16, 19, 82
Favreuil, 119, 121-123, 126-127, 129, 131-132
Fayet, 187, 189, 201, 203-204, 215-217, 253
Fécamp, 157
Fernandez, Captain, 196
Fins, 75, 108, 113-114, 150, 169
Flamicourt, 147
Flavy le Martel, 170, 176
Flers, 139
Fleury, 67
Foerster, Colonel, 124, 177, 193-194, 196, 207, 209, 212, 240
Fontaine les Clercs, 187, 214
Forges, 65, 67, 78, 81
Forgettes, 68
Foucaucourt, 82
Fouencamps, 39, 41, 46, 50
Fourichon, Admiral, 15-16
Fournier, Mayor M., 145
Foutrein, Commandant, 203-205, 242
Francilly, 201-203, 205, 214-217
Fransecky, Lieutenant General von Edouard von, 139
Franvillers, 98, 107
Fréchencourt, 93-94, 98, 161
Fresnoy, 40, 206
Freycinet, Charles de, 163-165, 185, 268
Fririon, General, 17

Gainville, 71, 157
Gambetta, Leon, 14-17, 19-20, 23-24, 35, 74-75, 163, 165, 227, 229
Garnier, Major, 111, 114-115, 145, 147, 149-152, 247-248
Gauchy, 187-188, 191-193, 207-208, 211

Gayl, Major General von, 157-158, 205, 215-216, 230, 237
Gentelles, 39-42, 44, 46-47, 54, 58
Gerhardt, Lieutenant, 147
Gien, 243-244
Giffécourt, 187, 199, 207-208
Gislain, Colonel de, 75-76, 180, 196, 199, 207, 211-212, 240
Gisors, 65, 68, 78
Givet, 32, 116
Glais-Bizoin, Alexandre, 15-16
Gneisenau, Major General Neidhardt von, 95, 97, 115, 233
Goeben, General August von, 26-27, 29, 31, 33, 40-42, 46, 48-54, 57-58, 67-74, 78-79, 82-83, 85, 87-90, 94-96, 98-99, 103-107, 112-113, 117-119, 122-123, 126, 129, 132, 136-145, 147-150, 156-157, 159, 161-166, 168-170, 172-176, 181, 183-184, 186, 189-192, 197-200, 205, 207-209, 211, 213-215, 217, 221-229, 233-235, 255
Gonesse, 139-140, 173, 184
Gournay, 65, 67-68, 81
Granville, Lord, 17, 79
Grévillers, 122-124, 126, 132
Gricourt, 203, 215-216
Groeben, Lieutenant General Georg von der, 31, 33, 35, 39-41, 48, 65-66, 76-78, 80-81, 111, 113, 121-123, 126-127, 132, 139, 159, 161, 169-170, 175-178, 181, 189, 192, 200, 203, 206, 214-217, 228, 234, 237, 255
Grugies, 187-188, 191-194, 196, 199, 207, 209-211, 217, 221, 251
Grumbrecht, Captain, 100
Guerbaville, 157
Guiscard, 33
Guise, 60, 137, 186-188, 255
Guyencourt, 168

Hailles, 41-42, 50
Halle, 143
Hallue, River, 84-86, 88-91, 93-94, 97, 99, 101, 103-106, 111-112, 114, 117-118, 161, 163-164, 168, 224
Ham, 22, 35, 37-38, 62, 76-79, 106, 112-113, 144, 147, 150, 164, 168, 170-172, 175-176, 183, 186-191, 201, 205, 223
Hamélincourt, 139
Hancourt, 178, 187, 251
Hangard, 41-43, 45-47
Happencourt, 176
Harfleur, 73, 108, 156-157
Harly, 211
Hassel, Major, 221, 233
Hébecourt, 39, 41, 49

INDEX

Hecquet, Commandant, 196, 240, 251
Hédauville, 168
Helfaut, 116
Hendicourt, 168
Henning, Lieutenant Colonel von, 90-91, 95, 233, 236
Herbecourt, 176
Hertzberg, Colonel von, 123, 126-127, 129, 192, 199, 209, 213, 235
Hoffbauer, Captain, 155
Holleben, Major, 169-170, 194
Holnon, 187-188, 203-205, 215
Holtzendorff, Lieutenant Colonel von, 197
Homblières, 211
Honfleur, 71
Howard, Sir Michael, 86-87, 141, 165, 198
Hubert, Captain, 81-82
Hüllesheim, Lieutenant Colonel von, 47
Hymmen, Colonel von, 192, 196, 199, 207, 217, 236

Isle, 186-188, 193, 197, 211, 212, 220
Isnard, Colonel, 162, 166, 168-170, 176, 188-190, 201, 203, 205, 215, 217, 242
Isneauville, 65, 69

Jeancourt, 176, 206
Jussy, 175-176, 238

Kargow, Colonel Beyer von, 49
Kising, Vice Sergeant Major, 96
Kluge, Captain, 144, 147, 151
Koppelow, Major, 46
Kraemer, Lance Corporal, 169
Krafft, Colonel, 62
Kummer, Lieutenant General Ferdinand von, 28-29, 48-50, 68, 73, 78, 80-82, 89-90, 93-94, 113, 117, 119, 121-124, 126-128, 131-132, 138-239, 144, 159, 175-176, 178, 180-181, 183, 189, 191-192, 197-198, 200, 202-203, 206, 214-215, 217, 225, 233, 236, 255

L'Epine de Dallon, 175, 213-214, 217, 222, 224
L'Equipée, 175
La Biette, 187, 212
La Bouillée, 87
La Fère, 28, 32-33, 35, 51, 53, 59-60, 62-63, 65-67, 76-77, 79, 110, 112, 145-147, 149, 159, 167, 175, 184, 186-191, 193, 196-197, 211, 223, 238, 255
La Ferté, 67
La Feuillée, 78
La Feuille, 68
La Grande Couronne, 71, 78, 108, 156
La Haye, 67

La Londe, 108, 153-155, 157
La Motte Brébière, 91
La Neuville, 89, 142
La Roquette, 108, 153
Lacoste, Colonel Delmas de, 60
Lagrange, Colonel de, 178-179, 201, 217
Lagrange, Commander, 75, 241
Lahoussoye, 103, 105, 107
Lamotte-Warfusée, 48
Lanchy, 180
Landrecies, 137, 225, 228
Laon, 31, 60, 63, 76, 159, 166-167
Lardiere, M J, 53
Lauriston, General, 108
Le Cateau, 213, 255
Le Catelet, 113, 137, 166, 212, 224, 255
Le Havre, 18, 70-74, 83-84, 103, 108, 156-157, 243
Le Mesnil, 144
Le Pontchu, 196, 199
Le Quesnel, 41
Le Thil, 68
Le Transloy, 123, 126, 129, 132, 145
Le Vergnier, 206
Lecointe, Lieutenant General Alphonse, 20-21, 36, 39, 42, 44, 46, 48, 53-54, 75-76, 82, 85, 88, 99-100, 126, 129, 176, 180, 188, 191-194, 196-198, 202, 207, 210-211, 213, 218, 220-221, 239
Legat, Colonel von, 153-155, 230
Lehndorf, 140
Lens, 79, 107-108
Lentze, Major, 214, 233
Les Alencons Farm, 83, 90-91
Les Andelys, 67, 70
Les Thilliers, 65
Lestien, Captain, 250
Lewinski, Major von, 92, 100-101
Licourt, 170
Liéremont, 147
Liffremont, 68
Ligny, 127, 129-130, 132
Lilien, Baron von, 119
Lille, 14, 18-20, 22, 24, 35-37, 48, 75, 84, 115, 128, 165-166, 227-228, 243
Lippe, General Count zur, 65-66, 113, 137, 142, 159, 168-170, 175-176, 184, 190, 196-197, 199, 211, 217, 228, 231, 236, 255
Lizerolles, 183, 191
Löe, Colonel von, 91-92, 100-101, 232-233
Longpré, 58, 89, 117
Longueau, 39
Longueval, 162
Louviers, 70
Loysel, General, 156

Luckowitz, Captain, 77
Lüderitz, Colonel von, 39, 234
Luetken, Lieutenant, 155
Lyons la Foret, 65, 67
Lyons, Lord, 17

Maison Brulée, 154
Maissemy, 206
Manteuffel, General Karl von, 25-26, 29-34, 37, 40-42, 44, 46-47, 50-52, 58-59, 63, 65-67, 69-72, 77-87, 91-92, 94, 99, 101, 104, 106, 108-109, 112-113, 115, 117-118, 123, 137-141, 145-148, 153, 197, 230, 243
Marcelcave, 42
Marchand, Lieutenant Colonel, 218, 241
Maretz, 137
Maricourt, 139
Marseille-le-Petit, 80-81
Marteville, 253
Martine, M, 76
Martinpuich, 161-162
Mecklenburg, Grand Duke of, 84, 158, 244
Memerty, Major General von, 142, 157, 159, 161, 163-164, 178, 180-181, 200, 205, 231
Mertens, Major, 121, 233
Mesnil St Laurent, 184, 187
Mettler, Colonel, 68, 98, 233
Metz, 16, 18-20, 22-23, 25, 27-30, 32, 34, 36-37, 76, 118
Mézières, 20, 28, 32, 35, 63, 82, 109, 143, 146-149, 162
Michelet, Lieutenant Colonel, 119, 178-179, 215-217, 241
Miraumont, 127, 138
Mirus, Major General von, 65, 81-83, 91, 99, 101, 106, 112-113, 115, 122, 127, 129, 234
Molliens Vidame, 117
Moltke, General Helmuth von, 25-26, 28, 32-33, 63, 67, 70-71, 77-78, 81-84, 87, 109, 139-142, 148, 157-158, 163-165, 172-175, 183-184, 222, 226, 228-229, 243-244
Mont St Quentin, 114, 143
Montdidier, 16, 33, 37, 40, 78, 80-82
Montescourt, 176, 183, 191
Montigny, 95, 97-98
Montivilliers, 71, 73, 156-157
Montmédy, 25, 27, 29, 63
Morcourt, 187
Moreuil, 37, 40-41, 50-51, 82, 87
Mory, 121-122, 126
Moulac, Admiral, 75, 82, 85-86, 88-89, 92, 99-100, 119
Moulineaux, 153-154
Moy, 79, 176, 240
Munk, Major, 203, 230

Nesle, 76, 113, 144-145, 170-172, 175, 238
Neuville St Amand, 184, 186, 196-197, 211
Nion, M, 72
Nouvion, 119
Noyon, 33-34, 37, 40, 79, 82
Nurlu, 147, 150, 166

Oestre, 214, 217
Olszewski, Major von, 94, 121-122
Omissy, 187
Orival, 108, 154, 156
Orleans, 37, 243-244

Pagenstecher, Captain, 147, 233
Palat, General (Pierre Lehautcourt), 41, 99-100, 106, 114, 133, 142, 149, 163-165, 179, 181-182, 184-186, 189-190, 201, 204
Paris, 15-18, 20, 22-23, 28, 33, 60, 78, 81, 84, 87, 110, 145, 148, 157-159, 163-166, 169-170, 174, 183, 228, 243
Patry, Léonce, 20, 22, 48, 75-77, 88, 97-98, 104, 106, 117, 119, 121, 124, 128-129, 132, 172, 176, 193, 196-197, 213
Pauly, Colonel, 171, 179, 189-190, 202, 215-218, 242
Paulze d'Ivoy, Lieutenant General, 37, 39, 48-49, 53-54, 56, 75, 82, 85, 88, 177-178, 180, 188, 191, 200-202, 217-218, 220, 241, 249
Payen, Captain, 75, 100, 119, 121-122, 124, 126, 129, 131-132, 161, 171, 177-179, 188, 201-202, 218, 220, 241, 249
Peletingeas, General, 156
Péronne, 22, 37-38, 48, 58, 66, 76, 78-80, 108-119, 123, 128, 132-134, 136-139, 142-152, 159-165, 169-170, 175, 178, 222-223, 237-238, 247-248, 255
Pertain, 82
Pestel, Lieutenant Colonel von, 89, 117-118, 123, 137, 178-180, 203, 234, 237
Peyre, Commandant, 149
Picquigny, 89, 117, 137, 238
Pierregot, 89
Pilsach, Major General Senfft von, 211, 236
Pittié, Colonel, 75, 126, 193, 207-208, 211, 240
Planche, Captain, 32, 60, 63
Poeuilly, 170-171, 175-181, 183, 200, 203
Poitevin, Lieutenant, 149
Pont Audemer, 70-71, 73, 155-157
Pont de l'Arche, 70, 78, 87
Pont Noyelles, 85, 90-91, 93, 95-97, 99-100, 102, 112, 118
Pontruet, 215, 225
Poulainville, 89
Pourtalès, Lieutenant von, 121

Pozières, 161, 163
Preinitzer, Major, 155
Pritzelwitz, Major General von, 42, 44, 70, 87, 157, 231
Puisieux, 13

Querrieux, 83, 85-86, 89-91, 93-95, 99, 101, 105, 161, 168
Quincampoix, 69
Quivières, 175

Rainneville, 89
Rancourt, 162
Reinecke, Lieutenant Colonel, 169-171, 175
Remicourt, 187
Remigny, 176
Réthel, 31
Rheims, 30-31
Rittier, Colonel, 22, 37
Robert le Diable, 109, 153-155
Roberts, Sir Randal,
Robin, Major General, 31, 33, 41-42, 51-52, 68-69, 74, 90, 95, 97, 107, 119, 128, 140, 151, 170-171, 175, 224, 228
Rocourt, 187-188, 217-218, 222, 224
Rocquencourt, 40
Roisel, 132, 142-144, 147, 171, 178, 249
Romancourt, 212
Roon, General Albrecht von, 26
Rosenzweig, Colonel von, 93, 126, 192-194, 198-199, 208, 210-211, 233, 235
Rothkirch, Lieutenant Count Karl Albrecht von, 183
Rougemontier, 155
Roupy, 76, 175-177, 180, 188, 191-192, 197, 200, 214, 217, 220
Rouvroy, 187
Roy, General, 153, 156
Roye, 37, 40-41, 77-79, 82, 113
Rubempré, 96
Rudolphi, Captain, 177, 200
Rumigny, 49

Sailly aux Bois, 132
Sailly-Saillisel, 108
Sains, 38, 50
Sapignies, 119, 121-122, 126, 131, 159
Saussier, General, 156
Savary, Sergeant Major, 57
Savy, 186-189, 200-203, 214, 217, 222
Scheffler, Colonel von, 175
Schell, Captain von, 124, 132, 145-146, 149, 172, 184, 190-191, 194, 206, 213-214, 217, 221-223, 226
Schmidt, Lieutenant, 112, 115

Schwartz, Lieutenant General von, 72, 140, 146, 230
Sedan, 20, 28, 63, 79, 85, 218
Selency, 203-206, 214-216
Senden, Major General Schuler von, 29, 32, 63, 83-84, 87-88, 106, 112-115, 143, 234, 243
Sequehaut, 225
Seraucourt, 176-177, 187, 191-192, 196-199, 211, 255
Serquigny, 72
Seton, Captain, 38, 85, 104, 191, 194, 208, 220
Soissons, 31-32, 60, 62, 146, 165
Somme, River, 14, 22, 37-38, 40-41, 47-48, 50, 53, 56-57, 62, 64, 66, 68, 71, 73, 75-76, 79-89, 91-92, 99-100, 103-104, 106, 109-113, 137-139, 142-146, 148, 150, 157, 159, 161, 163-164, 168, 170, 176, 184-188, 191, 202, 207, 210, 228, 233, 240, 248
Sommerfeld, Colonel von, 50, 233
Sorel, 169
Soyecourt, 179-181
Sperling, Major General von, 67, 87, 139-140, 175, 230
Spuller, Eugène, 16
St Aubin, 127-129, 131-132
St Denis des Monts, 78
St Fuscien, 50
St Gratien, 101
St Léger, 121
St Martin, 68, 186, 188-189, 202, 217-218
St Nicholas, 39, 41, 50-51
St Omer, 79
St Quentin, 25, 31-33, 38, 48, 60, 66, 76, 83-84, 87, 106, 113-114, 137, 142-143, 147, 159-160, 163-169, 172, 174-176, 179-189, 191-195, 197-203, 207-214, 216-226, 235, 239, 243, 249, 251, 253-256
St Saens, 68
St Sauflieu, 49, 51
St Simon, 76
St Valéry, 71
Ste Radegonde, 111
Steinmetz, General Karl von, 25, 27
Steverlynck, Captain, 249-250
Strantz, Major General von, 29, 113, 142, 147, 208, 234-235
Strubberg, Major General von, 49-51, 73, 90, 93, 119, 122-123, 126, 128-129, 176-178, 180-181, 200, 203, 217, 233
Sulzer, First Lieutenant, 80

Tailhade, Captain, 2066
Tergnier, 60, 62, 167, 173, 175, 184, 187, 190-191, 197
Tertry, 175

Testelin, Dr Achille, 14, 17-19, 22, 100, 152, 229
Thennes, 41-42, 44, 47
Thézy, 42
Thionville, 25, 27, 29, 63
Tiedemann, Major General von, 110-111
Tietzen, Colonel, 113, 231
Tilloy, 129-130, 132
Tincourt, 113, 144, 169-171
Tours, 15-17, 22-24, 35, 73, 84, 116, 243
Tourville, 156
Tous Vents,
Tramond, Major, 208
Trotha, Colonel von, 71

Ugny, 175
Urvillers, 187, 192, 196-197, 208, 251

Vadencourt, 85, 105
Valenciennes, 213, 224
Vaux, 122, 132
Vecquemont, 89, 91-92, 100-101
Velu, 126
Vendelles, 171, 179, 181, 206
Vendreuil, 176
Verdun, 28, 31-32
Vermand, 164, 169-172, 175-182, 184, 186-189, 200, 203-205, 249-250, 253
Vernon, 68, 70, 84, 157, 243
Vervins, 60, 137
Villeboisnet, General de la, 17

Villenoisy, Lieut Colonel Marrès de, 35-36, 53, 115-116, 165-166, 229, 239
Villers Bocage, 137
Villers-Bretonneux, 39-40, 42, 44, 46-47, 82
Villers-Carbonnel, 113
Villiers-St. Christophie, 76
Vogel, Captain, 26, 29, 57-59
Voigt, Lieutenant, 228
Voluet, Major, 116
Vouël, 62
Vraignes, 177-178, 180

Wagner, Lieutenant, 147
Warloy, 161
Wartensleben, Colonel Hermann von, 28, 35, 38, 40, 63-64, 67, 71, 79, 81, 86-87, 94, 99, 101, 104, 106, 110, 112, 114, 132, 134, 139, 230
Werder, Lieutenant General Karl von, 139, 231
William, King of Prussia, 25-26, 31, 183, 226
Wittich, Colonel von, 108, 126, 129, 150, 233
Witzendorff, Colonel von, 105, 159, 198, 215, 233
Woerhaye, Captain, 56, 58

Yvetôt, 72, 108

Zastrow, General Dietrich von, 27, 29, 32, 63, 139, 231, 244
Zédé, Commandant, 212, 240
Zglinitzky, Major General von, 51, 61-62, 231

Lightning Source UK Ltd.
Milton Keynes UK
UKHW020029260719
346828UK00002B/19/P